The Bank-Business Relationship

Paola Brighi · Maurizio Mussoni

The Bank-Business Relationship

Information Asymmetries, Relationship Lending, and Regulation

palgrave
macmillan

Paola Brighi
Department of Law "Cesare Beccaria"
University of Milan
Milano, Italy

Maurizio Mussoni
Department of Management
University of Bologna - Rimini Campus
Rimini, Italy

ISBN 978-3-031-91067-8 ISBN 978-3-031-91068-5 (eBook)
https://doi.org/10.1007/978-3-031-91068-5

No Cover credit line

This Palgrave Macmillan imprint is published by the registered company Springer Nature Switzerland AG
The registered company address is: Gewerbestrasse 11, 6330 Cham, Switzerland

Paola Brighi: To my husband and our daughters.
Maurizio Mussoni: To my beloved father, to whom I owe everything.

Acknowledgments

The authors wish to express their gratitude to the two anonymous referees for their valuable and constructive comments, as well as to the Publisher, Palgrave Macmillan-Springer Nature, the Executive Editor, Tula Weis, and the Production Editor, Supraja Yegnaraman, for their kind and attentive support during the final revision of this book.

Contents

List of Figures

List of Tables

CHAPTER 1

Overview

Relationship lending has emerged as a critical aspect of the bank-business relationship, particularly in the context of information asymmetries and financial constraints. The interplay between asymmetric information, switching costs, credit rationing, relationship lending, and bank lending behaviour constitutes a rich area of research within financial economics (Alessandrini et al., 2009; Beck et al., 2018; Berger & Udell, 1995b; Degryse & Ongena, 2008; Murro et al., 2023; Ongena & Smith, 2000; Udell, 2018; Vesala, 2007).

Within the context of the changes of the last two decades (financial crisis of 2007–2008, sovereign debt crisis of 2010–2011, pandemic crisis of 2020, advent of Fintech and shadow banking, Basel Accords update, etc.), our focus will be on the factors contributing to the transformation of the banks' lending function and corporate financial needs, and thus on the evolution of the bank-business relationship. To do that, we focus on how "market failures" characterizing the banking sector (asymmetric information, switching costs, etc.) affect the provision of financial services, and in this way, we investigate the bank-business relationship and its determinants. The aim is to analyze firms' competitive challenges towards a new entrepreneurial model, which requires innovative financial management, and how banks can respond to these renewed financial needs. Then we will analyze how regulatory environments shape lending decisions in the presence of information asymmetries and financial constraints.

P. Brighi and M. Mussoni, *The Bank-Business Relationship*,
https://doi.org/10.1007/978-3-031-91068-5_1

This book aims to analyze the rationales behind the recent banking system transformations, driven by both endogenous processes (the characterization of the financial and banking services as "credence goods" and their regulatory implications, the increasing technological innovations, and the "twin transition" towards digitalization and sustainability, the consolidation process to achieve greater operational efficiency) and exogenous factors (the many systematic crises of the last two decades and the resulting numerous regulatory changes). The book aims to comprehensively examine these dynamics, drawing upon the latest theoretical insights and empirical evidence.

The book begins by reviewing the foundational literature to provide a nuanced understanding of this field's conceptual underpinnings: asymmetric information between lenders and borrowers, credit rationing and financial constraints are the focus of Chapters 2 and 3. It then discusses how different institutional contexts influence the effectiveness of relationship lending mechanisms in mitigating financial constraints and shaping bank lending behaviour. Chapter 4 first analyzes the lending function and relationship lending as an internal way by which the financial system tries to overcome the costs due to asymmetric information, then presents the corresponding implications on the bank-business relationship and the evolution over time of corporate banking and bank lending behaviour. The policy implications for financial regulation, banking supervision, and public policy will be discussed by highlighting the role of regulatory frameworks in fostering relationship lending practices, enhancing access to credit for financially constrained firms, and promoting financial stability. Chapter 5 focuses on the banking regulation of financial risks and capital requirements—seen as an external solution to reduce credit rationing and its recent evolution in light of the many economic crises of the last two decades—in particular by delving into the forward-looking logic underlying the guidelines on Loan Origination and Monitoring (LOM), and the strengthening of the Basel Accords to enhance the banking system's stability. Chapter 6 analyzes the future implications of digital transformation and the Environmental, Social, and Governance (ESG) factors for banking risks. Finally, Chapter 7 concludes the book.

In more detail, Chapter 2, 'Asymmetric Information in Banking', analyzes the important role of information asymmetries in the bank-firm relationship, particularly concerning the lending function. Information asymmetries can lead to opportunistic behaviours, such as adverse selection and moral hazard, which in turn may result in banking market failures, like credit rationing.

Chapter 3, 'Credit Rationing and Financial Constraints', presents how credit rationing occurs when the demand for credit exceeds the supply; i.e., whenever the price of credit (the interest rate) is lower than the equilibrium, and borrowers are unable to obtain loans despite their willingness to pay higher interest rates. The challenge is to understand why banks, instead of increasing the interest rate on loans to bring the market back into equilibrium—as suggested by neoclassical price theory—prefer rationing part of the clientele. From an empirical standpoint, credit rationing remains a phenomenon that is difficult to quantify. Traditionally, credit rationing represents a problem for firms for both obtaining loans and bearing their costs, affecting both loan interest rates and the quantity of loans granted and utilized. In this way, credit rationing causes a certain rigidity in both loan quantities and prices, and therefore, the loan risk premium—the difference between the loans' interest rates and the risk-free rate—negatively correlates with market interest rates. The rigidity in interest rates implies that banks prefer not to increase the interest rate beyond a certain threshold to limit the potential risks of adverse selection and moral hazard. Several empirical studies suggest that credit rationing is particularly widespread among start-ups, small and young companies and firms investing in Research and Development (R&D). Financial constraints become more pronounced during economic crises, such as those that characterized the last decade (Bofondi et al., 2018; Brighi & Venturelli 2017).

Chapter 4, 'Relationship Lending, Transaction Lending and Corporate Banking', shows how a repeated and continuous relationship between a bank and a firm may alleviate these constraints and limit the impact of credit rationing on the firm's financing decisions. Relationship lending, or relational credit, is characterized by a relationship between a bank and a firm based primarily on confidential and non-codified information, known as soft information. This information is crucial for assessing the creditworthiness of clients characterized by informational opacity. Empirical evidence consistently highlights that a relationship developed on relational logic is associated with better lending conditions: higher credit quantities, lower interest rates, and reduced collateral requirements (Berger & Udell, 1995a; Petersen & Rajan, 1994).

However, the continuation of Chapter 4 shows how the relationship lending model does not preclude the use of more standardized and impersonal client relationships, such as transaction lending, which relies primarily on quantitative and objective information. Theoretical and empirical analyses suggest that these two models do not exclude but rather complement each other in what is referred to in the literature as the corporate banking model (Brighi et al., 2019; Udell, 2018). Relationship lending evolves into a more comprehensive and articulated model within corporate banking, characterized by different combinations of hard and soft information. Information asymmetry problems between banks and firms, and any consequent forms of credit rationing, can thus be mitigated through signalling mechanisms such as co-financing with own capital (Leland & Pyle, 1977) and the provision of collateral (Bester, 1987, 1994) or through the creation of an exclusive relationship with a specific bank, i.e., through relationship lending.

Chapter 5, 'Financial Risks and the Role of Banking Regulation', shows how supervisory authorities can introduce rules that discipline and incentivize banks to improve the borrowers' screening and monitoring in an attempt to mitigate information asymmetries and credit risk. This is one of the main reasons behind financial banking regulation and why it has become so special in recent years. In this chapter, we analyze some of the most important recent developments in financial risk regulation, i.e., the LOM guidelines and the Basel Accords. The recent EBA Guidelines on Loan Origination and Monitoring (EBA 2020) identify the processes and mechanisms for granting loans under robust and prudent standards. The LOM guidelines aim to enforce both a prudent loan bank's policy and fair customer protection and, at the same time, to ensure macroeconomic stability and resilience of the European banking system. The latest updates to the Basel Accords regarding bank capitalization aim to safeguard the banking system's stability. The three pillars of the Basel Accords establish (i) capital requirement for banks, (ii) prudential supervision, and (iii) market discipline. As part of the second pillar framework, we examine the Supervisory Review and Evaluation Process (SREP) through its four key components: (i) the business model, (ii) the Internal Capital Adequacy Assessment Process (ICAAP), (iii) the Internal Liquidity Adequacy Assessment Process (ILAAP), and (iv) governance.

In addition to credit and traditional risks, banks are subject to many other new financial risks. Among the new risks, Chapter 6, 'The Digital and Green Twin Transition: Data Governance and Risk Management', focuses on the new Information and Communication Technologies (ICT) risks and Environmental, Social and Governance (ESG) risks. The recent technological innovations are leading to a digital transformation of finance, such that banks are increasingly moving towards the so-called 'twin transition': the digital transition, referring mainly to Fintech and the Artificial Intelligence (AI) revolution, and the sustainability transition, referring mainly to the impact of ESG factors on banking risks. The United Nations 2030 goals, and the European commitment to the Green Deal opened the financial debate on non-financial risks, including ESG risks. Awareness about environmental protection and the corresponding governance sustainability represents a cross-cutting goal within financial intermediaries and beyond. ESG risks depend on the financial impacts of transitioning to a circular and more sustainable economy, and therefore they can have different degrees of significance in the short, medium and long term. The technological innovations of Fintech are creating new competitors for the banking system, such that traditional banks, to face this new competition, need to strengthen through aggregations with other banks that allow not only to achieve economies of scale and scope but also to innovate.

References

Alessandrini, P., Presbitero, A. F., & Zazzaro, A. (2009). Banks, distances and firms' financing constraints. *Review of Finance, 13*(2), 261–307.

Beck, T., Degryse, H., De Haas, R., & Van Horen, N. (2018). When arm's length is too far: Relationship banking over the credit cycle. *Journal of Financial Economics, 127*(1), 174–196.

Berger, A. N., & Udell, G. F. (1995a). Relationship lending and lines of credit in small firm finance. *The Journal of Business, 68*(3), 351–381.

Berger, A. N., & Udell, G. F. (1995b). Universal banking and the future of small business lending.

Bester, H. (1987). The role of collateral in credit markets with imperfect information. *European Economic Review, 31*, 887–899.

Bester, H. (1994). The role of collateral in a model of debt renegotiation. *Journal of Money, Credit and Banking, 26*(1), 72–86.

Bofondi, M., Carpinelli, L., & Sette, E. (2018). Credit supply during a sovereign debt crisis. *Journal of the European Economic Association, 16*(3), 696–729.

Brighi, P., Lucarelli, C., & Venturelli, V. (2019). Predictive strength of lending technologies in funding SMEs. *Journal of Small Business Management, 57*, 1350–1377.

Brighi, P., & Venturelli, V. (2017). Credit rationing and the role of non-performing loans: An empirical investigation on Italian SMEs. *Journal of Financial Stability, 33*, 36–47.

Degryse, H., & Ongena, S. (2008). Competition and regulation in the banking sector: A review of the empirical evidence on the sources of bank rents. In A. Thakor, & A. Boot (Eds.), *Handbook of financial intermediation and banking* (pp. 483–554). Elsevier Science.

European Banking Authority (EBA). (2020). Guidelines on loan origination and monitoring (LOM). EBA/GL/2020/06.

Leland, H. E., & Pyle, D. H. (1977). Informational asymmetries, financial structure and financial intermediation. *The Journal of Finance, 32*(2), 371–387.

Murro, P., Oliviero, T., & Zazzaro, A. (2023). Relationship lending and employment decisions in firms' bad times. *Journal of Financial and Quantitative Analysis, 58*(6), 2657–2691.

Ongena, S., & Smith, D. C. (2000). What determines the number of bank relationships? Cross-country evidence. *Journal of Financial Intermediation, 9*(1), 26–56.

Petersen, M. A., & Rajan, R. G. (1994). The benefits of lending relationships: Evidence from small business data. *The Journal of Finance, 49*(1), 3–37.

Udell, G. F. (2018). SME access to intermediated credit: What do we know and what don't we know? *Journal of Financial Intermediation, 32*, 34–49.

Vesala, T. (2007). Switching costs and relationship profits in bank lending. *Journal of Banking and Finance, 31*, 477–493.

CHAPTER 2

Asymmetric Information in Banking

2.1 Information Asymmetries in Banks' Lending Function

Early works in the field of asymmetric information date back to the 1950s, but the methodological approach was substantially reformulated with the advent of information theory in the late 1980s. Information theory is particularly applicable to markets and financial intermediaries, given the characteristics of informational asymmetries and uncertainty in which they operate.[1] The pioneering contributions of Akerlof (1970), Spence (1973), Stiglitz (1975) and Stiglitz and Rothschild (1976) analyze the problem of uncertainty about the quality of traded goods as a premise for the failure of markets for used cars, labour, education and insurance. These theoretical frameworks are also applicable to financial markets, which are characterized by the exchange of future promises of payment for the immediate availability of financial resources. The economic reliability of such promises and, indirectly, the efficiency of financial markets

[1] The concept of uncertainty plays a fundamental role in the study of financial markets. Its precise formalization dates back to Savage's pioneering contribution in 1954. Subsequent developments gave rise to the theory of decision-making under uncertainty: see Tirole (2010).

P. Brighi and M. Mussoni, *The Bank-Business Relationship*,
https://doi.org/10.1007/978-3-031-91068-5_2

crucially depend on two factors: (i) the imperfect distribution of information regarding the possibility that promises will be honoured, and (ii) the confidentiality of the information assets of each operator.[2]

These considerations are crucial for evaluating financial contracts. The reliability of a company presenting itself in the banking or securities market to raise funds influences the quality that potential creditors attribute to it. Furthermore, the availability of information—whether qualitative or quantitative[3]—affects the definition of the contractual form and, thus, the structure of the incentives incorporated into the contract.[4]

The literature on financial markets often resorts to information theory, focusing on the effects of adverse selection and moral hazard in situations of asymmetric information (see Sect. 2.2). The first application in the financial field of the theory of informational asymmetries and the so-called principal-agent model concerned the credit market and rationing problems, starting with the works of Jaffee and Russell (1976) and Stiglitz and Weiss (1981). In credit relationships, a situation of asymmetric information between the borrower (the agent) and the lender (the principal) is easily recognizable. In particular, the borrower often has superior information, both in terms of quantity and quality, about the investment project she intends to undertake, so that she has an informational advantage over the lender. It follows that the relationship between the parties is structurally characterized by an informational asymmetry to the disadvantage of the lender (the principal). This situation, known as ex-ante information asymmetry, or *adverse selection*, may result in pre-contractual opportunistic behaviour. Furthermore, once the

[2] It is well-known, indeed, that as soon as information becomes public, its value diminishes. See, for example, Pagano and Jappelli (1993) and Battacharya and Chiesa (1995). James and Wier's (1988, p. 49) example is illustrative: 'Companies may not wish to reveal to the public the information that lenders require. For example, suppose a firm is raising capital for an investment that involves a new marketing strategy, the value of which would be reduced if competitors learn of it prior to its introduction. Borrowing from insiders permits the firm to keep its strategy secret'. In contrast to public debt, extant research depicts privately placed debt as inside debt given the close proximity in the relation between the borrower and lender (Bhattacharya & Chiesa, 1995; Rajan, 1992).

[3] Liberti and Petersen (2019) writes: 'Hard information is quantitative, easy to store and transmit in impersonal ways, and its content is independent of the collection process. [...] Information which is difficult to completely summarize in a numeric score is what I will call soft information.'

[4] Examples of incentives incorporated in the contractual form of loans are collateral and covenants (Rajan & Winton, 1995).

exchange is made, an informational advantage remains, such that an ex-post information asymmetry or *moral hazard* arises, and the borrower may adopt post-contractual behaviour that deviates from the contractual agreements.[5]

Probably the most important aspect of banking that is affected by information asymmetries is the lending function, also known as the intermediation function, which consists of collecting funds from surplus units and transferring them to deficit units through loan-granting operations.[6] There are two primary issues related to the lending function: assessing the ability to repay borrowers (credit risk of individual transactions) and constructing a loan portfolio that balances risk and return.

Managing credit operations inherently involves credit risk, which is the risk that the counterparty may not fully or partially repay the interest and/or the funds received. Credit risk also includes the risk of market value losses in cash flows related to borrower positions due to macroeconomic factors (e.g., inflation, political crises) or unexpected deterioration in the creditworthiness of individual borrowers (Basel Committee on Banking Supervision, 2000). Bank losses due to credit risk can thus result from borrower default risk, involving bankruptcy and failure to repay the loan, and from creditworthiness deterioration risk or migration risk (Altman & Saunders, 1998).

These risks often stem from asymmetric information problems, which underlie the theory of financial intermediation and justify the existence of financial intermediaries. Asymmetric information is a fundamental issue in the banking sector, where lenders must often make decisions with incomplete information about borrowers' true ability to repay. Akerlof's (1970) theory of the "market for lemons" illustrates how quality uncertainty can

[5] Note that although this book analyzes the problem of information asymmetries from the bank's asset side—between the bank and the enterprise—similar issues also exist between the bank and the depositor. In the latter case, the 'weak' party of the contract is the depositor, as they do not have perfect information on the quality of the investment projects the bank will undertake. This form of information asymmetry lies at the core of bank run phenomena. For a deeper understanding, see the seminal work by Diamond and Dybvig (1983).

[6] The other functions performed by banks are: (i) the monetary function, which involves the production of currency and the provision of payment services, and (ii) the function of monetary policy transmission, which refers to the actions undertaken by the monetary authority through banks to guide and alter the quantity of money, credit, and finance in the system (see Mishkin & Eakins, 2024).

lead to market inefficiencies, a concept applicable also to bank lending. When banks cannot accurately distinguish between high- and low-risk (high- and low-quality) borrowers, they may either charge higher interest rates to all applicants or restrict lending altogether, creating a suboptimal allocation of resources and hindering economic growth (Stiglitz & Weiss, 1981).

In financial intermediation, access to information is essential, as information encompasses the set of knowledge related to a certain object and subject, its organization, processing, and dissemination (Greenbaum et al., 2019). Within the financial system, information serves as both input and output, and financial intermediaries are tasked with generating sufficient information on firms' economic situations at acceptable costs. Moreover, financial markets are characterized by the highest possible information asymmetries, both before and after the purchase of financial products, such that financial products are classified as *credence goods* (Darby & Karni, 1973; Inderst & Ottaviani, 2012a, b).[7] While some information in financial choices may be public and accessible to all operators, often, it is private and accessible only to a few (select) operators.

2.2 Adverse Selection and Moral Hazard in Banking Markets

Information asymmetries are classified into two main categories, which can both be described by the so-called principal-agent model. The first type of information asymmetries is represented by ex-ante asymmetries, where one party (the agent) has information that the other (the principal) cannot observe before the contract is concluded (hidden information) and can use it to her exclusive advantage. In the context of lending, banks often have less information than the borrowers themselves about their ability to repay the loan. Ex-ante information asymmetry can lead

[7] Credence goods are goods or services whose quality or effectiveness is difficult for consumers to evaluate, even after consumption. A typical example is medical services: when patients consult a specialist for treatment, they rely on the expert's knowledge to determine the appropriate cure. However, after receiving the treatment, patients—due to their lack of expertise—often cannot assess whether the improvement in their health is the result of the treatment or due to natural recovery. This uncertainty stems from information asymmetry between the provider and the consumer, a key characteristic of credence goods (Darby & Karni, 1973).

to valuation errors, known as ***adverse selection*** problems, occurring before the transaction. This happens when borrowers with a higher probability of undesirable outcomes (i.e., are less trustworthy) actively look for loans and are more likely to obtain them, potentially causing lenders to refrain from lending altogether—a market failure, as described by Akerlof (1970).

The second type of information asymmetries consists of ex-post asymmetries, where the parties involved in the exchange initially (ex-ante) have equal information regarding the relevant aspects of the contract. However, once the contract is concluded (ex-post), only one party (the agent) has access to certain information and can take potentially harmful actions (hidden action) that are not controllable by the other party (the principal). In fact, the information gathered to overcome adverse selection does not completely eliminate information asymmetry, which can reemerge ex-post after signing the contract. As a result, investors may not always be capable of assessing whether the borrower will behave as declared during the contract signing, leading to a potential opportunistic behaviour by the borrower, called ***moral hazard***. Moral hazard arises when the borrower engages in riskier actions ex-post, increasing the probability of default (Holmström, 1979), thus reducing the likelihood of loan repayment and potentially leading lenders to decide not to grant the loan. In both cases of adverse selection and moral hazard, the less informed party (the principal) needs to identify a mechanism (institutional tool) to avoid or manage the opportunistic behaviour of the counterpart (the agent), and this mechanism necessarily involves incurring costs. Recently, Park (2023) highlighted that asymmetric information between borrowers and lenders creates significant inefficiencies in investment in terms of either the exclusion of high-quality projects or the inclusion of low-quality projects. This dichotomy is crucial because it illustrates the dual challenges posed by information asymmetry: preventing good investments from receiving funding and allowing poor investments to proceed.

Since asymmetric information means that information is distributed unevenly among different economic agents, effective management of the lending function requires efficient information gathering, processing and systematization. According to the theory of ***delegated monitoring*** (Diamond, 1984), financial intermediaries (indirect financing channel) possess an informational advantage in managing information about borrowing customers compared to other financial operators (Leland &

Pyle, 1977), making them preferable to markets (direct financing channel) in transferring resources from surplus to deficit units. In fact, within the direct relationship between surplus and deficit units, savers/investors are at an informational disadvantage compared to the borrowing enterprise since they can rely only on publicly available information, which is inherently incomplete. On the contrary, borrowers have superior information on their economic, financial and asset situations, as well as precise knowledge of their economic activity's risks and future prospects (Mishkin, 2006).

The literature on informational asymmetries, starting with Leland and Pyle (1977), suggests that when the benefits derived from the greater information produced through economies of scale in ex-ante screening and ex-post monitoring—by financial intermediaries—exceed the costs enterprises and investors would incur for direct market financing and oversight, it becomes more advantageous to rely on banks rather than markets (Diamond, 1984). This reasoning is especially relevant for small and medium-sized enterprises (SMEs), where the costs of managing informational asymmetries are significantly higher than for large corporations. In fact, in economic systems with a high prevalence of SMEs, the presence of informational asymmetries between the lender (the bank) and the borrower (the enterprise) is particularly pronounced. These firms are subject to lower informational disclosure obligations compared to large corporations, which are typically structured as joint-stock companies.

In general, in a framework of informational asymmetries where the entrepreneur's risk and/or the investment project are not publicly known, addressing moral hazard and adverse selection risks through the banking system is undoubtedly less costly than direct finance. Financial intermediaries, through their evaluation of potential borrowers' projects, perform screening and monitoring functions that prevent the free-rider problem and offer differentiated contracts based on the selected borrower's type and risk. Additionally, banks are more effective in exerting pressure for debt repayment compared to atomistic markets (Diamond, 1984; Stiglitz & Weiss, 1981).[8] In fact, financial intermediaries, due to their specialization, can acquire the necessary information and assess its credibility, thereby reducing—though not eliminating—both ex-ante and ex-post information asymmetries. These activities fall under typical credit

[8] For further insights into the reasons that justify the existence and superiority of banks over markets in the theory of financial intermediation, refer to Greenbaum et al. (2019).

risk management activities of banks and primarily involve two instruments: (i) screening and monitoring individual credit operations, and (ii) assessing credit risk and diversifying the entire loan portfolio (Berger & Udell, 2006).

Informational problems primarily concern the selection of projects to finance—the so-called *screening* phase—and the subsequent monitoring of the financed entity's actions (the monitoring phase). Screening problems arise mainly from the difficulty external investors face in assessing the profitability of the financed project, as well as the potential for adverse selection phenomena during the information transmission process (Leland & Pyle, 1977). Specifically, potential investors find it challenging to distinguish between a 'good' quality enterprise, which issues shares in order to share the risk of a 'good' investment project with its partners, and a 'bad' quality enterprise, which aims to offload the excessive risk of its investment project onto third parties (the bank), similarly to the Akerlof's 'lemons' issue (1970). Screening therefore involves evaluating investment projects before loan granting and contractualization.[9] In fact, to mitigate the adverse selection risk, banks must select the best borrowers by acquiring information about the applicant and the feasibility of the project in order to estimate their default probability and reduce credit risks (Stiglitz & Weiss, 1981). As we will see, the necessary information for the screening phase can be gathered through means such as: (i) public credit registries (see Sect. 2.4); (ii) specialized external agencies, i.e., rating agencies and credit bureaus (see Sect. 2.4); (iii) internally by the bank based on its relationship history with the customer, i.e., by relationship lending (see Chapter 4).

Once the project selection problem is addressed and the firm is financed, *monitoring* the entrepreneur's behaviour becomes crucial. Monitoring aims to ensure that the entrepreneur's actions and the use of obtained funds align with the declared objectives, thereby preventing moral hazard (ex-post informational asymmetries). This can be achieved through: (i) enforcing behavioural rules; (ii) providing incentives for

[9] A different way to overcome the adverse selection problem is by initiative of the high-quality enterprises, which desire differentiating themselves from low-quality ones through signalling. Signalling entails costs that only high-quality firms are willing to bear to differentiate themselves from low-quality firms, in order to make their investment projects more attractive for external investors. This form of self-selection ensures that the signalling costs are too high for low-quality producers to imitate (Spence, 1973).

the enterprise to act in the bank's interests; and (iii) verifying that the economic outcomes and profits from the investment project are distributed according to the pre-established contractual agreements. Monitoring ensures, therefore, that borrowers maintain behaviours aligned with the agreed objectives, preventing moral hazard. Its purpose is to verify the continued conditions of creditworthiness assigned during loan granting: this goal can be achieved on one side through contractual clauses and on the other side through relationship lending, i.e., personalized, long-term relationships with customers (Boot, 2000). Contractual clauses encourage borrowers to maintain 'good' behaviours by setting minimum liquidity levels, financial burden coverage, or by sharing confidential information with the bank. Relationship lending allows the bank to mitigate at the same time both ex-ante (screening phase) and ex-post (monitoring phase) information asymmetries. In fact, knowledge of the past entrusted party's behaviour can facilitate monitoring, reducing the risk of moral hazard (Berger & Udell, 1995).

In summary, asymmetric information in banking means borrowers (the agents) have more information about their financial health and business prospects than lenders (the principals). This asymmetry can lead to adverse selection and moral hazard, resulting in many potential issues in lending decisions. Besides screening and monitoring functions, two other crucial mitigating factors affect the way banks can manage these informational asymmetries: trust and relational capital, both of which are strictly linked with relationship lending (see Chapter 4). Trust between the bank and the firm reduces the perceived risk associated with lending, allowing banks to make more informed decisions. Fukuyama (1995) highlights that trust can lower transaction costs and facilitate economic interactions. In banking, trust can be built through historical relationships, reputation and repeated interactions.

Consequently, when banks trust their customers, they are more likely to offer favourable lending terms as the perceived risk of default decreases (Guiso et al., 2004). Relational capital, which encompasses the value derived from relationships and networks, further enhances the lending process. Berger and Udell (1995) argue that relationship banking allows financial institutions to gather proprietary information over time, thus reducing the informational asymmetry. Long-term relationships enable banks to monitor customers more effectively, understand their financial needs and offer customized solutions. This relational capital becomes a competitive advantage, promoting more efficient credit allocation and fostering customer loyalty (Boot, 2000).

Empirical studies underscore the significance of relational capital in banking. For example, Petersen and Rajan (1994) found that firms with strong banking relationships benefit from better credit terms and increased access to capital. These relationships provide banks with insights into the borrowers' business cycles, cash flows and management quality, which are not readily available through formal financial statements alone. Such qualitative information, derived from relational capital, complements traditional credit assessment tools, leading to more nuanced lending decisions. Park (2023) adopts a general equilibrium framework to analyze investment efficiency across two sectors: opaque (where information is asymmetric) and transparent (where information is fully known). This approach allows for a nuanced understanding of how credit allocation between these sectors impacts overall investment efficiency and shows the need for improved information sharing among market participants to mitigate informational friction. Additionally, extending loan guarantee schemes and designing better-targeted subsidies could help mitigate the adverse effects of credit rationing and redlining. However, the paper cautions that these interventions must be carefully designed to balance efficiency gains with potential economic distortions.

More recently, Claessens et al. (2024) provide a nuanced analysis of how the length of firm-bank relationships influences the depth and nature of banks' private information, which in turn affects internal credit ratings and lending decisions. Their research reveals that as these relationships extend, banks acquire more profound insights into borrowers' financial health, peaking around the five-year mark. This accumulation of private information leads to more accurate internal credit assessments, which are instrumental in determining loan terms and conditions. Furthermore, the study highlights that the evolution of private information is particularly significant for smaller, leveraged firms and during periods outside of economic crises. These findings underscore the critical role of both soft information (e.g., qualitative assessments from ongoing interactions) and hard information (e.g., quantitative financial data) in the firm evaluation process (see Chapter 4). Integrating these information types enables banks to make more informed and effective lending decisions, reinforcing the importance of a complementary approach in credit risk assessment.

In another study, Beyhaghi and Weitzner (2023) use confidential regulatory data to show that banks' private information significantly impacts their internal credit ratings and lending decisions. Specifically, the study finds that when banks increase their expected loss estimates for a firm, this often precedes negative stock and bond returns in the subsequent quarter, as well as a higher likelihood of negative earnings surprises. This suggests that banks' internal evaluations contain valuable insights not immediately reflected in public markets. Furthermore, the research indicates that banks are more likely to update their risk assessments when they have greater loan exposure or when issuing new loans, highlighting the role of internal private information in shaping credit allocation decisions. These findings underscore the importance of banks' private information in their decision-making processes and the corresponding potential influence on broader financial market outcomes.

In conclusion, asymmetric information significantly challenges bank lending behaviour by introducing uncertainties about borrowers' ability to repay. Screening, monitoring, trust and relational capital serve as critical mechanisms to overcome these challenges. Screening increases the ex-ante probability of financing creditworthy investment projects, while monitoring ensures that borrowers maintain behaviours aligned with the agreed objectives. Trust reduces perceived risks and facilitates smoother financial transactions, while relational capital, built through long-term interactions, provides banks with valuable proprietary information (see Chapter 4).

2.3 Asymmetric Information and Agency Costs

The concept of agency costs derives from information asymmetries and is particularly linked to the moral hazard case in a framework where not only is there an asymmetric distribution of information between parties, but acquiring information incurs costs. Agency costs, in particular, are those incurred ex-post to manage possible moral hazard behaviour. Once again, the principal-agent model helps identify the scenario at hand: the principal, who does not have access to the information, 'hires' the agent to perform a task or activity in her interest so that there is a conflict of interest between them and the agent has exclusive access to reserved and private information. The agent, because of this informational advantage, may engage in opportunistic behaviour at the expense of the principal, potentially leading to a market failure (moral hazard). To avoid or manage the agent's opportunistic behaviour, the principal must identify a mechanism, such as monitoring or incentivizing the agent to act in her interest, which entails agency costs.

We analyze here two main typologies of agency costs: debt agency costs and equity agency costs. From the firm's point of view, debt agency costs specifically arise from the conflict of interest between its shareholders (the agent) and external investors (the principal). Shareholders have an interest in pursuing riskier investment projects because of their higher expected returns compared to those agreed upon with external investors. If the investment is successful, the firm (and thus the shareholders) appropriates the surplus, whereas if it fails, the costs are borne by the investors. In this framework, investors (the principal) have less information than the shareholders (the agent), who can, therefore, engage in opportunistic behaviour (undertaking riskier investments) to the detriment of the investors, leading to implicit agency costs for the latter. The consequence of this informational asymmetry is that some incentives are necessary for the investors to finance the firm, incentives that imply an increase in the cost of debt and make it more expensive than internal financing. Consequently, firms with high debt agency costs should reduce their level of debt financing.

Equity agency costs, as described by Jensen (1986), are associated with the conflict of interest between the firm's management (the agent) and shareholders (the principal). In fact, the management may take advantage of its control of free cash flow[10] by undertaking business initiatives that deviate from maximizing the firm's value to extracting its rents. In this case, the shareholders (the principal) have less information than the management (the agent), who may engage in opportunistic behaviour (initiating projects for personal gain) to the detriment of the shareholders, resulting in implicit agency costs for the shareholders. The tool available to shareholders to reduce these costs is leveraging debt, which removes resources from the control of management and can correct such opportunistic behaviour. Therefore, equity agency costs are inversely correlated with the degree of leverage—the ratio of debt to equity—that characterizes the firm's financial structure.

[10] Free cash flow consists of cash flows that exceed those required to finance all projects; i.e., cash flows with a positive net present value.

2.4 The Role of Public Credit Registries, Rating Agencies and Credit Bureaus

The public credit registries are centralized databases—essentially information archives—managed by central banks, which collect and store data on the credit exposures of households and businesses towards the banking and financial system; i.e., information on borrowers' credit history. These databases collect the information flows coming from financial intermediaries each time a customer requests a loan for an amount equal to or greater than a certain threshold value, which is reduced if the customer is in default.[11] The information includes the amount of credit requested and granted to the customer, besides the guarantees received, so that these registries provide financial institutions with detailed data to evaluate the ability to repay of potential borrowers, given that an accurate assessment of creditworthiness is crucial for reducing default rates and maintaining financial stability.

Central banks then provide feedback to intermediaries about the total credit exposures of their customers, the type of financing they have overall received, and whether their payments are regular. Intermediaries can also request information on potential customers who have submitted a loan application or are about to provide collateral in order to assess their ability to repay.

The main goal of public credit registries is to improve the process of creditworthiness assessment (Jones, 2019). The information retrieved from these registries provides a historical view of the customers, together with a detailed description of their behaviour in financial relationships. A second goal of the credit registries is to improve the quality of the credit granted by intermediaries and strengthen the stability of the financial system. Lastly, they facilitate access to credit for "creditworthy" customers since those with a good credit history are more likely to obtain financing at better conditions.

Jones (2019) finds that the use of credit registries significantly reduces information asymmetry between lenders and borrowers so that by accessing comprehensive credit histories, banks can make more informed lending decisions. As a result, credit registries affect lending decisions by

[11] Customers are classified as being in default when they experience severe difficulties in repaying their debt. This classification implies that the bank has assessed the customer's overall financial situation.

providing data on past defaults, current debts and repayment behaviour, and in this way, they allow banks to differentiate between high-risk and low-risk borrowers more effectively. With better information, banks can grant credit more confidently, potentially increasing the availability of credit to borrowers who might have been otherwise denied due to a lack of information. Moreover, access to credit register data is associated with lower default rates because banks can avoid lending to high-risk borrowers and can price loans more accurately based on the assessed risk.

Ultimately, credit registries enhance the transparency and efficiency of financial markets, in this way playing a crucial role in financial intermediation by improving the accuracy of creditworthiness assessments, thereby reducing the problems associated with information asymmetry. Financial institutions should always integrate credit register data into their credit assessment processes to improve loan performance and reduce the incidence of bad loans. At the same time, for savers, the use of credit registries can lead to fairer and more competitive lending rates, as banks can more accurately assess risk and reduce the premiums charged to offset unknown risks.

Besides credit registries, another important way for gathering the necessary information for the screening phase consists of credit bureaus, rating agencies and rating models. Rating agencies are specialized entities that gather and process detailed information on credit-borrowing enterprises. This information is independently analyzed to produce a rating that summarizes the quality of loans, i.e., the credit risk, in terms of the firm's risk of default. Among the most well-known rating models is the Altman model, also known as the Z-score model (Altman, 1968). However, in recent years, alternative models with improved predictive capabilities have been proposed in the literature.

The original Z-score model is based on a linear discriminant statistical analysis, which allows for classifying the statistical units into two groups, bankrupt and non-bankrupt companies, based on a set of known characteristics, i.e., by combining five financial ratios using a set of weights derived from statistical analysis. The initial study was conducted on a sample of publicly traded U.S. companies (sample period 1946–1965), resulting in the following formula:

$$Z_i = 1.2x_{i,1} + 1.4x_{i,2} + 3.3x_{i,3} + 0.6x_{i,4} + 0.99x_{i,5} \qquad (2.1)$$

where:

- $x_{i,1}$ = working capital/total assets.
- $x_{i,2}$ = retained earnings/total assets.
- $x_{i,3}$ = earnings before interest and taxes (EBIT)/total assets.
- $x_{i,4}$ = market value of equity/book value of total liabilities.
- $x_{i,5}$ = sales/total assets.

The result of this model is the Z-score of each borrower, which is compared to Altman's threshold value of 1.81. If the Z-score is above this value, the borrower is considered to be at low risk; if below, the borrower is deemed to be at high risk.[12] In the literature, there are alternative rating indicators proposed by other scholars,[13] but a first adaptation was proposed by Altman himself (Altman et al., 1998) for non-U.S. firms. In general, the original Z-score model was primarily designed for publicly traded manufacturing firms, while the subsequent adaptations, such as the Z'-score and Z''-score models, extended their applicability to non-manufacturing firms and private companies, respectively (Altman, 2000).

Another extension of the original Altman Z-score model is the ZETA® model, which addresses some limitations of the Z-score model by adapting it to a broader range of firms. Developed by Altman himself, together with Haldeman and Narayanan (1977), the primary goal of the ZETA® model was to improve the predictive power of bankruptcy models for a wider variety of firms, including both manufacturing and non-manufacturing firms and to provide a more comprehensive assessment over different economic cycles. The ZETA® model incorporates a broader set of financial ratios and variables compared to the original Z-score model and, in particular, includes seven financial ratios that were found to be significant predictors of bankruptcy through empirical research. While the exact formulation of the ZETA® model is proprietary, the key variables typically include Return on Assets (ROA), Stability of Earnings, Debt Service Coverage, Cumulative Profitability, Liquidity, Capitalization and Firm Size. These ratios and variables are combined using a proprietary

[12] Specifically, according to Altman's research, a *Z*-score above 2.99 indicates a low probability of bankruptcy, while a score below 1.81 suggests a high risk of financial distress (Altman, 1968).

[13] See Becchetti et al. (2010).

algorithm to generate a ZETA® score, which can be interpreted similarly to the *Z-score* in terms of assessing the likelihood of bankruptcy.[14]

Two different indicators commonly used in literature (see, among others, Brighi et al., 2019) are attributed to Zmijewski (1984) and Ohlson (1980), which work oppositely with respect to previous models; that is, a higher score is associated with higher default risk. The formula of the Zmijewski (1984) indicator is given by:

$$\begin{aligned} \text{Zm-Score}_i &= -4.336 - 4.513\left(\frac{\text{NI}}{\text{TA}}\right) \\ &\quad + 5.679\left(\frac{\text{TL}}{\text{TA}}\right) + 0.004\left(\frac{\text{CL}}{\text{CA}}\right), \end{aligned} \tag{2.2}$$

where TA represents total assets, NI net income, TL total liabilities, CL current liabilities and CA current assets. The formula of the Ohlson (1980) indicator is instead given by:

$$\begin{aligned} \text{O-score}_i &= -1.32 - 0.407\log(\text{TA}) + 6.03\left(\frac{\text{TL}}{\text{TA}}\right) \\ &\quad - 1.43\left(\frac{\text{WC}}{\text{TA}}\right) + 0.0757\left(\frac{\text{CL}}{\text{CA}}\right) \\ &\quad - 2.37\left(\frac{\text{NI}}{\text{TA}}\right) - 1.83\left(\frac{\text{FFO}}{\text{TA}}\right) + 0.285(D_{\text{Loss}}) \\ &\quad - 1.72(D_{\text{TL}-\text{TA}}) - 0.521\left(\frac{\text{NI}_t - \text{NI}_{t-1}}{|\text{NI}_t| + |\text{NI}_{t-1}|}\right), \end{aligned} \tag{2.3}$$

where TA = total assets, WC = working capital, TL = total liabilities, CL = current liabilities, CA = current assets, NI = net income, FFO = funds from operations, D_{Loss} is a dummy variable equal to 1 if the firm has had losses in the last two years and $D_{\text{TL}-\text{TA}}$ is a dummy variable if total liabilities exceed total assets.

In general, the introduction of the Altman Z-score model marked a significant advancement in the field of credit risk assessment. It provided

[14] The ZETA® model has been widely adopted by financial institutions, credit rating agencies and regulatory bodies due to its enhanced accuracy and broader applicability. It has been particularly useful in assessing the financial health of large corporations and conglomerates, which may not fit neatly into the categories for which the original *Z*-score model was designed.

a robust, statistically validated tool for predicting corporate bankruptcy, which has been widely adopted by financial institutions, investors and regulators. Among the various validations and refinements to which the Z-score model has been subjected over the years, it is also noteworthy that Hillegeist et al. (2004) compared the predictive power of the Z-score model with other models, such as the Ohlson O-score and the neural network approaches, and found that while the Z-score remains valuable, integrating multiple models can enhance its accuracy. Another recent alternative model is the Campbell et al. (CHS) model (2008), which uses a broader set of predictors, including firm leverage, profitability and stock return volatility to estimate bankruptcy probabilities. The authors estimated the probability of corporate failure by using a dynamic logit model and by incorporating both accounting and market-based variables to predict financial distress. Key predictors include high leverage, low profitability, small market capitalization, poor past stock returns, high stock return volatility, low cash reserves, high market-to-book ratios and low stock prices. The CHS model has been shown to be more accurate than leading alternative measures of corporate failure risk[15] and has thus become a significant tool in financial research, offering insights into the determinants of corporate failure and the pricing anomalies associated with financially distressed stocks.

Recently, other researchers expanded on the Altman Z-score model and various credit rating methodologies, introducing adaptations and exploring new applications. An example is the application of the Z-score model as an early warning indicator for financial distress leading to bankruptcy and delisting, specifically focusing on firms listed on the Johannesburg Stock Exchange (Matanga & Holman, 2024). Other examples are the application of the Altman Z-score to predict financial distress in the nursing home industry, utilizing a modified version of the model tailored to this sector (Lord et al., 2020), and an extensive review that

[15] An intriguing finding from their research is that, since 1981, stocks with higher estimated failure probabilities have delivered anomalously low returns. Despite exhibiting higher standard deviations, market betas and loadings on value and small-cap risk factors, these financially distressed stocks underperform compared to those with lower failure risk. This pattern is particularly pronounced among stocks with potential informational or arbitrage-related frictions. These results challenge the notion that value and size effects in stock returns are compensation for financial distress risk.

delved into the evolution and diverse applications of the Altman Z-score model across various industries, highlighting its modifications and relevance in different sectors (Rashid et al., 2024).

In recent years, the rise of machine learning techniques and artificial intelligence (see Chapter 6) has led to the development of credit scoring models that leverage large datasets and complex algorithms to enhance predictive power. Models such as Support Vector Machines (SVM), random forests and neural networks have demonstrated superior performance in distinguishing between financially stable and distressed firms, particularly in the context of large-scale credit assessment applications. Some other examples of advancements in credit rating models are synthetic credit ratings, which use publicly available accounting and market-based information (Nissim, 2023), multi-modal deep learning, which integrates structured and unstructured data to enhance prediction accuracy (Tavakoli et al., 2025), and finally, Markov models for rating migration which account for economic state fluctuations and their impact on default probabilities (Kalkbrener & Packham, 2024). These alternative models provide improved predictive accuracy compared to traditional models, and their integration into risk assessment processes is essential for modern financial institutions.

Nevertheless, the Z-score model's simplicity and transparency have contributed to its enduring popularity. Despite the advent of more sophisticated techniques, including machine learning and artificial intelligence, the Z-score model remains a benchmark for evaluating financial distress and has profoundly influenced the development of credit risk assessment methodologies in banking. Its enduring relevance attests to its robustness and practical utility: as financial markets continue to evolve, the principles underpinning the *Z*-score model will likely remain integral to the development of new and improved rating models.

A similar job to that of rating agencies is done by credit bureaus, even if they serve slightly different purposes in the credit assessment ecosystem. Rating agencies evaluate the creditworthiness of companies, financial instruments and even sovereign nations; they assign credit ratings (e.g., AAA, BBB, junk status) to reflect the risk of default on bonds or loans, and their assessments influence investment decisions in capital markets (examples are Moody's, S&P Global, Fitch Ratings). Credit bureaus, on the other hand, collect and maintain credit information on individuals and businesses; they focus primarily on consumer and business credit history, compiling reports based on data from financial institutions, lenders, and other entities, and they provide credit scores (e.g., FICO, VantageScore) that summarize an individual's or business's ability to repay (examples are Equifax, Experian, TransUnion).

References

Akerlof, G. A. (1970). The market for 'lemons': Quality uncertainty and the market mechanism. *The Quarterly Journal of Economics, 84*(3), 488–500.

Altman, E. I. (1968). Financial ratios, discriminant analysis and the prediction of corporate bankruptcy. *The Journal of Finance, 23*(4), 589–609.

Altman, E. I. (2000). *Predicting financial distress of companies: Revisiting the Z-score and ZETA® models*. Stern School of Business, New York University.

Altman, E. I., Haldeman, R. G., & Narayanan, P. (1977). ZETA analysis: A new model to identify bankruptcy risk of corporations. *Journal of Banking & Finance, 1*(1), 29–54.

Altman, E. I., Hartzell, J., & Peck, M. (1998). Emerging market corporate bonds—A scoring system. In R. M. Levich (Eds.), *Emerging market capital flows. The New York University Salomon Center Series on Financial Markets and Institutions* (Vol. 2). Springer.

Altman, E. I., & Saunders, A. (1998). Credit risk measurement: Developments over the last 20 years. *Journal of Banking & Finance, 21*(11–12), 1721–1742.

Barbieri, L., Bofondi, M., Carpinelli, L., & Sette, E. (2020). Credit supply and productivity growth. *Journal of the European Economic Association, 18*(3), 1363–1393.

Basel Committee on Banking Supervision. (2000). Principles for the management of credit risk.

Becchetti, L., Castelli, A., & Hasan, I. (2010). Investment–cash flow sensitivities, credit rationing and financing constraints in small and medium-sized firms. *Small Business Economics, 35*, 467–497.

Berger, A. N., & Udell, G. F. (1995). Relationship lending and lines of credit in small firm finance. *Journal of Business, 68*(3), 351–381.

Berger, A. N., & Udell, G. F. (2006). A more complete conceptual framework for SME finance. *Journal of Banking & Finance, 30*(11), 2945–2966.

Beyhaghi, M., & Weitzner, G. (2023). *Are banks really informed? Evidence from their private information* (Working paper), Richmond Federal Reserve Bank.

Bhattacharya, S., & Chiesa, G. (1995). Proprietary information, financial intermediation, and research incentives. *Journal of Financial Intermediation, 4*(4), 328–357.

Boot, A. W. A. (2000). Relationship banking: What do we know? *Journal of Financial Intermediation, 9*(1), 7–25.

Brighi, P., Lucarelli, C., & Venturelli, V. (2019). Predictive strength of lending technologies in funding SMEs. *Journal of Small Business Management, 57*, 1350–1377.

Brighi, P., & Venturelli, V. (2017). Credit rationing and the role of non-performing loans: An empirical investigation on Italian SMEs. *Journal of Financial Stability, 33*, 36–47.

Campbell, J. Y., Hilscher, J., & Szilagyi, J. (2008). In search of distress risk. *The Journal of Finance, 63*(6), 2899–2939.

Claessens, S., Ongena, S., & Wang, T. (2024). 'If You Don't Know Me By Now...'. Banks' Private Information and Relationship Length, Swiss Finance Institute, Research Paper Series, 23-01.

Cowan, K., Drexler, A., & Yañez, Á. (2015). The effect of credit guarantees on credit availability and delinquency rates. *Journal of Banking & Finance, 59*, 98–110.

Darby, M. R., & Karni, E. (1973). Free competition and the optimal amount of fraud. *The Journal of Law and Economics, 16*(1), 67–88.

Diamond, D., & Dybvig, P. (1983). Bank runs, deposit insurance and liquidity. *Journal of Political Economy, 9*, 401–419.

Diamond, D. W. (1984). Financial intermediation and delegated monitoring. *The Review of Economic Studies, 51*(3), 393–414.

Fukuyama, F. (1995). Trust. In *The social virtues and the creation of prosperity*. Free Press Paperbacks.

Greenbaum, S. I., Thakor, A. V., & Boot, A. W. (2019). *Contemporary financial intermediation*. Academic Press.

Guiso, L., Sapienza, P., & Zingales, L. (2004). The role of social capital in financial development. *The American Economic Review, 94*(3), 526–556.

Hillegeist, S. A., Keating, E. K., Cram, D. P., & Lundstedt, K. G. (2004). Assessing the probability of bankruptcy. *Review of Accounting Studies, 9*(1), 5–34.

Holmström, B. (1979). Moral hazard and observability. *The Bell Journal of Economics, 10*(1), 74–91.

Inderst, R., & Ottaviani, M. (2012a). Competition through commissions and kickbacks. *American Economic Review, 102*(2), 780–809.

Inderst, R., & Ottaviani, M. (2012b). How (not) to pay for advice: A framework for consumer financial protection. *Journal of Financial Economics, 105*(2), 393–411.

Jaffee, D. M., & Russell, T. (1976). Imperfect information, uncertainty, and credit rationing. *The Quarterly Journal of Economics, 90*(4), 651–666.

James, C., & Wier, P. (1988). Are bank loans different? Some evidence from the stock market. *Journal of Applied Corporate Finance, 1*, 46–54.

Jensen, M. C. (1986). Agency costs of free cash flow, corporate finance, and takeovers. *American Economic Review, 76*(2), 323–329.

Jones, A. (2019). Assessing creditworthiness: The use of credit registers in financial intermediation. *International Journal of Bank Marketing, 37*(4), 879–895.

Kalkbrener, M., & Packham, N. (2024). A Markov approach to credit rating migration conditional on economic states, arXiv:2403.14868 [q-fin.RM].

Leland, H. E., & Pyle, D. H. (1977). Informational asymmetries, financial structure, and financial intermediation. *The Journal of Finance, 32*(2), 371–387.

Liberti, J. M., & Petersen, M. A. (2019). Information: Hard and soft. *The Review of Corporate Finance Studies, 8*(1), 1–41.

Lord, J., Landry, A., & Savage, G. T. (2020). Weech-Maldonado R. predicting nursing home financial distress using the Altman Z-Score. *INQUIRY: The Journal of Health Care Organization, Provision, and Financing, 57*.

Matanga, N., & Holman, G. (2024). Adapting Altman Z-score models for early warning signals: Evidence from delisted mining stocks on the Johannesburg Stock Exchange. *Investment Analysts Journal, 53*(3), 249–261.

Mishkin, F. S. (2006). *The economics of money, banking, and financial markets*. Addison Wesley.

Mishkin, F. S., & Eakins, S. (2024). *Financial markets and institutions, global edition* (10th ed.). Pearson.

Nissim, D. (2023). *Synthetic credit ratings and the inefficiency of agency ratings* (Columbia Business School Research Paper, 17–81).

Ohlson, J. A. (1980). Financial ratios and the probabilistic prediction of bankruptcy. *Journal of Accounting Research, 18*(1), 109–131.

Pagano, M., & Jappelli, T. (1993). Information sharing in credit markets. *Journal of Finance, 48*, 1693–1718.

Park, S. (2023). Government lending as a tool to mitigate the effect of asymmetric information. *Public Finance Review, 51*(5), 688–715.

Petersen, M. A., & Rajan, R. G. (1994). The benefits of lending relationships: Evidence from small business data. *The Journal of Finance, 49*(1), 3–37.

Rajan, R., & Winton, A. (1995). Covenants and Collateral as Incentives to Monitor. *The Journal of Finance, 50*(4), 1113–1146.

Rajan, R. G. (1992). Insiders and outsiders: The choice between informed and arm's-length debt. *Journal of Finance, 47*, 1367–1400.

Rashid, F., Khan, R. A., & Qureshi, I. H. (2024). A comprehensive review of the Altman Z-Score model across industries.

Savage, L. J. (1954). *The foundations of statistics*. Wiley.

Spence, M. (1973). Job market signaling. *The Quarterly Journal of Economics, 87*(3), 355–374.

Stiglitz, J. E. (1975). The theory of 'screening', education, and the distribution of income. *American Economic Review, 65*(3), 283–300.

Stiglitz, J. E., & Rothschild, M. (1976). Equilibrium in competitive insurance markets: An essay on the economics of imperfect information. *The Quarterly Journal of Economics, 90*(4), 629–649.
Stiglitz, J. E., & Weiss, A. (1981). Credit rationing in markets with imperfect information. *American Economic Review, 71*(3), 393–410.
Tavakoli, M., Chandrab, R., Tiana, F., & Bravo, C. (2025). Multi-modal deep learning for credit rating prediction using text and numerical data streams. *Applied Soft Computing, 171*, 112771.
Tirole, J. (2010). *The theory of corporate finance*. Princeton University Press.
Zmijewski, M. E. (1984). Methodological issues related to the estimation of financial distress prediction models. *Journal of Accounting Research, 22*, 59–82.

CHAPTER 3

Credit Rationing and Financial Constraints

3.1 Equilibrium Credit Rationing Under Symmetric and Asymmetric Information

Several empirical studies suggest that credit rationing is particularly widespread among start-ups, small and young companies, and firms investing in Research and Development (Xu et al., 2020). Furthermore, financial constraints become increasingly important during periods of economic downturn, like those characterizing the last decade (Bofondi et al., 2018; Brighi & Venturelli, 2017). In this chapter, we investigate the main theories of credit rationing in order to understand why banks prefer rationing some of their customers instead of increasing interest rates on loans so that the market returns to equilibrium, as suggested by the neoclassical price theory.

A primary element in specifying the definition of credit rationing stems from the nature of the imbalance between supply and demand for funds. If the excess demand is temporary and due to delays in adjusting the credit price, we observe a *short-term disequilibrium rationing*. On the contrary, if some institutional constraints are introduced, this adjustment may be hindered, resulting in *long-term disequilibrium rationing*.[1] Finally,

[1] See Stiglitz and Weiss (1981, p. 393): 'On the other hand, long-term unemployment (above some 'natural rate') or credit rationing is explained by governmental constraints such as usury laws or minimum wage legislation.'

P. Brighi and M. Mussoni, *The Bank-Business Relationship*,
https://doi.org/10.1007/978-3-031-91068-5_3

if the excess demand persists regardless of exogenous constraints, we observe what is called *equilibrium rationing*, primarily attributable to imperfections in the credit market.

The research about the latter (equilibrium rationing) dates back to Hodgman's pioneering contribution in 1960, where the author showed that assuming the existence of insolvency risk, the supply curve of funds for some customers can bend backward with respect to the interest rate. Hodgman argued that as the loan size increases, so does the insolvency risk and, consequently, the interest rate; however, beyond a certain loan size, an increase in the interest rate is not sufficient to prevent the insolvency risk, leading banks to stop lending regardless of the interest rate.

Freimer and Gordon (1965) provided an initial critique of Hodgman's model, noting that a bank's search for a risk premium based on loan size is not an optimal policy. They proposed a model in which the bank sets an interest rate for each borrower and refuses to grant credit at any interest rate other than the established one. This situation is termed *strong rationing*, in contrast to Hodgman's *weak rationing*. In other words, they showed that the loan size deemed optimal by the bank depends on the interest rate applicable to that customer, considering the opportunity cost given by the loan plus the expected losses from the potential customer's insolvency. The result is a backward-bending supply curve: initially, as the interest rate increases, so does the loan size, reaching a maximum at a certain interest rate; beyond this point, for higher interest rates, the supply curve bends backward, and the loan size offered begins to decrease.

In a 1969 contribution, Jaffee and Modigliani challenged the models *à la* Hodgman by questioning the assumption of perfectly competitive credit markets, which implied that the market interest rate solely determined the demand for credit. In order to prove the existence of rationing, it was necessary to show an excess demand for credit relative to supply and thus explicitly consider the demand function.[2] Jaffee and Modigliani assumed that banks face a negatively sloped demand function and tend to behave as discriminating monopolists. In a framework where banks can

[2] Jaffee and Modigliani (1969, p. 851), write: 'It should be clear that information on the supply curve alone will generally not be sufficient to derive implications about credit rationing. For this reason, the development of our theoretical model of credit rationing integrates the demand for credit and the determinants of the loan rate with the supply of loans.'

freely set the interest rate on loans, it is crucial to understand whether it can be optimal to set it at a level where there is an excess of demand over supply, resulting in rationing. In such a framework, equilibrium rationing is essentially attributable to limited or imperfect discrimination. In fact, if banks could perfectly discriminate among their customers, they would apply a different interest rate to each one, rationing would no longer be convenient, and each customer would never be charged an interest rate below the one at which supply meets demand.

In reality, even if banks are fully aware of each customer's risk level, they might be compelled to apply uniform interest rates to different customers due to institutional constraints or simply to avoid losing market share.[3] In this case, the profit maximization problem differs from that of a discriminating monopolist: banks classify customers into clusters, applying to each a common interest rate. The optimal interest rate for each customer group lies between the highest and the lowest interest rate a discriminating monopolist would apply to that group of customers. Based on these assumptions, it may be convenient for banks to ration (exclude) customers for whom the optimal interest rate under discriminatory monopoly conditions is higher than the uniform interest rate applied. The probability of rationing is positively correlated with the heterogeneity of interest rates within each group of customers.

Jaffee and Modigliani's formulation extended Hodgman's model by introducing the interactions between demand and supply of funds. However, while advancing in this regard, they regressed in another: their explanation of credit rationing and banks' incapability to perfectly discriminate among customers depended on exogenous factors, which Hodgman believed should be disregarded.[4] Hence, the need to look for solutions that could endogenize the factors making customers' discrimination 'imperfect'. Nevertheless, their research proved to be problematic, and only by removing some basic assumptions, such as the perfect and symmetric information of economic agents, was it possible, starting from

[3] See Jaffee and Russell (1976, p. 651): 'The discussion of credit rationing has largely stressed institutionally given aspects of loan markets such as usury ceilings, borrower-lender "relationships", risk standards and various constraints on price setting.'

[4] See Hodgman (1963, p. 147): '[...] But there seems to be an impression that credit rationing sometimes may occur in the absence of regulated or conventional interest ceiling. My purpose is to discuss credit rationing of this latter type.'

the mid-1970s, to set up models that could endogenize credit rationing within the framework of banks' behavioural function.

In the models discussed above, it is assumed that the uncertainty (i.e., the probability) regarding the outcome of the financed investment projects is objective and that both the bank and the customer have the same information on the probability of success or failure of the projects; i.e., there is symmetry of information. In reality, information distribution is imperfect, and in particular, the contracting parties have different levels of knowledge about the quality of the 'goods' (the loans) being negotiated. Given this assumption, even equilibrium credit rationing can be explained by Akerlof's (1970) model, wherein a market with asymmetric information in equilibrium, low-quality goods drive out high-quality ones (adverse selection). This market failure can be particularly present in credit markets,[5] where, to the strong informational asymmetries, the probability of default is an increasing function of the interest rate r, and consequently, the bank's expected profit increases in a non-monotonic way with respect to r. This implies the existence of a critical interest rate r^* at which the bank's expected profit reaches its maximum level, such that the existence of equilibrium rationing arises because, in the presence of excess demand, it is not convenient for the bank to grant credit at interest rates that are higher than the critical one (r^*).

Therefore, it is important to take into consideration the potential factors that can affect the bank's expected profit and subsequently analyze how these factors may be affected by variations in r. Based on these assumptions and their actual occurrence in the real world, Keeton (1979) introduced a new specification of the rationing phenomenon by distinguishing between: (i) Type I rationing, where some or all customers receive a smaller amount of credit than desired at the prevailing interest rate; and (ii) Type II rationing, where banks deny credit to some customers while granting it to others who are otherwise indistinguishable from those rationed.

[5] Similar markets include the labour and insurance markets. In Akerlof's original model, the example used was the market for used cars: 'lemons' are cars in poor condition. Adverse selection problems are more likely to arise in such a market, where the frequency of transactions is low, compared to a market where the information structure regarding quality is perfect.

3.2 Credit Rationing Models: Type I and Type II Credit Rationing

The introduction of asymmetric information into the analysis of credit markets can be traced back to Jaffee and Russell (1976). Their model formally introduces the impossibility of screening—unlike Jaffee and Modigliani's (1969) model, which assumed screening capabilities—by considering the (excessively high) costs of assessing borrowers' default probabilities. Credit markets are assumed to be perfectly competitive,[6] and borrowers are classified as either 'honest' or 'dishonest'.[7] Ex-ante banks cannot distinguish between them and can only infer their probability distribution, whereas the borrower's true nature is revealed ex-post. The demand for credit is a decreasing function of the interest rate and is identical for both honest and dishonest borrowers; otherwise, dishonest borrowers would be perfectly distinguishable ex-ante. However, dishonest borrowers face bankruptcy costs in case of default,[8] which alters their utility function compared to honest borrowers. Honest borrowers accept only loan contracts they are certain they can fulfil, while dishonest borrowers repay only if bankruptcy costs exceed the repayment amount. If bankruptcy costs are lower, dishonest borrowers derive higher utility from defaulting rather than repaying. Based on these assumptions, Jaffee and Russell (1976) identify three possible market equilibria.

The first equilibrium corresponds to a scenario where the demand and supply of funds are equal (see point *S* in Fig. 3.1).[9] In this case, the

[6] Unlike the model of Jaffee and Modigliani (1969), which places particular emphasis on the existence of a monopolistic market structure, this model shows that credit rationing can also occur in a perfectly competitive framework.

[7] In this model, 'honest' agents are those who accept a credit contract only if they are capable of honouring its terms, whereas 'dishonest' agents choose to go bankrupt whenever the costs associated with their default are sufficiently low.

[8] By assumption, bankruptcy costs differ among dishonest borrowers, so the proportion of insolvent customers varies according to the repayment value of the loan. Specifically, the authors posit that there is a minimum loan repayment level below which all borrowers are solvent. As the repayment value increases, the proportion of solvent borrowers decreases and that of insolvent borrowers increases.

[9] Hess (1984) shows that Jaffee and Russell (1976) confuse the supply curve under perfect competition with the locus of points where profits are zero. Hess shows that if the supply curve is appropriately corrected, the perfectly competitive model of Jaffee and Russell (1976) is no longer compatible with the conclusion that credit rationing is profitable for the bank in both the short and long term.

interest rate is higher than the opportunity cost of bank deposits, but only by an amount sufficient to cover the default risk. Within this equilibrium, it is as if honest borrowers pay a premium to offset the default risk posed by dishonest borrowers.

In the second equilibrium, honest borrowers maximize their utility subject to a constraint that incorporates the presence of dishonest borrowers (see point *E* in Fig. 3.1). Due to the adverse selection mechanism inherent in credit markets, which attracts dishonest agents, honest borrowers opt for rationing, choosing to pay an interest rate at which they would have preferred to demand more credit in the absence of dishonest borrowers. This scenario is defined by Keeton (1979) as ***Type I credit rationing*** (see point *A* in Fig. 3.1). The equilibrium featuring credit rationing (point *E*) is preferred to the one without rationing (point *S*) because at point *E* borrowers achieve a higher utility level than at point *S*, despite credit restrictions.

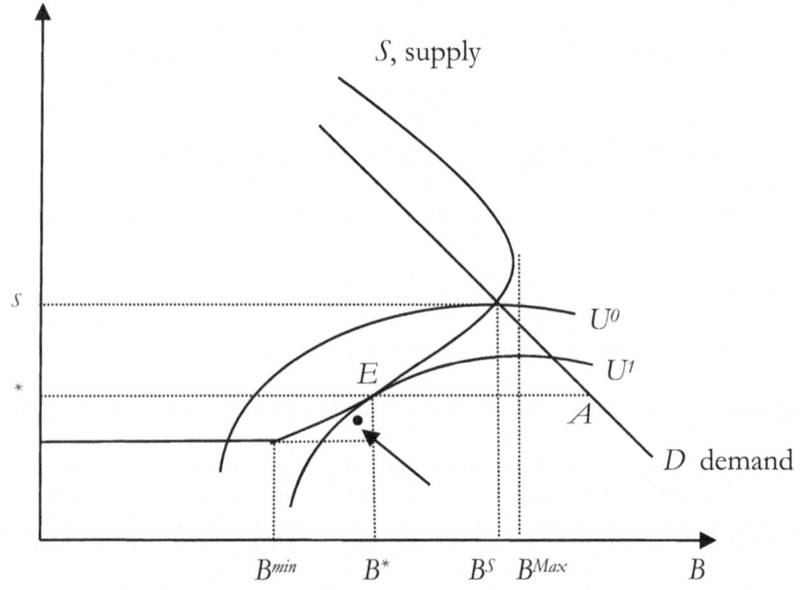

Fig. 3.1 Equilibrium credit rationing of first type (*Source* Jaffee and Russel [1976, pp. 659–661])

The third equilibrium considers the possibility of multiple contractual solutions. Suppose a new bank enters the market and offers a more favourable loan contract (see point H in Fig. 3.1). In that case, all honest borrowers will switch to the new contract, leaving dishonest borrowers with the less favourable contract (point *E*). Under these conditions, the original bank will incur losses, leading to the withdrawal of the less favourable contract *E* from the market. Consequently, dishonest borrowers will also switch to the new contract *H*, ultimately causing losses for the new bank as well. This dynamic results in an unstable equilibrium, in which banks will cease to offer contracts catering to dishonest borrowers, thereby making all loan contracts unprofitable. In other words, the bank will only offer 'honest' contracts on the market, and all borrowers (both honest and dishonest) will be forced to request those contracts, which ultimately prove to be unprofitable. In such a market, if the differences between the groups are sufficiently small, a stable equilibrium with multiple contracts cannot exist. A solution to this problem could derive from a different competitive market structure. The authors show that, for example, in a monopolistic market, the bank could offer a greater quantity of loans compared to the perfect competition framework. However, this would come at the expense of a higher interest rate, leading even honest borrowers to prefer the previous solution, with *Type I rationing*.

Keeton (1979) was the first to introduce the concept of *Type II rationing*, which arises when some borrowers, otherwise indistinguishable from others, are denied credit. This form of rationing stems from rigidities in the supply of funds, interest rate constraints, entry barriers or specific conditions of moral hazard. Keeton's primary contribution lies in his observation that in the presence of moral hazard, borrowers respond to interest rate increases by selecting riskier projects. As a result, banks may find it unprofitable to lend at higher interest rates since the associated risks reduce their expected profits.

This approach was further refined by Stiglitz and Weiss (1981), who demonstrated that credit markets experience interest rate effects that diverge from the bank's expected returns, which also depend on the probability of repayment by the borrowers. They argued that as the interest rate increases, the bank's expected return is subject to two opposing effects: a direct effect, whereby higher interest rates increase returns, all else being equal, and an adverse selection effect, which leads riskier borrowers to seek credit disproportionately. In fact, Stiglitz and Weiss show that if a bank increases the interest rates, the pool of potential borrowers tends to undertake an increasing number of high-yield/high-risk projects, since borrowers willing to pay higher interest rates are more inclined to invest in riskier projects (i.e., projects with higher expected returns). The latter effect reduces the bank's expected profitability because higher-risk borrowers are more likely to default.

Meanwhile, borrowers who plan to undertake low-yield, low-risk investment projects will not demand loans from the bank, as they cannot afford or are unwilling to pay high interest rates, given that the low expected returns of their projects would be insufficient to repay the loan. Consequently, as the interest rate rises, the average riskiness of the customers increases, and the bank's expected profits can be presumed to decrease. Additionally, a moral hazard effect emerges as higher interest rates incentivize borrowers to undertake riskier projects, further diminishing the bank's expected profits. In fact, as the interest rate increases, the behaviour of the customers changes (adverse incentive or moral hazard effect). Stiglitz and Weiss show that a higher interest rate increases the propensity to invest in riskier projects. This occurs because an increase in the interest rate reduces the expected return for the borrower investing in low-yield, low-risk projects much more than for those investing in high-yield, high-risk projects. Thus, an increase in the interest rate can lead borrowers to undertake riskier projects, further reducing the bank's expected profit.

On the contrary, if the interest rate is sufficiently low, the positive direct effect outweighs the adverse selection and moral hazard effects, leading to an increase in the bank's expected profit. However, beyond a certain threshold, the negative effects dominate, causing the expected return to decline. The optimal interest rate is the point at which the bank's expected profit Φ is maximized (see r^* in Fig. 3.1). At this rate, excess demand for credit remains unmet, leading to equilibrium credit rationing: this represents an equilibrium because banks may rationally refuse to lend to borrowers willing to pay higher interest rates due to the increased default risk associated with such loans, implying that at interest rates above r^* the bank's expected profit would decrease.

In the Stiglitz and Weiss model, it is assumed that the bank identifies a group of projects, and for each project, the distribution of returns is known. Additionally, the bank can distinguish between groups of investment projects with different average returns, but does not know the risk associated with each project. In case the average expected returns between the two projects are equal, the first is assumed to be riskier than the second one if all risk-averse investors prefer the second to the first. A borrower's insolvency depends on her ability to repay the loan, and she will be in default whenever the returns on the investment project plus any collateral[10] are not sufficient to repay the loan; i.e., when the following condition holds:

$$C + R \leq B(1 + r) \tag{3.1}$$

where C stands for collateral, R is the returns on the investment project, B is the loan amount, and r is the interest rate charged by the bank. Therefore, the bank's profit function will be determined by the minimum value between the loan repayment amount and the return on the project plus any collateral,[11] expressed as:

$$\Phi(R, r) = \min(C + R; B(1 + r)) \tag{3.2}$$

which is a concave function of the project's returns.

Similarly, for the borrower, the profit is given by the higher value between the return on the project net of the repayment amount and the negative value of the collateral, which is a convex function of the project and can be expressed as:

$$\Pi(R, r) = \max(R - B(1 + r); -C). \tag{3.3}$$

Based on these preliminary considerations, Stiglitz and Weiss state several theorems that show the existence of a competitive equilibrium with credit rationing.

Theorem 3.1 For a given interest rate r, there is a critical value q^* such that a firm borrows from the bank if and only if $q > q^*$.

Theorem 3.2 As the interest rate increases, the critical value of q^*, below which individuals do not apply for loans, increases.

[10] Collateral is an exogenous variable in the model. Bester (1985a) also endogenizes this variable.

[11] It is possible to distinguish between internal collateral (assets of the firm) and external collateral (assets of the entrepreneur) as well as between real collateral (pledge, lien and mortgage) and personal collateral (guarantee, endorsement, etc.). In the Stiglitz and Weiss (1981) model, although not specified, it can be inferred that the type of collateral they refer is a real collateral.

These first two theorems imply that a firm goes to the credit market only if the riskiness of its project exceeds a certain threshold value and that, due to adverse selection, this critical value increases with the bank's interest rate.

Theorem 3.3 The expected return on a loan to a bank (i.e., the bank's expected profit Φ) is a decreasing function of the riskiness of the loan.

Theorem 3.4 If there are a discrete number of potential borrowers (or types of borrowers), each with a different risk level q, the bank's expected profit Φ will not be a monotonic function of r.

Theorems 3.3 and 3.4 state, in other words, that an increase in the interest rate produces, besides a positive direct effect, a negative indirect effect due to adverse selection. If this latter effect prevails, the bank's expected profit is a non-monotonic function of the interest rate (see Fig. 3.2, Quadrant II).

Theorem 3.5 Whenever the bank's expected profit function is an interior mode (i.e., it has an interior maximum solution), there exist supply

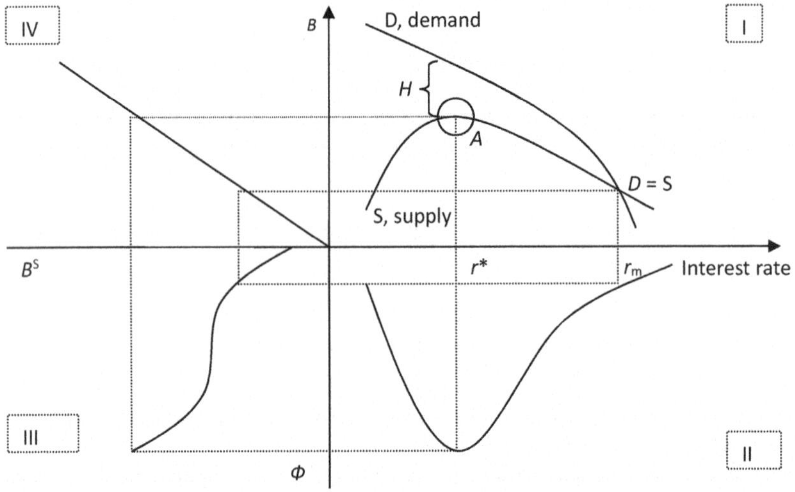

Fig. 3.2 Equilibrium credit rationing of the second type (*Source* Stiglitz and Weiss [1981, p. 397])

functions of funds such that the competitive equilibrium entails credit rationing.

Theorem 3.5 can be effectively illustrated through a graphical representation (see Fig. 3.2). The supply curve for loans is built by defining: (i) the relationship between the interest rate on loans r and the bank's expected profit Φ (Quadrant II); (ii) the relationship between the supply curve B^S and Φ (Quadrant III); and (iii) the relationship between B and r (Quadrant I). Figure 3.2 also shows that at the optimal interest rate r^*, the demand for credit exceeds the supply by the amount H. It is also important to note that there is an interest rate, r_m, at which the supply equals the demand for credit. However, the interest rate r_m is not an equilibrium one: the bank prefers to charge an interest rate r^* lower than r_m, in this way attracting at least the same number of customers and achieving higher expected profits.[12]

Theorem 3.6 If the bank's expected profit function Φ has several modes (i.e., it has multiple interior maximum solutions), market equilibrium could either be characterized by credit rationing (i.e., a single interest rate equal to or lower than the equilibrium interest rate) or by two interest rates, with an excess demand for credit in the lower one.

According to Theorem 3.6, in case $r^* > r_m$ (see Fig. 3.3), two interest rates can be applied, r_1 and r_2, for which $\Phi(r_1) = \Phi(r_2)$. Given the decreasing demand for credit, there is an excess demand at r_1, leading to credit rationing unless $r_1 = r_m$. Borrowers with a reservation interest rate $\geq r_2$ will demand credit at higher interest rates, and those who did not obtain credit at r_1 can obtain it at the higher interest rate r_2 (where there is an excess supply). A bank loan at an interest rate r_3 where $\Phi(r_3) < \Phi(r_1)$ will not be granted, while no bank will lend at interest rates between r_1 and r_2. Finally, a bank offering loans at an interest rate r_4 where $\Phi(r_4) > \Phi(r_1)$ will not attract any borrower because for $r_4 > r_2$ there is no excess demand.

Theorem 3.7 If, at a given nominal interest rate r, a risk-neutral firm is indifferent between two investment projects, an increase in the interest rate may lead the firm to undertake the project with a higher probability of failure.

[12] Theorem 3.5 predicts the possibility of the bank's expected profit function having two or more interior maxima. See Stiglitz and Weiss (1981).

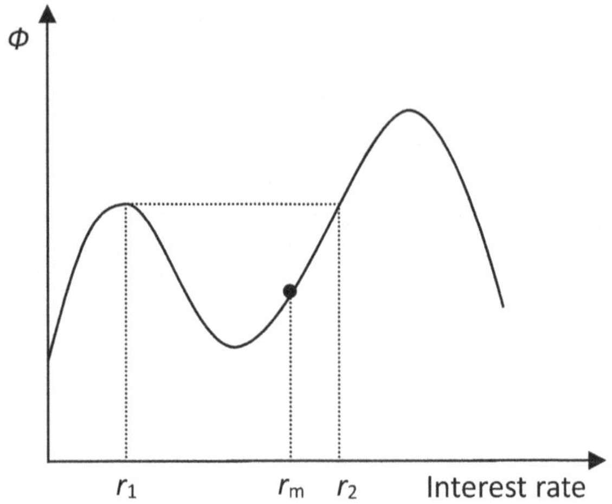

Fig. 3.3 Bank's expected profit function (*Source* Stiglitz and Weiss [1981, p. 398])

In other words, a moral hazard effect prevails, negatively impacting the bank's expected profit similarly to the adverse selection case, in this way inducing the bank, in the presence of an excess demand, to ration credit rather than increase the interest rate.

Although Stiglitz and Weiss (1981) address some limitations of previous models, first among all, the assumption of perfect information, it has some flaws that weaken its theoretical formulation and empirical implications.[13] One major issue is the strength of the adverse selection and moral hazard effects via the interest rate. It should be noted that in this model, equilibrium rationing is only a possibility and not a need. In particular, if there were a multitude of investment projects uniformly distributed across the entire range, the adverse selection effect via the interest rate might never occur, or it may occur only at very high interest rates. Additionally, suppose customers could be classified into a number of groups observable (ex-ante) by the bank. In that case, Type II rationing might occur only for the marginal group; i.e., the one with the lowest

[13] Note that in this brief presentation we have shown only the first seven theorems of the Stiglitz and Weiss (1981) model. However, our considerations remain valid even if we extend the analysis to the other seven theorems of the model.

expected profit, while the demands of the supra-marginal groups would be fully satisfied.

A second weakness of the Stiglitz and Weiss (1981) model lies in the bank's inability to recognize the risk level of firms' projects. This becomes particularly significant in a dynamic framework: since, in the long run, both adverse selection and moral hazard effects are eventually observable, the bank can learn some relevant information to identify the risk level of its customers. In fact, the bank has at its disposal screening and monitoring tools that allow it to assess the quality of its customers, albeit imperfectly, both ex-ante and ex-post. While riskier customers sometimes try to 'mimic' the behaviour of more reliable customers, this behaviour is marginal.

The third weakness of the model is due to the fact that Stiglitz and Weiss do not distinguish between the number of loans granted and their amounts; i.e., they consider the loan size as constant. In this way, the authors do not investigate the effects of an increase in loan size on a bank's expected profit. Bester (1985a) observes that the single-contract equilibrium of the Stiglitz and Weiss model is not sustainable when different types of contracts are allowed. In fact, different types of contracts can be used, through a sort of self-selection mechanism, to discriminate among different levels of customer risk. Introducing different contracts of varying sizes, durations, collateral clauses, etc., in a competitive framework like the one assumed by Stiglitz and Weiss creates the conditions for positive profits for banks offering them. Introducing different contractual clauses creates separating equilibria: for example, the bank can vary the interest rate and the collateral to select different groups of customers, easing the adverse selection effect and, thus, credit rationing.

In this way, Bester (1985a) introduces the role of collateral and interest rates as screening mechanisms, demonstrating that credit rationing could be mitigated through self-selection contracts. By varying interest rates and collateral requirements, banks can differentiate between borrowers with varying risk profiles. This mechanism weakens the adverse selection problem and reduces the extent of credit rationing. Furthermore, if we interpret Bester's (1985a) model in terms of contract theory, we can say that while in the Stiglitz and Weiss model—where the collateral is fixed and equal for all customers—the debt contract is identified by the interest rate, in Bester's model the collateral level is a choice variable too. Based on these assumptions, concerning the bank's ex-ante screening policy, it emerges that the optimal contractual form might not be a debt contract at all, or it might be a debt contract without rationing. Lastly, the assumption of single-period contracts appears unrealistic, as the bank–customer relationship generally extends over multiple periods. However, it should be noted that even in a multi-period framework with asymmetric information,[14] adverse selection and moral hazard potentially continue to exist, although the contracting parties have tools to mitigate the corresponding negative effects.

Similarly to Bester (1985a), Freixas and Rochet (2008) emphasize the role of modern banking mechanisms, such as credit scoring and dynamic contract structures, in alleviating information asymmetry and reducing rationing inefficiencies. Other recent empirical studies, such as those by Jiménez et al. (2017) and Banerjee et al. (2019), have provided further evidence of credit rationing in contemporary financial markets. Jiménez et al. (2017) found that credit rationing is particularly pronounced in periods of financial distress when banks tighten lending standards. Banerjee et al. (2019) examined microfinance institutions and highlighted the persistence of credit constraints for small borrowers, reinforcing the significance of asymmetric information in lending markets.

To conclude this brief review of the theoretical literature on credit rationing, it is essential to highlight some fundamental differences between the competitive model of Jaffee and Russell (1976) and the monopolistic model of Stiglitz and Weiss (1981), which represent the foundation for the modern credit rationing literature. First of all, the definition of rationing adopted by Jaffee and Russell corresponds to what Keeton (1979) calls *Type I rationing*, where credit rationing occurs whenever the bank sets a loan interest rate at which the supply of funds is lower than the demand. This definition includes both a notion and a rule for rationing, where the rationing rule suggests that all potential borrowers have equal access to credit markets but may receive loans smaller than requested. Moreover, the competitive model of Jaffee and Russell leaves two questions open: the first concerns the determination of the amount of credit granted to each customer; the second regards the criterion by which the 'rationing rule' is applied. These problems are partially addressed in the contribution of Stiglitz and Weiss (1981), who adopt a different definition of rationing that can be traced back to Keeton (1979), *Type II*

[14] In a multi-period framework, the notion of relationship lending prevails, whereby a long-term and repeated relationship reduces informational asymmetries, facilitating the assessment of the riskiness of investment projects (see Chapter 4).

rationing. In this case, rationing occurs whenever some borrowers, seemingly indistinguishable from others, do not receive credit at all. Although the rationed customers would be willing to accept more onerous contractual conditions, the bank, based on an ex-ante assessment of the riskiness of their projects, considers them too risky and rationally decides not to grant credit.

In conclusion, the theoretical and empirical literature on credit rationing has evolved significantly since Jaffee and Russell (1976) and Stiglitz and Weiss (1981). While early models emphasized the role of asymmetric information, recent research has explored mechanisms to mitigate credit rationing, including collateral requirements, credit scoring and improved banking regulation. The persistence of credit rationing across different economic contexts underscores the complexity of financial intermediation and the importance of continued research in this field.

3.3 Bibliometric Analysis of Credit Rationing Literature

The foundational work by Stiglitz and Weiss (1981) initiated a series of studies analyzing credit rationing under different assumptions. Stiglitz and Weiss showed that equilibrium credit rationing could arise in a non-regulated market due to adverse selection and moral hazard. These issues stem from asymmetric information about borrower characteristics and behaviour. In general, on the one hand, adverse selection models assume that lenders have no information on borrower types, leading to credit rationing or the use of signalling mechanisms (e.g., collateral requirements) to sort borrowers. On the other hand, moral hazard models typically operate within a single-period framework, assuming that borrower defaults have no future repercussions, but this assumption was challenged by studies suggesting that multi-period models better capture the dynamics of borrower behaviour.

The following contribution of Bester (1985a, 1985b) demonstrated that simultaneous optimization of interest rates and collateral requirements by banks could achieve perfect sorting of borrowers, thereby eliminating credit rationing. His models indicated that collateral requirements could effectively screen borrowers based on risk, reducing the incidence of adverse selection. Further, Milde and Riley (1988) showed similar results when loan amounts were used as a screening device instead of collateral.

Various assumptions have been tested to understand the dynamics of credit rationing. For example, Besanko and Thakor (1987a, 1987b) showed that under perfect competition and certain distribution assumptions, collateral would not be used as a screening device if borrowers had sufficient wealth. These studies explored how the distribution of returns (first-order stochastic dominance) influenced the use of collateral in competitive versus monopolistic lending markets. They highlighted that collateral is more likely to be used under competitive conditions. Bester (1987) extended this by showing that rationing would still occur if collateral requirements were constrained by borrower wealth. These models typically consider both risk-neutral and risk-averse borrowers and examine different market structures (competitive versus monopolistic lenders).

Milde and Riley (1988) extended the screening mechanisms to include loan amounts, showing that smaller loan sizes could also serve as a screening tool to mitigate credit rationing. Schmidt-Mohr (1997) analyzed scenarios where risk aversion among borrowers influenced the use of collateral, showing that under risk aversion, collateral would not be used if technologies were divisible, and screening could occur through loan size instead.

The literature also explores how information sharing between lenders affects credit markets. Pagano and Jappelli (1993) and Padilla and Pagano (2000) extended basic rationing models by considering scenarios where lenders utilize past credit information on borrowers and share this information publicly. These models typically assume that lenders can optimize contracts using this shared information, which can mitigate adverse selection and moral hazard problems. In particular, Pagano and Jappelli (1993) showed that information sharing among lenders could mitigate adverse selection by allowing better differentiation between high-risk and low-risk borrowers. Their model assumed that lenders could fully inform themselves about immigrant borrowers, which led to increased lending volumes for previously rationed safe borrowers. Padilla and Pagano (2000) extended the discussion to include moral hazard by modelling a two-period framework where borrower effort levels influenced loan repayment probabilities. They showed that sharing default information could mitigate moral hazard by incentivizing borrowers to exert higher effort to avoid being labelled as high-risk.

According to Flatnes (2021), contrary to some theoretical models, the empirical evidence suggests that lenders widely use collateral as a screening and incentive mechanism. Collateral requirements not only protect lenders against default losses but also incentivize borrowers to exert effort to avoid losing their pledged assets. In fact, including collateral in models of credit information sharing changes the dynamics significantly because it implies that reducing collateral requirements through improved information sharing can decrease credit rationing by making loans accessible to borrowers with limited wealth. Thus, empirical evidence showed how allowing for collateralized contracts in models can provide a more accurate representation of real-world credit markets.

Furthermore, Flatnes (2021) contrasts the effects of private utilization of default information by individual lenders with public information sharing via credit bureaus. Private information utilization may still lead to suboptimal outcomes, as borrowers can switch lenders to avoid worse terms. In contrast, public sharing creates a more comprehensive incentive structure, reducing both adverse selection and moral hazard. His analysis extends to scenarios where borrowers are fully aware of how lenders use past credit information. This awareness can influence borrower behaviour positively, as they are incentivized to maintain good credit standing to access better loan terms in future periods.

In general, by performing a bibliometric analysis, we can see how the literature on credit rationing developed over the years. We selected from the database Web of Science (WOS) all the publications on the topic 'credit rationing' published from 1985 to 2024 (the widest data range available on WOS) by searching in the fields 'title', 'abstract' and 'author keywords', and as a result we found a total of 880 articles. Then, to refine the data, we applied two primary filters:

i. The publication must fall within the research categories of Economics, Business Finance, Business, Management, Development Studies, Environmental Sciences, Agriculture, Urban Studies, Mathematical Methods in Social Sciences, and Operations Research Management.
ii. The publications must be written in English and in the form of regular articles, articles published as early access, proceedings papers, book chapters and reviews.

The final sample consists of 748 articles, the majority of which (see Fig. 3.4) are in the fields of Economics, Business Finance, Management and Business.

Table 3.1 provides an overview of the primary data structure utilized in this study. The publication data spans from 1985 to 2024 and encompasses 748 documents. These documents have been published in 290 journals and authored by 1,421 researchers. Of the total articles, only 212 are attributed to single authors, indicating a prevailing trend of collaboration within the topic of credit rationing. The average citation level for these articles is approximately 25 citations per paper. This signifies the growing impact and interest in this field of research, as reflected by the substantial number of citations received (18,936).

Regarding keywords, the selected articles are associated with 1,504 author-suggested keywords (provided below the abstract of each article) and 952 database-generated keywords known as 'keywords plus'. As we will see in the remainder of this section, these keywords collectively contribute to a comprehensive understanding of the themes and topics explored within the credit rationing literature.

Figure 3.5 depicts the research papers' temporal distributions and average citation levels over time. We observe that the research on this

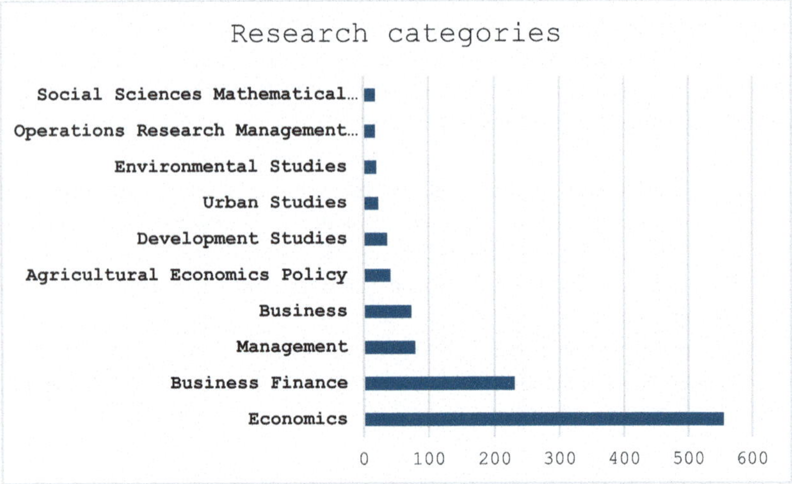

Fig. 3.4 Research categories (*Source* Web of Science Core Collection)

Table 3.1 Descriptive statistics

Description	*Results*
Main information about data	
Timespan	1985–2024
Sources (Journals, Books, etc.)	290
Documents	748
Annual growth rate %	4.85
Document average age	13.1
Average citations per Doc	25.74
References	18,936
Document contents	
Keywords Plus (ID)	952
Author's Keywords (DE)	1,504
Authors	
Authors	1,421
Authors of single-authored docs	212
Authors collaboration	
Single-authored docs	239
Co-authors per Doc	2.19
International co-authorships %	28.88
Document types	
Article	667
Article; book chapter	2
Article; early access	7
Article; proceedings paper	31
Proceedings paper	40
Review	1

Source Web of Science Core Collection

topic in the first period (1985–1998) started growing continuously, then remained pretty much stable in the second period (1999–2012), and finally started growing again at a strong pace in the last period (2013–2022). Regarding the citations, we observe a continuously growing path from the very beginning of the observed period until 2022. Both indicators signal a continuously growing interest in this topic in the academic arena.

Figure 3.6 presents prominent journals that publish research on credit rationing. Most published literature on credit rationing belongs to the journal categories of finance and economics, with a notable exception for a journal belonging to the field of entrepreneurship and small business management.

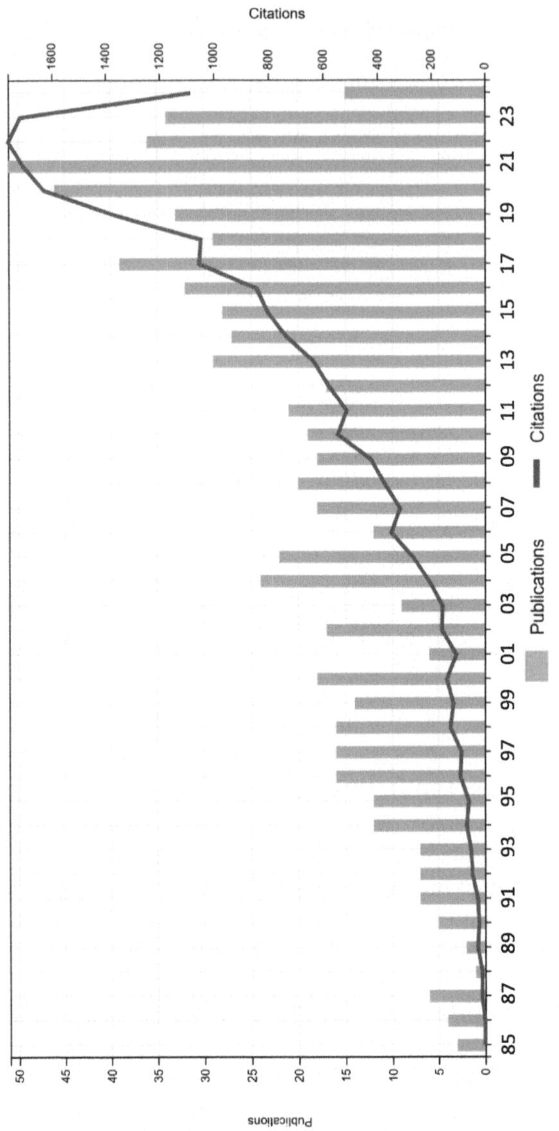

Fig. 3.5 Publication growth: number of publications and citations per year (*Source* Web of Science Core Collection)

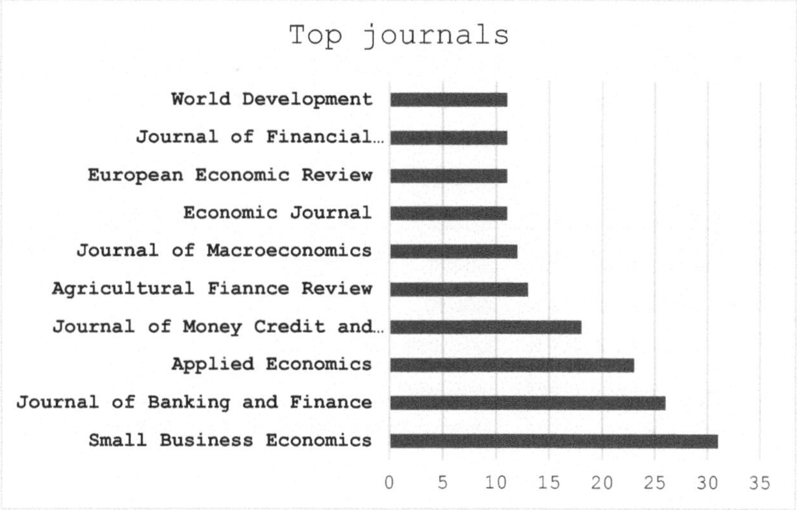

Fig. 3.6 Top journals (*Source* Web of Science Core Collection)

Figure 3.7 presents a comprehensive overview of the most highly cited authors, considering their total citations. Within this index, called 'Most Local Cited References', Bibliometrix counts the local citations, that is, the citations that a reference (a document included in at least one of the bibliographies of the articles in our sample) has received from publications included in our sample. The reference lists include all documents from bibliographies, and when a reference is also part of the sample, it is called a 'cited document'. So, 'local citations' are citations received from a reference article internally to our sample.[15]

The ranking of authors serves two primary purposes: firstly, to identify prominent contributors and the leading articles in the field of credit rationing, and secondly, to acknowledge their significant impact on the existing body of literature. The foremost authors in this ranking are Stiglitz and Weiss (1981), with 350 citations, which maintains by far the

[15] On the contrary, within the 'Most Global Cited Documents', Bibliometrix includes the total 'global citations', that is, the citations that an article, included in the sample, has received from documents indexed on a bibliographic database (WoS, Scopus, etc.). So, global citations are those received by a selected article 'all over the world'.

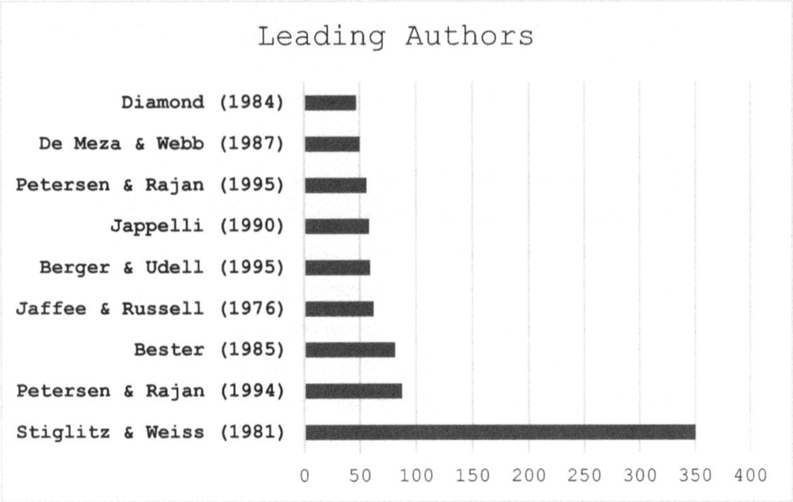

Fig. 3.7 Leading authors (*Source* Web of Science Core Collection)

top position, followed by Petersen and Rajan (1994) with 87 citations, Bester (1985a) with 81, Jaffee and Russell (1976) with 81, and Berger and Udell (1995) with 62 citations.

Figure 3.8 represents graphically the same picture of the most highly cited authors by a so-called 'references spectroscopy', which depicts the patterns, frequencies and characteristics of citations and references within our sample of publications. In particular, the black line represents the number of cited references, while the red line shows the deviation from the 5-year median. As we can see, there has been an increasing number of citations during the first period (1957–1980), followed by an important peak in 1981 due to the seminal work of Stiglitz and Weiss (1981) and an increasing pattern of citations in the following years (1982–2010), and finally a decreasing path in the last years (2013–2022).

Following prior literature (Chiaramonte et al., 2023; Dervi et al., 2022; Van Eck & Waltman, 2010), we now employ cartographic/keyword and trend analyses to provide a comprehensive depiction of the development and progression of the literature concerning credit rationing. Keyword analysis highlights the literary landscape within various clusters identified by different colours. Trend analysis, on the

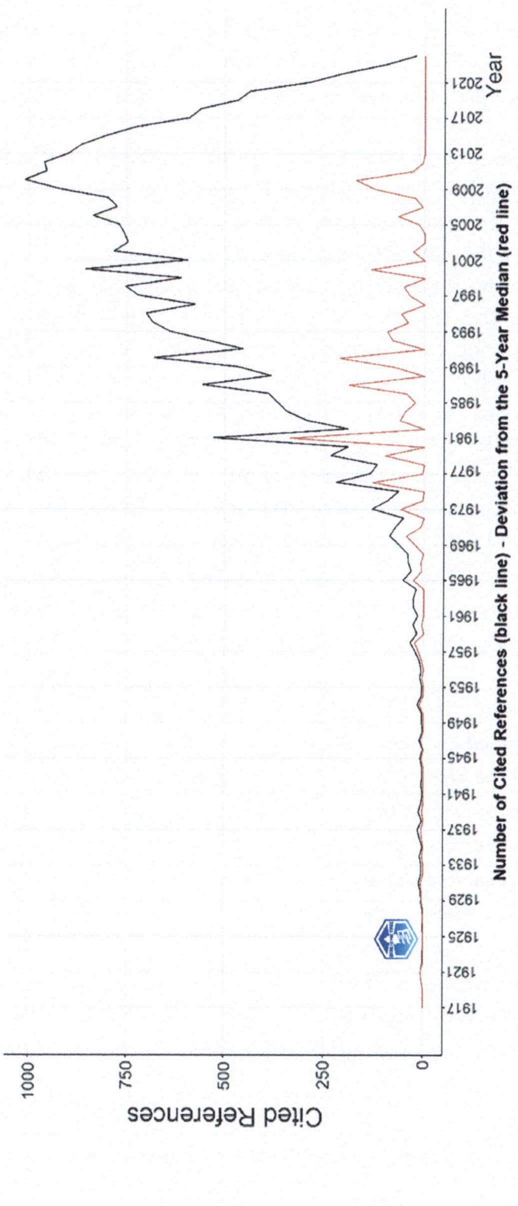

Fig. 3.8 References Spectroscopy (*Source* Web of Science Core Collection)

other hand, helps to understand the evolution of literature over different periods. To conduct these analyses, we establish a minimum inclusion threshold of five occurrences for a specific keyword (Chiaramonte et al., 2023; Khan et al., 2022). Figures 3.9 and 3.10 present the obtained results for the keyword analysis, while Fig. 3.11 presents the results for the trend analysis.

Figure 3.9 shows that ‘credit rationing’, ‘credit’, ‘rationing’ and ‘asymmetric information’ are the most frequent keywords. The keyword analysis confirmed that the literature mainly centred on the topic of credit rationing and the role played by asymmetric information.

Figure 3.10 shows instead the co-occurrence between the different keywords, that is, the number of publications in which two keywords occur together and the corresponding clusters. We can see that the most important cluster (blue colour), as expected, is represented by the group of keywords linked to the ‘credit rationing’ and ‘asymmetric information’ topics, while the other clusters are those of ‘SMEs’ and ‘credit constraint’ (purple colour), the ‘financial crisis’ (orange colour), the ‘banking’ and ‘financial intermediaries’ (light blue colour), the ‘credit’ and ‘rationing’ (yellow colour), and finally, the ‘microfinance’ (green colour).

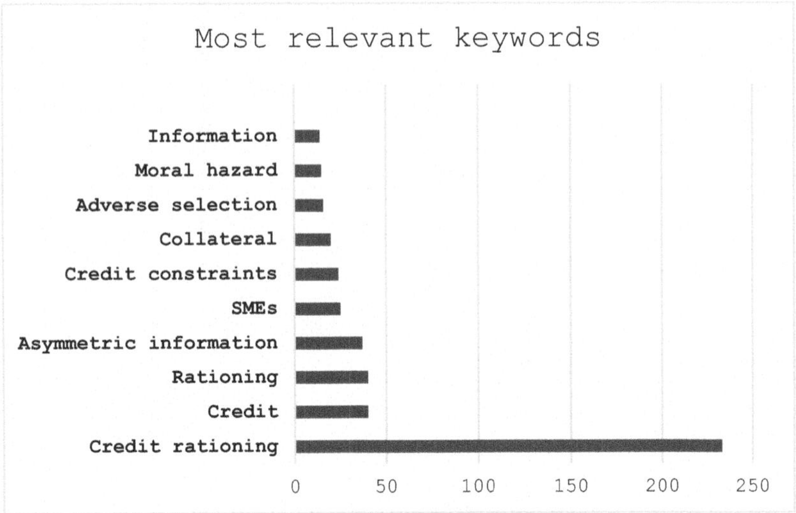

Fig. 3.9 Most relevant keywords (*Source* Web of Science Core Collection)

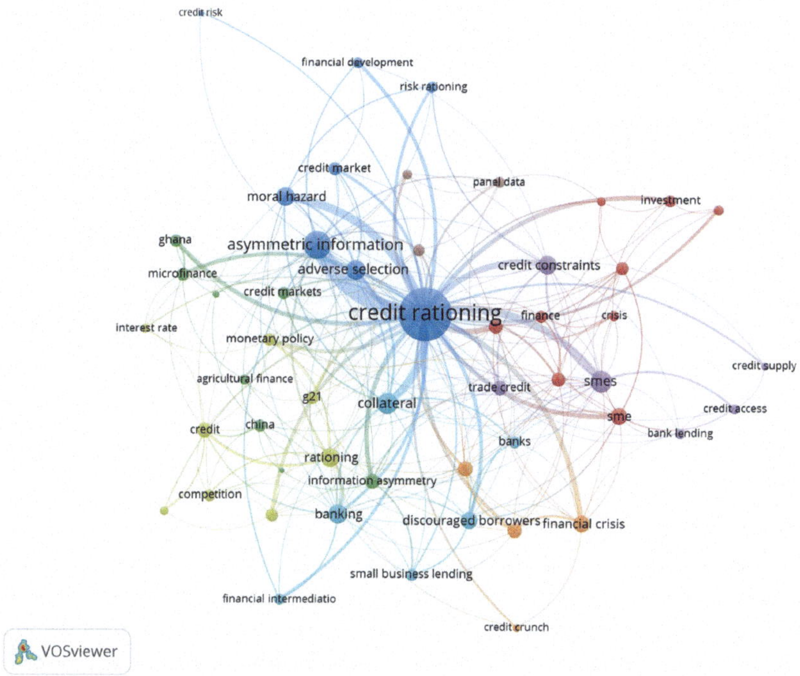

Fig. 3.10 Keyword analysis (*Source* Web of Science Core Collection)

Figure 3.11 shows the trend analysis; that is, the thematic evolution over time. In particular, Fig. 3.11 reveals how early literature (1985–1999) started concentrating solely on credit rationing itself, while the following phase (2000–2007) started linking the topic to asymmetric information and guarantees. The third phase (2008–2013) follows the big financial crisis of 2007–2008, so the literature started talking of transition, collateral, interest rates, SMEs and financial crisis. In the fourth phase (2014–2017), the literature started concentrating on SMEs, asymmetric information and fiscal policies, while in the fifth phase (2015–2021), the literature turned to information and credit constraints and crisis due to COVID-19 and the ongoing Russia–Ukraine war. In the last years (2022–2024), literature seems to go back to its origins, talking mainly of credit rationing, SMEs and credit risk.

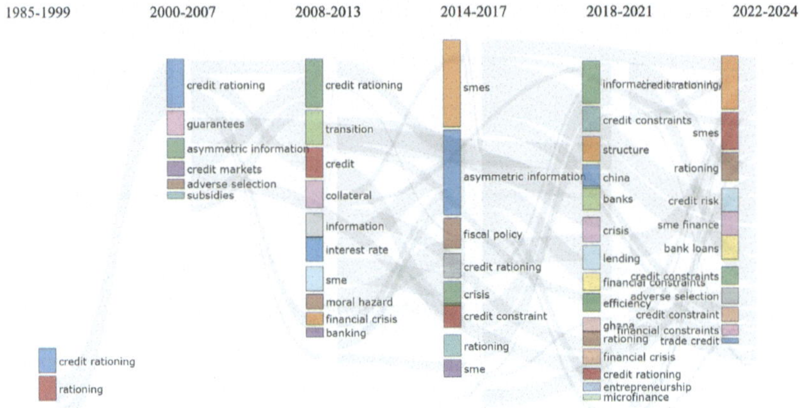

Fig. 3.11 Trend analysis (*Source* Web of Science Core Collection)

The last step of this bibliometric analysis consists of the so-called stream analysis, composed of a thematic map and a coupling map. A thematic map in bibliometrics is a visual representation used to illustrate the conceptual structure of a research field by highlighting the relationships between different topics, themes or keywords within a body of literature. These maps are typically generated through techniques like co-word analysis or cluster analysis, which help in identifying and visualizing the main themes and their connections within a set of academic publications.

Figure 3.12 shows the clusters of themes, where each cluster represents a group of related themes or topics that frequently co-occur in the literature. These clusters can reveal the main areas of research within a field and how they are related to one another. The vertical axis represents the 'density', which refers to how closely related the themes within a cluster are to each other, whereas high-density clusters indicate well-developed and mature themes. In the horizontal axis, it is represented the 'centrality', which refers to the importance of a theme in connecting different clusters or in the overall research field, where themes with high centrality are often considered core topics within the field. In this way, we have a strategic diagram, which helps in identifying which themes are motor themes (high centrality and high density), basic themes (high centrality but low density), emerging or declining themes (low centrality and low density), and niche themes (low centrality but high density). As we can see, and as expected, the motor themes are those of credit rationing, asymmetric information and SMEs, while the niche themes are those of credit access, financial development, microfinance and capital structure.

Figure 3.13 shows the coupling map, where the primary objective of bibliographical coupling of literature is to elucidate the dimensions and trends of literature within a particular research field. Bibliographic coupling occurs when two documents cite the same references. The coupling map shows how closely related different documents are based on the number of shared references they have. Documents that are strongly coupled (i.e., share many references) tend to cluster together on the map, and these clusters can indicate groups of related research or subfields within a broader research area. In this way, bibliographic coupling maps help reveal the intellectual structure of a research field by showing how different works or researchers are connected through shared references. This can provide insights into how knowledge is organized and how different areas of research are interrelated.

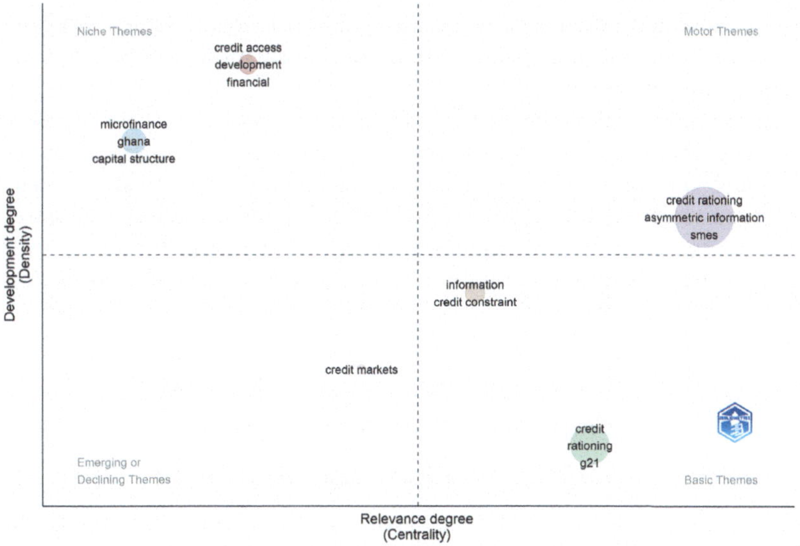

Fig. 3.12 Thematic map (*Source* Web of Science Core Collection)

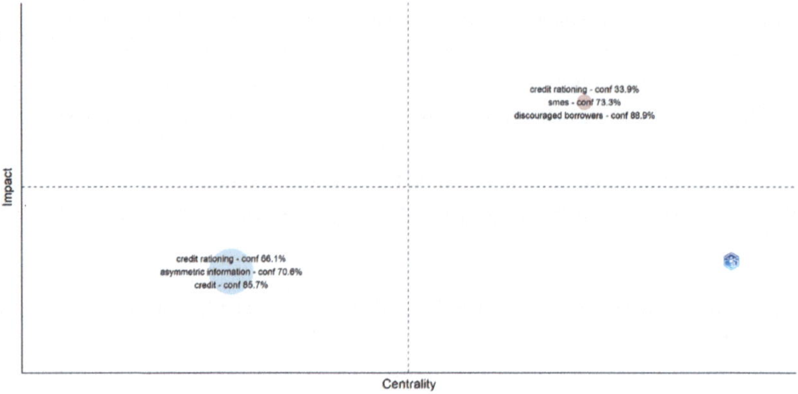

Fig. 3.13 Coupling map (*Source* Web of Science Core Collection)

The outcomes of our bibliographical coupling analysis show the two current main research streams in the literature about credit rationing. The most important stream in recent years links credit rationing, SMEs and discouraged borrowers, while the traditional stream, which links the topics of credit rationing and asymmetric information, has become the second most important.

In summary, after the seminal work of Stiglitz and Weiss (1981), different theoretical models have addressed the challenges of credit rationing through various mechanisms, including interest rates, collateral requirements and information sharing. All these models emphasize the importance of dynamic models that capture borrower behaviour over multiple periods and the significant role of collateral and information sharing in improving credit market efficiency and reducing rationing.

3.4 Credit Rationing in Specific Frameworks and Scenarios

3.4.1 Increasing Interest Rates and Increasing NPL Ratio

We present now some specific frameworks and scenarios where the credit rationing issued proved to be particularly relevant. The first interesting scenario is the rising inflation rate that followed the COVID-19 pandemic of 2020 because of many factors, so as a response, the main central banks started increasing the market interest rates. As seen in Sect. 3.2, according to Stiglitz and Weiss (1981), higher interest rates can lead to increased default risk—in a framework of moral hazard and Type II credit rationing—so within the recent scenario of increasing market interest rates, we would expect a corresponding increase in default risk. In the last years, we have indeed observed an increase in default risk, particularly among speculative-grade and lower-rated issuers, so this may represent empirical evidence of the validity of the Stiglitz-Weiss model.

In the United States, the speculative-grade corporate default rate has seen a significant rise. As of December 2023, the default rate stood at 4.8%, the highest level since May 2021. This increase is attributed to the challenging financing conditions and tighter funding liquidity that have particularly affected the lowest-rated borrowers. A notable example includes several high-profile defaults such as Envision, Venator, QualTek, and Monitronics (S&P Global Ratings, 2023a, 2023b). In Europe, the speculative-grade corporate default rate is expected to rise to 3.75% by September 2024. The increase in defaults is partly due to the rising costs of debt as yields continue to climb despite narrowing spreads. This rise in the costs of debt makes it more difficult for companies, especially those with lower credit ratings, to refinance existing debt or service new debt (S&P Global Ratings, 2023c).

Among the factors that may have contributed to this increased default risk, we can surely include the global economic conditions, since tightened credit conditions and slower economic growth have increased the financial strain on companies. The overall economic slowdown has particularly impacted sectors like consumer products, media and entertainment, chemicals, packaging, and environmental services (S&P Global Ratings, 2023c). Because of that, in the United States, the speculative-grade bond spread suggests an increasing default rate, with the distress ratio indicating significant credit stress among lower-rated issuers. Moreover, various economic indicators, such as the yield curve inversion, declining corporate profits and tightening bank lending conditions, signal heightened financial stress and potential for increased defaults over the next 12 months (S&P Global Ratings, 2023b). A significant example is represented by the consumer/service sector, which globally experienced the highest number of defaults, with significant defaults occurring in leisure time/media sectors. In the US, this sector led with 96 defaults, indicating the sector's vulnerability to economic shifts and interest rate hikes (S&P Global Ratings, 2023a). In Europe, the high-yield bond market has faced increased pressure: the high costs of debt have led to higher default risks, especially as a large portion of speculative-grade debt matures in 2025.

A second interesting scenario concerning the credit rationing phenomena is the generalized and strong increase in the Non-Performing Loans (NPL) ratio of banks that has particularly developed at a global level starting from the 2007–2008 global financial crisis. The academic literature provides significant insights into the link between credit rationing and the NPL ratio. We have seen that credit rationing occurs when banks limit the amount of credit available to borrowers, regardless of the interest rate, and this situation often arises due to asymmetric information, leading banks to restrict lending to minimize potential losses. Credit rationing implies a decrease in the total volume of loans (the denominator of the NPL ratio) because when banks restrict credit, fewer loans are granted, but the number of non-performing loans (the numerator) may not decrease at the same rate, leading to an increase in the NPL ratio. This is because the existing bad loans remain on the books while new lending is curtailed.

Regarding the empirical evidence, Goyal et al. (2023) indicate that banks with higher capital adequacy ratios and adequate loan loss provisions tend to experience fewer losses from NPLs. This relationship underscores the risk management strategies banks employ in response to rising NPL ratios, which can include credit rationing to control potential defaults. Klein (2013) also noted that NPLs are inversely related to capital adequacy, highlighting that banks with lower capital are incentivized to take on riskier loans, which often leads to higher NPLs. If we take into consideration the macroeconomic and institutional factors, the work of Tanaskovic and Jandric (2023) found that higher credit growth is often associated with increased credit risk and higher NPL ratios, especially in environments with lax loan underwriting standards. Additionally, institutional quality, governance and regulatory oversight play crucial roles in moderating the relationship between credit rationing and NPL ratios. Effective regulatory frameworks and institutional quality can thus mitigate the negative impacts of credit rationing by ensuring better credit risk management and more stringent loan approval processes.

These studies collectively highlight the intricate dynamics between credit rationing, bank capital adequacy, and the NPL ratio, providing a comprehensive understanding of how restricting credit can inadvertently increase the proportion of non-performing loans in the banking sector. Because of this, it is not easy to understand how much the increase in the NPL ratio observed after the 2007–2008 global financial crisis is due to an increase in the NPL ratio numerator or to a decrease in the NPL ratio denominator. In fact, to understand the changes in the NPL ratio after the global financial crisis, it is necessary to examine the percentage changes in both the numerator (non-performing loans) and the denominator (total loans). Here we report a summary based on recent data:

- from 2007 to 2008, we observed an NPL ratio increase of 138.64%, with an increase in the numerator of 104.55% and a decrease in the denominator of –14.29%; during the first year of the global financial crisis, the NPL ratio increased significantly, and the increase in NPL (numerator) was the major contributor, and the decrease in total loans (denominator) also contributed to the increase in the NPL ratio;
- from 2008 to 2009, we observed an NPL ratio increase of 41.18% due to an increase in the numerator equal to 33.33% and a decrease in the denominator of –5.56%; in the second year after the financial crisis, the NPL ratio further increased, and the increase in NPL was the primary driver, while the decrease in total loans contributed to a lesser extent;
- from 2009 to 2010, we started observing a reversal of the trend, with a decrease of the NPL ratio equal to –11.46% due to a decrease in the numerator of –16.67% and a decrease in the denominator of –5.88% in the third year, the NPL ratio fell because of a decrease both in the NPL and in total loans.

In conclusion, the increase in the NPL ratio observed after the 2007–2008 financial crisis was primarily driven by a substantial increase in the numerator (Non-Performing Loans), while the decrease in the denominator (Total Loans) also contributed to the rising NPL ratio, but to a lesser extent compared to the increase in Non-Performing Loans.

3.4.2 SMEs, Start-Ups and R&D-Oriented Firms

The credit rationing issue is particularly acute for specific firms, e.g., small and medium-sized enterprises (SMEs), start-ups, and firms strongly investing in Research and Development (R&D), as these entities face unique challenges that exacerbate informational asymmetries and perceived risks by lenders. This subsection examines the literature on credit rationing as it pertains to these specific types of firms, highlighting key findings and implications for policy and practice.

Start-ups and young firms often struggle with credit rationing due to their lack of established credit history and financial performance records. Studies such as those by Petersen and Rajan (1994) indicate that start-ups and young firms have limited access to external finance, largely because they cannot provide sufficient information to reassure lenders about their ability to repay. This lack of information increases the risk of adverse selection and moral hazard, making banks hesitant to grant credit. Keeton (1979) further elaborates on this by explaining how start-ups facing higher interest rates may resort to riskier projects, thus perpetuating a cycle of credit denial.

SMEs face similar challenges. Due to their size, they often have limited collateral and a narrow asset base, which makes securing loans more difficult. Beck et al. (2005) find that small firms in developing countries are particularly disadvantaged in accessing credit. The limited scale of their operations means that they are perceived as high-risk borrowers, leading to higher interest rates or outright credit denial. Additionally, small firms often lack the negotiating power to secure favourable loan terms, further exacerbating their credit access issues. More recently, Kallandranis et al. (2023) provide a detailed examination of credit rationing dynamics among Eurozone SMEs, and in particular, they highlight the importance of considering both rejected and discouraged borrowers (i.e., borrowers who do not apply for loans due to fear of rejection) to understand the financial barriers faced by SMEs fully. The study calls for targeted policy actions to alleviate these constraints and promote a more inclusive financial environment for SMEs. In particular, they find that smaller and younger firms are systematically discouraged from applying for loans, indicating that the frequency of discouraged firms cannot be ignored in credit market analyses. Moreover, they show how credit rationing probabilities decrease with firm size, confirming that larger firms face fewer financial constraints, while regarding firm age, the probability of being credit rationed follows an inverse U-shaped pattern, with start-ups facing the highest rejection rates, followed by middle-aged firms, while older firms experience lower rejection probabilities. Finally, their analysis reveals a general decline in rejection rates over time, although the discouragement rate does not show a clear trend; this result suggests that while banks may be rejecting fewer applications, the underlying fear of rejection among SMEs remains persistent.

Firms investing heavily in R&D are particularly susceptible to credit rationing. R&D projects typically involve high uncertainty and long gestation periods before generating returns. As a result, banks are often reluctant to finance these projects due to the higher risk and the difficulty in evaluating the potential outcomes. According to Hall and Lerner (2010), the intangible nature of R&D assets complicates collateralization, making it harder for these firms to secure traditional loans. This situation is further compounded by the fact that R&D-intensive firms often operate in highly competitive and rapidly changing markets, adding to the uncertainty and perceived risk.

Addressing credit rationing for start-ups, small and young companies, and R&D-investing firms requires targeted policy interventions. Governments and financial institutions can play a crucial role by developing credit guarantee schemes that reduce the risk for lenders. According to the OECD (2014), such schemes can significantly enhance credit access for SMEs and innovative firms by providing partial guarantees that cover a portion of the loan defaults. Additionally, fostering a robust venture capital ecosystem can provide alternative financing sources for high-risk, high-reward projects typically shunned by traditional banks (Gompers & Lerner, 2001).

Credit rationing remains a significant barrier for start-ups, small and young companies, and R&D-intensive firms. The unique challenges faced by these entities necessitate specialized financial products and supportive policies to bridge the financing gap. By reducing informational asymmetries and perceived risks, policymakers and financial institutions can facilitate better access to credit, thereby supporting innovation and economic growth.

3.4.3 Economic Crises and Downturns

Credit rationing, where borrowers are denied loans despite being willing to pay higher interest rates, often intensifies during economic crises. This phenomenon can have severe implications for economic stability and recovery. This review explores the literature on credit rationing during economic downturns, focusing on the mechanisms driving this issue and its broader economic impacts.

Economic crises exacerbate the problem of credit rationing due to increasing uncertainty and risk aversion among lenders. According to Stiglitz and Weiss (1981), asymmetric information plays a crucial role in credit rationing. During economic downturns, the adverse selection problem intensifies as the pool of borrowers appears riskier overall, leading banks to restrict lending to avoid potentially high default rates. Banks also face increased difficulty in distinguishing between high-risk and low-risk borrowers, further tightening the supply of funds (Mishkin, 1991).

Additionally, banks' balance sheets deteriorate during crises, reducing their capital base and lending capacity. Bernanke and Lown (1991) highlight the 'credit crunch' phenomenon, where banks, experiencing capital shortfalls, drastically cut back on lending. This contraction is compounded by regulatory capital requirements, which become binding constraints during downturns, forcing banks to limit credit extension even further.

Credit rationing during economic downturns disproportionately affects SMEs and new ventures, which are typically more reliant on external financing. Beck et al. (2005) find that SMEs in developing countries are particularly vulnerable to credit constraints, which impede their ability to invest, expand and survive during downturns. This is because SMEs often lack the collateral and credit history required to secure loans, making them less attractive to risk-averse lenders in periods of economic downturn.

The contraction in credit availability can lead to a significant slowdown in economic activity. According to Koo (2008), a 'balance sheet recession' occurs when firms prioritize debt repayment over investment due to the inability to secure financing, leading to prolonged economic stagnation. This phenomenon was notably observed during the Japanese economic crisis of the 1990s and the global financial crisis of 2007–2008.

Policymakers have employed various measures to mitigate the impact of credit rationing during economic crises. Central banks often engage in monetary easing to lower interest rates and increase liquidity in the banking system. However, Mishkin (2009) argues that during severe economic crises, traditional monetary policy tools may be insufficient. Therefore, unconventional measures, such as quantitative easing and targeted lending facilities, are necessary to support credit markets.

Government guarantees and direct lending programmes are also crucial in alleviating credit constraints. The Troubled Asset Relief Program (TARP) implemented during the 2007–2008 financial crisis is a prominent example, where the US government injected capital into banks to stabilize the financial system and encourage lending (Veronesi & Zingales, 2010). Similarly, the Paycheck Protection Program (PPP) during the COVID-19 pandemic provided forgivable loans to SMEs to maintain employment and business continuity (Granja et al., 2020).

Credit rationing intensifies during economic crises due to increased risk aversion, deteriorating bank balance sheets and heightened information asymmetries. This leads to significant adverse effects on SMEs and overall economic activity. Policymakers must employ a mix of traditional and unconventional monetary policies, along with government guarantees and direct lending programmes, to mitigate the impact of credit rationing and support economic recovery.

3.5 Concluding Remarks

Informational asymmetries between banks and firms can lead to a phenomenon known as credit rationing. Theoretically, we distinguish between Type I rationing (Jaffee & Russell, 1976) and Type II rationing (Stiglitz & Weiss, 1981). In Type I rationing, all potential borrowers have equal access to the credit market but may receive a loan smaller than requested. Conversely, in Type II rationing, some borrowers, who appear indistinguishable from others, do not receive any credit. Despite being willing to accept more onerous contract terms, the bank's ex-ante assessment deems their projects too risky and, based on a rational choice, decides not to extend credit to them.

While the theoretical definition of rationing appears straightforward, empirically quantifying it is challenging. Traditionally, for firms, credit rationing represents both a problem of the quantity of credit obtained and the cost incurred. Empirically, this involves measuring interest rate trends on loans and the amounts of credit issued and utilized. In the presence of rationing, a certain rigidity in both the quantity and price of credit is expected. Specifically, the risk premium on loans, defined as the difference between the loans' interest rates and the risk-free rate, is negatively correlated with market interest rates. Additionally, banks provide a form of quantity insurance by offering new non-revocable credit lines (loan commitments) in response to generalized market interest rate increases (Berger & Udell, 1992).

Further insights into empirically identifying credit rationing can be obtained through surveys, measuring constraints on credit provision and acquisition from both the supply side (Bank Lending Survey by the ECB) and the demand side (Survey on the Access to Finance of Enterprises-SAFE). These surveys help to capture any restrictions on granting or obtaining credit.

References

Akerlof, G. A. (1970). The market for 'lemons': Quality uncertainty and the market mechanism. *The Quarterly Journal of Economics, 84*(3), 488–500.

Banerjee, A., Breza, E., Duflo, E., & Kinnan, C. (2019). *Can microfinance unlock a poverty trap for some entrepreneurs?* (NBER Working Paper Series, 26346).

Beck, T., Demirguc-Kunt, A., & Maksimovic, V. (2005). Financial and legal constraints to growth: Does firm size matter? *Journal of Finance, 60*(1), 137–177.

Berger, A. N., & Udell, G. F. (1992). Some evidence on the empirical significance of credit rationing. *Journal of Political Economy, 100*(5), 1047–1077.

Berger, A. N., & Udell, G. F. (1995). Relationship lending and lines of credit in small firm finance. *Journal of Business, 68*(3), 351–381.

Bernanke, B. S., & Lown, C. S. (1991). The credit crunch. *Brookings Papers on Economic Activity, 1991*(2), 205–247.

Besanko, D., & Thakor, A. V. (1987a). Collateral and rationing: Sorting equilibria in monopolistic and competitive credit markets. *International Economic Review, 28*, 671–689.

Besanko, D., & Thakor, A. V. (1987b). Competitive equilibrium in the credit market under asymmetric information. *Journal of Economic Theory, 42*, 167–182.

Bester, H. (1985a). Screening vs. rationing in credit markets with imperfect information. *The American Economic Review, 75*(4), 850–855.

Bester, H. (1985b). The level of investment in credit markets with imperfect information. *Journal of Institutional and Theoretical Economics, 141*, 503–515.

Bester, H. (1987). The role of collateral in credit markets with imperfect information. *European Economic Review, 31*, 887–899.

Bofondi, M., Carpinelli, L., & Sette, E. (2018). Credit supply during a sovereign debt crisis. *Journal of the European Economic Association, 16*(3), 696–729.

Brighi, P., & Venturelli, V. (2017). Demand and Supply Determinants of Credit Availability: Evidence from the Current Credit Crisis for European SMEs. In *Financial Markets, SME Financing and Emerging Economies* (pp. 41–70). Cham: Springer International Publishing.

Chiaramonte, L., Dreassi, A., Piserà, S., & Khan, A. (2023). Mergers and acquisitions in the financial industry: A bibliometric review and future research directions. *Research in International Business and Finance, 64*, 101837.

De Meza, D., & David C. Webb. (1987). "Too much investment: A problem of asymmetric information." *The quarterly journal of economics 102*(2), 281–292.

Dervi, U. D., Khan, A., Saba, I., Hassan, M. K., & Paltrinieri, A. (2022). Green and socially responsible finance: Past, present and future. *Managerial Finance, 48*(8), 1250–1278.

Diamond, Douglas W. (1984). "Financial intermediation and delegated monitoring." *The review of economic studies 51*(3), 393–414.

Flatnes, J. E. (2021). Information sharing and rationing in credit markets. *American Journal of Agricultural Economics, 103*(3), 944–960.
Freimer, M., & Gordon, M. J. (1965). Why bankers ration credit. *The Quarterly Journal of Economics, 79*(3), 397–410.
Freixas, X., & Rochet, J. C. (2008). *Microeconomics of banking*. The MIT Press.
Gompers, P., & Lerner, J. (2001). The venture capital revolution. *Journal of Economic Perspectives, 15*(2), 145–168.
Goyal, S., Singhal, N., Mishra, N., & Verma, S. K. (2023). The impact of macroeconomic and institutional environment on NPL of developing and developed countries. *Future Business Journal, 9*(45).
Granja, J., Makridis, C., Yannelis, C., & Zwick, E. (2020). Did the *Paycheck protection program hit the target?* (NBER Working Paper, No. 27095).
Hall, B. H., & Lerner, J. (2010). The financing of R&D and innovation. *Handbook of the Economics of Innovation, 1*, 609–639.
Hess, J. D. (1984). Imperfect information and credit rationing: Comment. *The Quarterly Journal of Economics, 99*(4), 865–868.
Hodgman, D. R. (1960). Credit risk and credit rationing. *The Quarterly Journal of Economics, 74*(2), 258–278.
Hodgman, D. R. (1963). *Commercial bank loan and investment policy*. Champaign.
Jaffee, D. M., & Modigliani, F. (1969). A theory and test of credit rationing: Reply. *American Economic Review, 59*(5), 852–856.
Jaffee, D. M., & Russell, T. (1976). Imperfect information, uncertainty, and credit rationing. *The Quarterly Journal of Economics, 90*(4), 651–666.
Jappelli, Tullio. (1990). "Who is credit constrained in the US economy?." *The Quarterly Journal of Economics 105*(1), 219–234.
Jiménez, G., Ongena, S., Peydró, J.-L., & Saurina, J. (2017). Macroprudential policy, countercyclical bank capital buffers, and credit supply: Evidence from the Spanish dynamic provisioning experiments. *Journal of Political Economy, 125*(6), 1723–2245.
Kallandranis, C., Anastasiou, D., & Drakos, K. (2023). Credit rationing prevalence for Eurozone firms. *Journal of Business Research, 158*, 113640.
Keeton, W. R. (1979). *Equilibrium credit rationing*. Garland Publishing.
Khan, A., Goodell, J. W., Hassan, M. K., & Paltrinieri, A. (2022). A bibliometric review of finance bibliometric papers. *Finance Research Letters, 47*(A), 102520.
Klein, N. (2013). *Non-performing Loans in CESEE: Determinants and impact on macroeconomic performance* (IMF Working Paper No. 13/72). Washington, DC: International Monetary Fund.
Koo, R. C. (2008). *The holy grail of macroeconomics: Lessons from Japan's great recession*. Wiley.

Milde, H., & Riley, J. G. (1988). Signaling in credit markets. *Quarterly Journal of Economics, 103*, 101–129.
Mishkin, F. S. (1991). *Asymmetric information and financial crises: a historical perspective* (NBER Working Paper, No. 3400).
Mishkin, F. S. (2009). Is monetary policy effective during financial crises? *American Economic Review, 99*(2), 573–577.
OECD. (2014). *Financing SMEs and entrepreneurs 2014: An OECD scoreboard.* OECD Publishing.
Padilla, A. J., & Pagano, M. (2000). Sharing default information as a borrower discipline device. *European Economic Review, 44*, 1951–1980.
Pagano, M., & Jappelli, T. (1993). Information sharing in credit markets. *Journal of Finance, 48*, 1693–1718.
Petersen, M. A., & Rajan, R. G. (1994). The benefits of lending relationships: Evidence from small business data. *The Journal of Finance, 49*(1), 3–37.
Petersen, M. A., & Rajan, R. G. (1995). "The effect of credit market competition on lending relationships." *The Quarterly Journal of Economics 110*(2), 407–443.
Schmidt-Mohr, U. (1997). Rationing versus collateralization in competitive and monopolistic credit markets with asymmetric information. *European Economic Review, 41*, 1321–1342.
S&P Global Ratings. (2023a). Default, transition, and recovery: 2023 annual global corporate default and rating transition study.
S&P Global Ratings. (2023b). Higher rates for even longer could Push the U.S. speculative-grade corporate default rate to 5% by September 2024.
S&P Global Ratings. (2023c). Elevated interest rates could Push the European speculative-grade corporate default rate to 3.75% by September 2024.
Stiglitz, J. E., & Weiss, A. (1981). Credit rationing in markets with imperfect information. *American Economic Review, 71*(3), 393–410.
Tanaskovic, S., & Jandric, M. (2023). Impact of financial development and financial inclusion on banking stability: Evidence from ASEAN countries. *Future Business Journal.*
Van Eck, N., & Waltman, L. (2010). Software survey: VOSviewer, a computer program for bibliometric mapping. *Scientometrics, 84*(2), 523–538.
Veronesi, P., & Zingales, L. (2010). Paulson's gift. *Journal of Financial Economics, 97*(3), 339–368.
Xu, B., Yang, J., & Dasí-Rodríguez, S. (2020). Determinants of credit availability for high-tech start-ups. *International Entrepreneurship and Management Journal, 16*(4), 1483–1501.

CHAPTER 4

Relationship Lending, Transaction Lending and Corporate Banking

4.1 Costs-Benefits Analysis of Relationship Lending and Multi-banking

In a pioneering contribution, Hodgman (1963) emphasized the importance of relationship lending, understood as a continued and repeated credit relationship over time, as a crucial factor in determining the contractual terms of bank loans. Subsequently, Hester (1977), using a sample of 1,072 loans granted by 62 US banks in 1972, empirically tested Hodgman's intuition. The results suggest that pre-existing and long-lasting customer relationships facilitate the establishment of more favourable contractual terms for clients. Since then, numerous studies have been developed to identify, on the one hand, a shared definition—still not achieved—of relationship lending and, on the other, some empirical regularities.

From a theoretical perspective, the literature on informational asymmetries (see, among others, Diamond, 1984, 1991; Sharpe, 1990) suggests that banking intermediaries exist because they benefit from economies of scale and/or comparative advantages in producing information on borrowers. Specifically, if the benefits in terms of greater information produced exceed the costs, it will be more advantageous to resort to banks rather than the market. Banks derive benefits from the economies of scale realized in conducting ex-ante screening and ex-post monitoring operations. The costs are twofold and include those that firms would incur to

P. Brighi and M. Mussoni, *The Bank-Business Relationship*, https://doi.org/10.1007/978-3-031-91068-5_4

convince investors to finance them and those that the latter would incur to monitor them (Diamond, 1984). Informational asymmetries characterizing the bank–firm relationship, particularly pronounced in the case of SMEs, find a possible solution in establishing continuous and repeated customer relationships through which the bank acquires an exclusive and lasting informational asset. These advantages are further accentuated in the case of local banks. The deep root in the local community provides these banks with a series of advantages evident both in the screening and monitoring phases. Better knowledge of customers, improved management of information flows during the credit relationship, and greater risk control through the activation of social sanctions against debtors—feasible only within a local community (peer monitoring, see Stiglitz, 1990; Varian, 1990)—imply a reduction in the screening and monitoring costs for SMEs. These advantages are added to those traditionally derived by the bank from operating under monopoly conditions in the payment services and from establishing long-term contractual relationships, the so-called relationship lending.

According to the most recent literature on financial intermediation, relationship lending is characterized by an implicit long-term contract between a bank and a borrower. Through repeated interactions with the firm, the bank accumulates private information (soft information) that reduces informational asymmetry. Numerous theoretical studies have highlighted the superiority of this form of relationship compared to the more fragmented, transaction-based approach. In the latter case, the relationship between the bank and the firm is limited to a single transaction, whose risk-return evaluation is based solely on accounting data and publicly available information (hard information). While relationship lending represents a mechanism through which the bank can mitigate informational asymmetries in financing SMEs, it does not exclude the possibility for this category of firms to access transaction lending services (leasing, mortgages, etc.) offered by larger banks (Berger & Udell, 2002). According to the so-called 'current paradigm', large banks tend to specialize in loans to larger, less opaque firms from an informational perspective, using hard information; smaller banks are more specialized in financing SMEs due to a comparative advantage in possessing soft information (Berger & Black, 2011). Subsequent literature (Udell, 2018) transcends the dichotomous approach—relationship lending vs. transaction lending—and identifies lending technologies differentiated by the varying degrees of hard and soft information they encompass (see Table 4.1).

The phenomenon describing a continuous and long-term relationship between a bank and a firm is identified using terms that are sometimes interchangeable, such as relationship banking and relationship lending. However, it is challenging to find a universal definition in literature. Relationship banking is characterized by features that extend beyond those of relationship lending, as it includes not only the provision of credit, but also other financial services. Additionally, this practice can be associated with both investment banks and non-bank financial intermediaries. A more suitable term to describe the bank–firm relationship, according to Boot (2000), is 'relationship intermediation', which encompasses the provision of financial services under two conditions:

- The financial intermediary makes costly investments to acquire confidential information on each financed client, which often becomes the exclusive property of the intermediary.

Table 4.1 Lending technologies

Technology	*Type*	*Borrower*	*Information*
Relationship lending	Relationship	Opaque	Soft
Financial statement lending	Transaction	Transparent	Hard
Asset-based lending/ discounting	Transaction	Opaque	Hard
Factoring	Transaction	Opaque	Hard
Equipment lending	Transaction	Opaque and transparent	Hard
Leasing	Transaction	Opaque and transparent	Hard
Real estate-based lending	Transaction	Opaque and transparent	Hard
Small businesses' credit scoring	Transaction	Opaque	Hard
Crowdfunding	Transaction	Opaque	Hard
Trade credit	Transaction and relationship	Opaque and transparent	Soft and hard

Source Elaboration by the Authors, based on Udell (2018)

- The profitability of these informational investments and the opportunity to repeat them over time are verified through multiple and repeated interactions, either in terms of time or the number of services used, with each client.

Freixas (2005) identifies relationship banking as an investment activity in the provision of financial services that allows for a series of repeated contractual operations with the same client. The investment in customer relationships differs depending on the type of underlying financial contract. However, since the standard investment is the one made by the bank in the various stages of the credit investigation to acquire information on the borrowing firm, the term relationship banking has often become synonymous with relationship lending, a restriction widely used in the literature. In order to meet the definition of relationship banking, according to Freixas (2005), the following conditions must be met:

- The bank must be able to offer financial services to its clients on more favourable contractual terms than its competitors, and this competitive advantage should consolidate over time.
- Loan contracts are incomplete. In other words, long-term contingent loan contracts are not available, and if they were, they would not be superior to non-contingent ones.

The first condition suggests a superiority of banks in gathering information that goes beyond the relatively more objective data, such as financial statements, collateral and other public information, which constitute the core of the so-called soft information. The information obtained is confidential and not accessible to competitors. The second condition implies that a higher degree of integration due to, for example, a merger or acquisition between the bank and the firm is impossible. It also excludes long-term conditional loan contracts that provide two options: (i) the contract is regularly completed; (ii) the contract is renewed but is tied to a predetermined interest rate (Freixas, 2005).

The literature on relationship lending identifies many benefits but also some costs associated with this practice. From a theoretical perspective, Bornheim and Herbeck (1998) suggest that the net benefit curve of relationship lending has a monotonically decreasing shape and intersects the x-axis at a certain threshold value of the duration of the banking relationship (see Fig. 4.1).

The benefits of relationship lending primarily include more favourable contractual terms, the ability to rely on stable interest rates in the face of counter-cyclical monetary policies, and greater flexibility during both the negotiation and renegotiation phases to the advantage of the firm. The bank, thanks to the informational advantage acquired during the relationship, reduces the ex-ante risk of evaluating the firm. Furthermore, the firm is protected against credit rationing risk through continuous and implicit renewal of the loan contract (Petersen & Rajan, 1995). The re-negotiability of the loan contract prevents internal financial tensions related to temporary negative shocks (Boot et al., 1993; Greenbaum & Thakor, 1995; von Thadden, 1995). The exclusivity of the relationship with a bank creates the conditions for an implicit insurance service—the

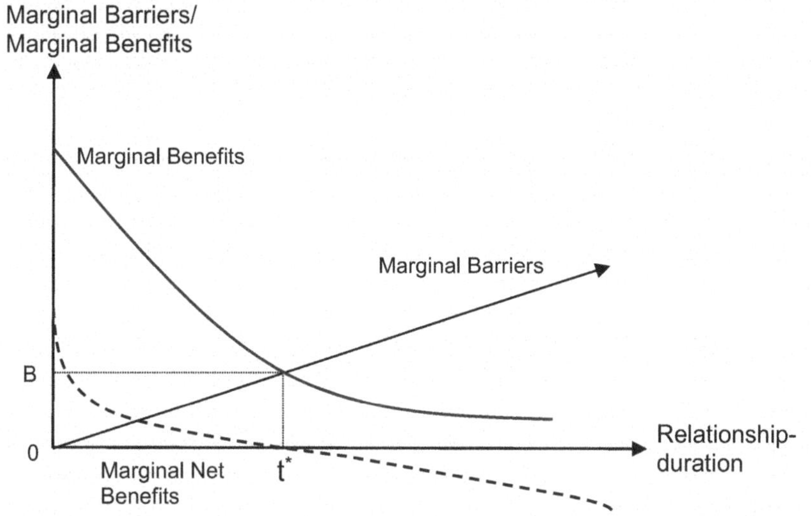

Fig. 4.1 Benefits and costs of relationship lending (*Source* Bornheim & Herbeck [1998, p. 328])

bank is ready to provide emergency credit lines if the firm faces temporary liquidity crises or to shield it from sudden generalized interest rate increases (interest rate smoothing, Berlin & Mester, 1999).

Moreover, the bank tends to relax collateral requirements (Berger & Udell, 1996; Boot & Thakor, 1994). Specifically, Boot and Thakor (1994) show that correct behaviour by the firm and successful investment projects enhance the firm's reputation, signalling its good quality, which allows it to obtain more favourable contractual terms from the bank in subsequent periods. Firms that survive in the market and accumulate a series of regular payments significantly reduce the liquidity constraints resulting from informational asymmetries (Holmstrom & Tirole, 1997). In summary, an exclusive and long-lasting relationship provides the bank with privileged information that enables a better assessment of the borrower and the application of more advantageous contractual terms.

Conversely, the costs affect both the bank and the client. In the event of a potential default by the firm, the bank might renew the credit in an attempt to recover previous loans. This situation is referred to as the soft-budget constraint problem, where the bank is 'captured' by the client. In scenarios where it would have been optimal to liquidate the firm, the bank, hoping to recover prior loans, proceeds with an inefficient renegotiation of the existing loan contract. Anticipating such behaviour from the bank, the firm might take excessive risks ex-ante, failing to exert the necessary effort to avoid bankruptcy (Bolton & Scharfstein, 1996; Dewatripont & Maskin, 1995).

In a credit-based system, the bank tends to exert influence over the firm's internal decisions, fostering the establishment of close bilateral ties between the two parties. Given the costly nature of information production, economies of scale lead to a natural monopoly in providing credit to a particular entity, creating conditions for rent extraction through the application of higher interest rates: this is the debtor hold-up issue (Greenbaum et al., 1989; Rajan, 1992; Sharpe, 1990). However, this risk can be mitigated through borrowing from multiple banks (Thakor, 1996; von Thadden, 1992, 1995). Von Thadden (1995) demonstrates that a relationship with two banks is sufficient to restore competition among intermediaries, reducing the risk of ex-post increases in the cost of credit. One way to alleviate the informational monopoly resulting from relationship lending is through information sharing with other banks. If banks enjoy an informational monopoly, firms lack the incentive to invest in high-quality projects because they fear banks will reduce the returns through high interest rates. Therefore, banks have an incentive to commit to sharing information with other banks. The theoretical model by Padilla and Pagano (1997) suggests that information sharing generates Pareto superior equilibria compared to non-sharing.

Informational rent extraction could also result from a virtuous mechanism among market power, relationship lending, credit conditions and availability, as suggested by Petersen and Rajan (1995). Greater market power exercised by an intermediary can lead to increased investments in acquiring long-term customer relationships, which in turn generate informational rents and a greater supply of credit at the beginning of the banking relationship. Initially, if the credit market is concentrated, banks tend to offer lower interest rates relative to the average quality of the borrower. Once the banking relationship is consolidated and the borrower's good quality is confirmed, the bank tends to charge higher interest rates. The dynamic analysis of credit conditions relative to the average quality of the borrower is efficient, as it reduces credit rationing. Specifically, the model predicts that if the market concentration is high: (i) the number of financed firms increases; (ii) the average quality and cost of credit for financed firms decrease; (iii) the cost of credit decreases more slowly as the quality of the financed firm increases.

An alternative theory explaining the benefits of relationship lending is related to switching costs; i.e., the costs a customer incurs when moving from one intermediary to another. These costs influence adverse selection mechanisms and, consequently, the competitive structure of the banking system. Vesala (2007) demonstrates that if switching costs are low, the banking market is contestable, making it easy for any customer, even those of 'poor' quality, to change banks. The resulting threat of adverse selection limits price competition and discourages competing banks (outsiders) from making overly aggressive offers. Consequently, it is easier for an insider bank to offer favourable terms to retain its customers, especially if they have proven to be of 'good' quality over time. The risk of adverse selection diminishes as switching costs increase, allowing only 'good' quality customers to switch intermediaries. The consequence is that competing banks become more aggressive, and for the insider bank, it becomes more challenging to retain its customers without increasing risk propensity, resulting in reduced profits. However, above a certain threshold, the adverse selection effect disappears completely, competing banks' offer conditions do not change, and higher switching costs associated with a more concentrated credit market produce an unequivocal positive effect on the markup that the insider bank can charge. Therefore, there is a non-monotonic 'V-shaped' relationship between insider bank profits and switching costs. In summary, Vesala (2007) demonstrates that the bank benefits from relationship lending in two extreme market situations: (i) when switching costs are very low and the market is highly contestable; (ii) when switching costs are high and the market is highly concentrated.

Ioannidou and Ongena (2010) analyze how a customer's decision to switch from one intermediary to another can influence bank behaviour and the credit conditions offered. Specifically, the authors demonstrate that when switching from an insider bank to a competing bank, a firm can obtain significantly more favourable terms. The new bank initially lowers the loan interest rate but sharply increases it after a few years, following a strategy consistent with the existence of hold-up costs. Ornelas et al. (2022) achieve similar results in a study on the relationship between market concentration and loan spreads, finding a positive relationship. They also confirm the hold-up practice, but only in the case of private banks. Public banks, as the relationship with the firm strengthens, reduce the loan spread.

A summary of the main benefits and costs of relationship lending discussed in this section is presented in Table 4.2.

Relationship lending can also take the form of 'multi-banking' or 'multi-lending'; that is, the situation where a firm has more banking relationships. As previously seen, this model can be adopted by firms as a strategy to mitigate the adverse effects of hold-up posed by banks, but other theoretical arguments help elucidate the rationale behind multi-banking. According to Detragiache et al. (2000), firms tend to diversify their credit relationships to reduce the risk that their primary bank, due to a sudden shortage of funds, is unable to refinance the firm's investment projects. In other words, if a firm maintains an exclusive relationship with one bank and that bank suddenly faces a liquidity crisis, the firm will need to seek financing from another bank, with which it has less informational transparency. This situation, characterized by informational asymmetries, increases the risk of credit rationing. To avoid this, firms diversify their funding sources ex-ante among multiple banks, hoping that ex-post, at least one will be able to refinance their investment projects. Based on this reasoning, the authors develop a theoretical model to determine the optimal number of banking relationships. They conclude that multiple banking relationships are optimal for borrowers who seek to safeguard

Table 4.2 Benefits and costs of relationship lending

Benefits	*Costs*
Better contractual terms Relationship lending allows firms to obtain more favourable loan conditions, such as lower interest rates, reduced collateral requirements, and greater credit availability (Berger & Udell, 2002; Boot, 2000)	**Informational monopoly position (hold-up problem)** The lending bank may exploit its superior knowledge about the borrower, limiting the firm's ability to seek alternative financing sources (Sharpe, 1990; von Thadden, 2004)
Interest-rate smoothing Protection of firms, in terms of interest rates, against restrictive monetary policies by providing a counter-cyclical function (Gambacorta & Mistrulli, 2014)	**Soft-budget constraint/bank capture** Banks may continue financing struggling firms in an attempt to recover previous loans, leading to inefficient credit allocation (Boot & Thakor, 2000; Ioannidou & Ongena, 2010)
Greater flexibility in negotiations Relationship lenders provide more lenient repayment terms and are more willing to renegotiate loan conditions in times of distress (Petersen & Rajan, 1995)	**Higher cost of financing in the long run** Borrowers may face higher interest rates over time due to reduced competition among lenders (Ongena & Smith, 2001)
Enhanced reputation and market signal Successfully securing a loan from a relationship lender signals creditworthiness to other market participants, potentially easing access to other forms of financing (Berger et al., 2001)	**Switching costs** Firms may find it costly to change banks due to informational lock-in, leading to suboptimal financing decisions and banks' capture of the client (Farinha & Santos, 2002)
Increased credit availability for SMEs Small and medium enterprises benefit from stronger relationships with banks, which can compensate for their lack of credit history (Beck, 2013; Degryse & Van Cayseele, 2000)	**Potential reduction in credit supply during crises** Relationship lending can expose banks to higher credit risk, making them more reluctant to extend new loans in financial downturns (Bofondi et al., 2018)

Source Elaboration by the Authors

against the risk of rationing due to the liquidity and capital constraints of their primary bank. Conversely, single banking is optimal only when informational asymmetries are so minor that adverse selection risks are negligible for any bank.

Detragiache et al. (2000) argue that more advanced financial systems from a regulatory standpoint facilitate arm's-length relationships rather than relationship lending. Furthermore, they show that more efficient distressed loan recovery systems encourage exclusive banking relationships, disincentivizing multi-banking. The bank–firm relationship is modelled on the premise that banks acquire information on the firm's quality, which is not shared with other financial intermediaries. A relationship bank, having incurred significant costs to produce private information on the borrower's quality, may be inclined to use this information for rent extraction. Ex-post rent extraction by creditors can distort the ex-ante incentives of entrepreneurs, leading to suboptimal investment project choices. In such circumstances, establishing a second banking relationship can restore competition among lenders and limit ex-post rent extraction, as suggested by empirical studies.

In the case of large firms, Carletti et al. (2007) argue that multi-banking can be seen as a strategy adopted by the bank rather than the firm to build a diversified asset portfolio and limit counterparty risk. Banks, while performing their lending function, face regulatory (e.g., minimum capital requirements) and managerial constraints (e.g., customer distance), where multi-banking may be the optimal solution for financing multiple projects and achieving greater diversification, which is particularly true for smaller banks relative to the size of the project being financed. Banks engage in multi-banking more intensively when they have high overall exposure, are relatively small compared to the investment project, and when firms show low profitability and poor loan repayment reliability. An additional advantage of multi-banking is the greater stability it provides for the banking system, making it particularly attractive for banks with stringent capitalization levels, high monitoring costs and relationships with low-profitability firms.

Another argument supporting multi-banking is provided by Hart (1995) and Bolton and Scharfstein (1996). They suggest that multiple banking relationships can limit opportunistic behaviour by the firm's management, which could lead to the firm's default. With multiple bank creditors, coordinating a debt restructuring plan in case of default becomes more difficult and costly, potentially incentivizing firms to avoid default. Therefore, firms may be motivated to maintain multiple banking relationships in environments where bankruptcy costs are low, creditor rights are weak and the legal system's efficiency is uncertain.

Boot and Thakor (2000) argue that the preference of a banking institution for one type of relationship over another is influenced by competitive mechanisms within the financial system. For instance, increased competition within the banking system may make relationship lending more attractive, as it serves as a buffer against potential stock price fluctuations. Conversely, greater competition from the capital market reduces the expected profitability of credit, disincentivizing new entrants into the banking system. Consequently, in the face of increased capital market competition, banks tend to weaken relationship lending, reducing opportunities for firms to establish multiple banking relationships.

Braggion and Ongena (2011) document a significant shift from single to multiple banking relationships over the past two decades. They analyze this transition through a historical lens, providing insights into the evolving nature of firm-bank interactions and the factors driving firms to diversify their banking connections. Refait-Alexandre and Serve (2020) investigate why small and medium-sized enterprises (SMEs) opt for multiple banking relationships. Their study, based on a survey of French SMEs, reveals that larger, high-performing and innovative firms are more inclined to engage with multiple banks. Notably, the research highlights that a CEO's mistrust of their primary bank significantly increases the likelihood of the firm establishing multiple banking relationships, emphasizing the role of trust in banking decisions.

Cappelletti and Mistrulli (2023) offer an interesting reinterpretation of multi-banking during the pandemic crisis years. They highlight the role of multi-banking in reducing liquidity risk for debtors and propose that the interaction between multi-banking and liquidity risk, along with solvency and liquidity requirements imposed by regulators on the banking system, could have implications for financial stability. Their findings suggest that in the absence of other, or affordable, liquidity sources for banks, multi-banking could become perilous due to the contagion effect it might generate among multi-bank institutions, thereby jeopardizing financial stability. These results are particularly relevant for understanding how macroeconomic shocks such as the recent COVID-19 pandemic might impact the real economy and for assessing the implications of alternative bank resolution mechanisms in the face of systemic liquidity crises.

Finally, Fracasso et al. (2024) examine how a firm's social connections impact its banking relationships. Utilizing data from Italian manufacturing firms, the researchers developed text-based measures to assess firm connectedness and found that firms with extensive networks tend to engage with a higher number of banks. This suggests that well-connected firms may leverage their networks to secure more diversified banking partnerships.

These studies collectively enhance our understanding of the factors influencing firms' decisions to maintain multiple banking relationships, including social connectedness, historical trends, trust dynamics and strategic financial considerations.

4.2 The Determinants of Relationship Lending

Relationship lending, or the client relationship between a bank and a firm, is not directly observable. Thus, various variables are used in empirical analysis to approximate this relationship.

(i) The ***duration of the relationship*** between the bank and the firm. The longer the relationship between the bank and the client, the more private and confidential information the bank accumulates (Berger & Udell, 1995; Ongena & Smith, 2001; Petersen & Rajan, 1994). Concerning this variable, empirical evidence yields mixed results. Early US studies on relationship lending suggest that as the duration of the credit relationship increases, contractual terms improve either because the interest rates charged by the bank decrease (Berger & Udell, 1995) or because the amount of credit granted increases (Berger & Udell, 1995; Petersen & Rajan, 1994). Other studies suggest that the accumulation of private information allows the bank to engage in informational capture of the client (hold-up), resulting in informational rent obtained by charging higher interest rates (Angelini et al., 1998; López-Espinosa et al., 2017; Stein, 2015). Angelini et al. (1998) focus on the lending behaviour of cooperative banks: in Italy, these institutions are generally small, have a different governance model than non-cooperative banks, and operate in areas limited to their municipality and neighbouring ones. The results indicate that price discrimination occurs only when the bank lends to non-member clients. Stein (2015) primarily observes discriminatory pricing for SMEs, which, due to their greater informational opacity, rely almost exclusively on banks and thus have lower bargaining power. López-Espinosa et al. (2017) demonstrate that the increase in interest rates is only temporary: the interest rate has a concave shape concerning the duration of the relationship. Unlike previous studies, the authors show that acquiring confidential information (soft information) reduces informational asymmetries, allowing the bank to lower the cost of the greater risk assumed at the beginning of the relationship and consequently reduce the interest rate charged. Finally, other studies (Berger & Udell, 1995; Cole, 1998) show that the duration of relationship lending is highly correlated with the firm's age and positively impacts credit availability. While the first variable reflects private information exclusively acquired by the bank over time, the firm's age accounts for public information that indirectly measures the firm's reputation and survival capacity. Correlated with the definition of the duration of the banking relationship is also the intensity of the relationship in terms of breadth, i.e., the number of products and/or services acquired by the same client through repeated interactions with the bank (Boot, 2000).

(ii) The ***number of banking relationships*** of a firm. An exclusive banking relationship, so-called 'single banking', promotes the development of a close relationship between the bank and the firm, creating conditions for less competition among banks, greater informational monopoly and easier loan contract renegotiation. A higher number of banking relationships—so-called 'multiple banking' (see Sect. 4.1)—can, on the one hand, mitigate the hold-up phenomenon attributable to the bank's capture of the firm and, on the other, the risk of soft-budget constraint; i.e., the bank's capture by the client (Rajan, 1992; Sharpe, 1990). In order to verify whether multiple banking mitigates these risks, it would be necessary to know the interest rate charged by the bank to the client, a variable that is often not available for such analyses (Santikian, 2014). In line with Detragiache et al. (2000), multiple banking can mitigate the impact of banks' liquidity shocks on borrowers. Cappelletti and Mistrulli (2023) demonstrate that this result holds only in normal times when the liquidity market functions smoothly. Conversely, during a crisis, when financial markets are compromised, multiple loans can lead to contagion and threaten financial stability. One possible reason might be that borrowers, facing an unexpected demand for loan repayment, might draw on available credit lines from other banks to avoid premature liquidation of their projects. In such a scenario, contagion and a generalized systemic liquidity crisis may occur. Finally, Elsas (2005) demonstrates that single banking is neither a necessary nor sufficient condition for relationship lending; however, a negative correlation between the number of banking relationships and the incidence of relationship lending seems plausible.

(iii) The ***share of debt*** with the main bank (***hausbank***), i.e., the degree of exclusivity of the bank-client relationship. As the share of total debt financed by a bank (main bank) increases, the probability of relationship lending increases. Various metrics are used to approximate the exclusivity of a relationship: (a) the Herfindahl index of loan concentration, calculated as the sum of the squared credit shares of each bank (Ongena et al., 2012); (b) the ratio of the credit granted by a single bank to the credit granted by the banking system as a whole (Brighi et al., 2019); (c) the ratio of 'relational' loans to total debt, where relational loans are defined as those obtained from local or regional banks (city, regional or second-tier regional banks) in which the main financing bank is among the ten largest shareholders (Aoki, 2023). The risk associated with the degree of exclusivity of the bank–firm relationship is that of the soft-budget constraint (Boot, 2000; Elsas & Krahnen, 1998).

(iv) The ***distance*** between the bank and the firm. The distance between the borrower and the bank is another factor characterizing relationship lending, influencing both credit supply and interest rates. In the literature, the bank–firm distance can be defined in three ways: (a) geographic distance (Degryse & Ongena, 2004, 2005); (b) functional distance (Alessandrini et al., 2009); (c) hierarchical distance (Stein, 2002).

Geographic distance is the physical distance (measured in kilometres) between the bank and the borrower. The loan's contractual terms depend on the distance separating the client from the lending bank and the distance from competing banks. Based on horizontal spatial differentiation models like Hotelling (1929) or circular Salop (1979), firms incur transportation costs to reach the bank's branch. If the bank cannot observe the client's geographic location, it applies a uniform price (interest rate) for all clients (regardless of their geographic location). Conversely, if the bank knows the client's geographic location, it implements a policy of spatial price discrimination (interest rates); specifically, if the clients bear transportation costs, the bank charges a higher interest rate to clients closer to the bank. Nearby borrowers face higher total transportation costs if they want to switch to a competing bank (further away than their current bank), creating conditions for greater market power for the bank. Similarly, a monopolist bank charges a higher loan rate to nearby borrowers, as these borrowers incur lower total transportation costs. Consequently, spatial price discrimination based on the client's geographic location (and related transportation costs) implies, for a given number of banks, a negative relationship between the loan rate and the bank–firm distance and a similar positive relationship between the loan rate and the distance between the firm and the nearest competing bank (see Table 4.3).

Screening (ex-ante) and monitoring (ex-post) costs associated with informational asymmetries between the bank and the firm can also depend on geographic distance. The accuracy of the firm evaluation process decreases as the distance between the bank and the firm increases. In this context, Hauswald and Marquez (2003) developed a model where the precision of the signal regarding the borrower's quality received by the bank diminishes with increasing distance. As the distance between the bank and the firm increases, adverse selection problems intensify. Consequently, a locally operating bank may have an informational advantage and charge higher interest rates to closer firms (hold-up). Therefore, a negative (positive) relationship prevails between the interest rate and the distance between the bank and the financed firm (Degryse et al., 2005).

In a subsequent contribution, Hauswald and Marquez (2006) highlight that the greater informational asymmetries associated with geographically distant clients increase the probability of credit rationing. Other

Table 4.3 Relationship lending and geographical distance

	Impact on interest rates due to	
Theory	*Distance from lending bank*	*Distance from competing banks*
Transportation costs (for the firm)	–	–
Uniform distribution	No	No
Spatial price discrimination	Negative	Positive
Transportation costs (for the bank)	–	–
Marginal price	Positive	No

Source Elaboration by the Authors, based on Degryse et al. (2005)

studies confirm that credit rationing is more prevalent in areas characterized by a high concentration of branches of large banks. As the distance between the bank and the firm increases, it becomes more difficult to assess the borrower's quality. In this regard, firms located in functionally distant credit markets, even if large and transparent, are more rationed compared to firms located in credit markets largely populated by functionally closer banks (Alessandrini et al., 2009; Brighi & Venturelli, 2017; Degryse et al., 2018; Presbitero et al., 2014).

Another line of research has investigated the relationships between distance, the internal organization of banks and lending policies. Berger et al. (2005) show that large banks lend at greater distances compared to small banks, as they are better equipped to handle hard information. Mian (2006) confirms that local banks are much more focused on SMEs that are opaque in terms of information and for which soft information is more relevant than hard information in the credit granting process. The higher credit risk associated with the greater distance of financed clients can also influence the strategy for opening new branches, which are more profitable if concentrated closer to the headquarters (Lim & Nguyen, 2021). Recent advancements in Information and Communication Technologies (ICT) have reduced the importance of transportation and informational costs between the bank and the client, increasing the availability and timeliness of information and enhancing the availability of impersonal loans from geographically distant banks (Felici & Pagnini, 2008; Mocetti et al., 2017). Nonetheless, part of the literature agrees that in the case of SMEs, relationship lending continues to be an advantageous lending technology for closer banks, which can obtain soft information at lower costs (Berger et al., 2011; Petersen & Rajan, 2002).

Functional distance is defined as the distance between the bank's decision-making centre and the branches distributed across the territory where information is gathered and client credit practices are initiated. Alessandrini et al. (2009) define functional distance as the ratio of 'locally distributed branches weighted alternatively by the physical, economic, and socio-cultural distance separating them from the bank's headquarters, and the total number of branches', according to the following formula:

$$\text{Functional Distance}_i = \frac{\sum_{z_p=1}^{P_i} \left[\text{Branches}_{iz_p} \times \ln(1 + D_{iz_p})\right]}{\sum_{z_p=1}^{P_i} \text{Branches}_{z_p}}, \tag{4.1}$$

where:

- $z_p = 1, \ldots, P_i$ are the provinces where the bank's branches are located.
- $D_{iz_p} = \sqrt{(X_{z_p} - X_{HQ_i})^2 + (Y_{z_p} - Y_{HQ_i})^2}$ is the Euclidean distance between the province z_p (where the branch is located) and the province (where the bank *i*'s headquarters, HQ_i, are situated).

Over the last 20 years, the banking system has been influenced by technological innovation, deregulation and consolidation, which have profoundly changed the geography of the banking industry. On the one hand, the first two factors—technological innovation and deregulation—have significantly increased the operational proximity of banks to local economies. On the other hand, banking consolidation has exacerbated the functional distance between decision-making centres and local communities. Empirical evidence suggests that a greater functional distance between banks and firms has negative effects on both financed firms and lending banks. Firms, especially SMEs located far from decision-making centres, experience a higher probability of credit rationing (Alessandrini et al., 2009). Banks report lower performance and higher risk (Brighi & Venturelli, 2014); moreover, locally oriented banks (such as cooperative credit banks) are disadvantaged in terms of cost efficiency, negatively impacting the economic development rate of their respective territories (Bernini & Brighi, 2018).

Hierarchical distance is a measure closely related to functional distance, considering the management of information within the bank's organizational structure. Stein (2002) suggests that a bank, depending on its organizational structure, will utilize different types of information. For a large and hierarchically complex organization, collecting soft information at the local level may be too costly due to high delegation costs. A large bank distant from its branches tends to dissipate the soft information collected locally, increase the monitoring costs of local managers' activities, and impede the effective transfer of best practices from operational branches to decision-making centres, focusing only on transferring efficiency from the latter to the former. Conversely, small banks decentralized across the territory, characterized by high proximity between the headquarters and branches, may have a comparative advantage in lending to small, more opaque firms, where collecting soft information is crucial in both the granting and monitoring phases.

Numerous studies analyze how the hierarchical structure of banks can influence: (i) the type of lending technology to adopt (Alessandrini et al., 2010; Presbitero & Zazzaro, 2011); (ii) the likelihood and amount of financing (Cotugno et al., 2013); (iii) the probability of making the correct financing decision (Brighi et al., 2019; Calcagnini et al., 2018).

Firstly, some studies analyze how banks, based on the hierarchical distance between the operational branches and decision-making centres, develop either a transaction-based or relationship-based approach. Large banks with a complex hierarchical structure should respond to competitive pressure by focusing efforts and resources on transaction-based technology. In contrast, smaller banks with a simpler hierarchical structure should concentrate on relationship-based technologies. Specifically, Presbitero and Zazzaro (2011) demonstrate that if the local credit market is predominantly populated by 'hierarchical' banks (large and distant), relationship lending is expected to weaken with increasing competitive pressure. Conversely, if the organizational structure of the local credit market consists of non-hierarchical banks (small, local, and cooperative banks), relationship lending strengthens with increasing competitive pressure.

Moreover, other studies investigate how hierarchical distance can influence the decision, the amount of financing and the probability of default. In this regard, Cotugno et al. (2013) studied how the bank's organizational structure and hierarchical distance within the bank affected credit availability during the 2007–2008 financial crisis; their results suggest that the greater the hierarchical distance between the branch where the loan originates and the hierarchical level that approves the financing, the lower the amount of credit granted.

Finally, other studies examine how hierarchical distance influences the correctness of financing decisions. Calcagnini et al. (2018), with reference to a regional bank's clientele, demonstrate that the probability of loan default increases with greater hierarchical distance, confirming the superiority of the proximity-based relationship model over the transaction-based model. Brighi et al. (2019) analyze how the probability of making the correct decision in terms of loan acceptance or rejection negatively depends on the collegiality of the decision-making body. In other words, the probability of making the correct decision negatively depends on the hierarchical distance between the branch manager, who meets the client, and the board of directors, who makes the final decision.

4.3 Effects of Relationship Lending on Contractual Conditions

In this section, we delve into the link between credit contractual conditions—interest rates, credit availability and collateral requirements—and relationship lending by comparing the main empirical findings in the literature. In the empirical studies reviewed herein, the dependent variable is represented by the contractual conditions, while the independent variables are represented by proxies of relationship lending, such as the duration or the number of banking relationships. These analyses are particularly salient for SMEs, which, in contrast to larger firms, typically encounter greater challenges in accessing direct market financing due to heightened informational opacity. Relationship lending serves as a mechanism to mitigate these information asymmetries (between banks and SMEs) and alleviate the associated issue of credit rationing.

Empirical evidence from the United States, Europe, and Italy reveals heterogeneous and sometimes contradictory findings regarding the influence of relationship lending on contractual terms offered by banks to SMEs. In the United States, for instance, Petersen and Rajan (1994) find that relationship lending enhances credit supply and reduces interest rates. However, an increase in the number of banking relationships is associated with higher interest rates. In a subsequent study, Petersen and Rajan (1995) investigate the link between interest rates and banking market structure, finding, counterintuitively, that more concentrated credit markets tend to offer lower interest rates to SMEs. Berger and Udell (1995), analyzing the same dataset but focusing on 'lines of credit', observe that relationship lending results in lower interest rates and collateral requirements for SMEs. Cole (1998) reinforces the finding that banks are more inclined to lend to firms with which they have established relationships. The volume of credit supplied is positively correlated with relationship intensity and inversely correlated with the number of banking relationships. Notably, relationship duration appears to have a limited effect on improving contractual conditions, since banks quickly acquire the confidential information of the firm, in contrast to Berger and Udell's (1995) assertion that long-term relationships are necessary to accrue such benefits.

Using a sample of 766 US firms, Brick and Palia (2007) examine the joint effects of relationship lending on explicit interest rates and implicit contractual elements such as collateral, distinguishing between real and personal guarantees. Their findings indicate a significant negative relationship between relationship lending and both adjusted interest rates and real collateral. Moreover, they identify a prevailing strategic interplay between interest rate setting and the use of personal guarantees, with the latter positively influencing interest rate levels.

Research on small banks further elucidates the implications of relationship lending, and in particular, whether relationship lending can change the behaviour of small banks in the process of evaluating non-performing loans. Kang et al. (2013) find that small banks in Texas, particularly in smaller counties, demonstrate a greater commitment to supporting clients during periods of financial distress. This leads to reduced profitability and heightened risk for small banks but provides substantial support to borrowers, especially during financial difficulties, yielding a wealth transfer from lenders to borrowers. The importance of relationship lending in times of crisis is further studied by Dewally and Shao (2014), who show that during the 2007–2008 financial crisis, firms with established banking relationships maintained better liquidity and profitability, obtained new credit and achieved higher leverage levels. Finally, regarding the pandemic crisis, James et al. (2021) underscore the enduring importance of community banks in financing small businesses during the pandemic, affirming their role despite the rise of digital credit evaluation technologies. This work aligns with literature concluding that community banks continue to play a significant role in financing SMEs despite the advent of new information management technologies and credit scoring models (Berger et al., 2014), and supporting the view that there is an inverse relationship between bank size and their propensity to lend to small businesses (Mkhaiber & Werner, 2021).

There is also extensive empirical evidence on relationship lending in major European countries. Elsas and Krahnen (1998) study the German concept of the *hausbank* and its alignment with relationship lending, focusing on the differences between *hausbank* and other banks in corporate lending policies. Their findings confirm the idea that the concept of *hausbank* is closely related to the theoretical principle of relationship lending, and in particular, indicate that *hausbanks* provide a stabilizing role by extending credit even during firm downturns, although they do not offer more favourable pricing terms. In other words, *hausbanks*, unlike regular banks, increase the volume of credit granted in case of deterioration of the firm's quality, thereby providing implicit insurance against potential negative shocks, although subject to the risk of a soft-budget constraint. However, there are no price differences between *hausbanks* and other banks, suggesting that, in this case, relationship banking does not seem to create price advantages for SMEs.

Another in-depth study on the bank–firm relationship in Germany is represented by Harhoff and Körting (1998), who find that longer relationships and exclusivity reduce collateral requirements but do not influence interest rates or credit volume. They focus on the duration of the credit relationship as a proxy for relationship lending and find a positive effect in terms of lower collateral requirements but no benefit in the amount of credit granted and the interest rates applied. If instead the number of established banking relationships is used as a proxy for relationship lending, similar results are obtained. Firms that tend to have an exclusive credit relationship benefit from this relationship in terms of lower collateral requirements, while the effect on interest rates and supply of credit is not statistically significant. Finally, in case mutual trust between the bank and the firm is considered as an additional proxy for relationship lending, the results suggest a positive effect in terms of more favourable interest rates. The conclusion is that, all else being equal, firms with exclusive and long-lasting customer relationships enjoy better contractual conditions, with more significant benefits in terms of lower collateral requirements rather than more favourable interest rates or higher credit supply. Another study conducted by Lehmann and Neuberger (2001) presents partially contrasting results, noting that transparency may lead to higher interest rates due to hold-up concerns, while relationship stability enhances pricing conditions. In other words, the presence of a continuous and transparent information flow would increase the interest rates applied, creating the conditions for a hold-up problem. Conversely, the stability of the banking relationship, even during crises, would benefit firms through more favourable pricing conditions.

Memmel et al. (2008), using an extensive dataset, confirm the persistence and quantitative significance of relationship lending in Germany. Their results suggest that within the German banking system, despite the evolution of automated processing of both quantitative and qualitative information in bank credit risk management, relationship lending remains a widespread and quantitatively significant phenomenon. Consistent with theoretical literature, the authors demonstrate that customer relationships are crucial in reducing informational asymmetries between banks and firms, leading to an easing of credit rationing problems, particularly for SMEs and R&D-focused startups. Regarding this last category of firms, the authors show that, contrary to Detragiache et al. (2000) but consistently with Bhattacharya and Chiesa (1995), there is a preference for exclusive and unfragmented credit relationships. Another result they find is that firms of higher quality tend to prefer exclusive relationships, suggesting a self-selection mechanism so that firm quality influences the probability of relationship lending. This result implies a sort of self-selection over time, where good-quality firms remain tied to a specific bank, while lower-quality firms tend to change banks more often.

Stein (2015) finds that a higher share of debt with a main bank reduces financing costs, although long relationship durations may incur hold-up costs. He demonstrates that a firm's financing costs decrease as the share of bank debt held by the main bank increases. Conversely, these costs tend to increase with the duration of the relationship, thus generating hold-up costs. Changing banks initially results in only a small discount on the interest rate, which increases for borrowers with strong relationships with their previous bank. The study confirms the theory that relationship lending can generate both costs and benefits. Flögel (2018), in a study comparing a regional savings bank and a large national German bank, finds that the functional distance is shorter in the larger bank for about 50% of the processed credit decisions. This result holds for loans up to 1 million euros to SMEs with good credit scores. Conversely, smaller banks continue to enjoy an informational advantage for lending decisions to financially distressed SMEs.

In Belgium, Degryse and Van Cayseele (2000) analyze the effects of relationship lending on interest rates and collateral. They find that relationship duration is positively correlated with interest rates in both the short and long term. However, relationship intensity with a main bank reduces them: if the relationship intensity—measured by the main bank's weight—is considered, the result is reversed. The presence of a main bank, from which the firm obtains not only credit but also other financial services, creates advantages in terms of lower interest rates. This result is statistically significant and dominates the previous one. On the other hand, the exclusivity of the customer relationship increases collateral demands, possibly due to the informational advantage enjoyed by the bank. Although the reasons for this result are unclear, the authors associate it with the informational advantage the bank gains over the firm's activities, which are thus more easily captured as collateral. In our view, the reason could also be that the bank's greater exposure to the firm subjects it to higher risks, which it can control by increasing the collateral demand.

Hernández-Cánovas and Martínez-Solano (2006, 2010) examine Spanish SMEs and find that longer and exclusive relationships lead to higher interest rates and collateral requirements: firms that operate exclusively with one bank tend to be subject to higher collateral requirements. However, firms with fewer banking relationships benefit from lower interest rates. The authors also explore the relationship between relationship lending and firm riskiness, concluding that riskier firms would benefit from lower interest rates if they relied on a smaller number of banks. This result implies that exclusive banking relationships, by reducing loan uncertainty—thanks to greater negotiation flexibility, better monitoring of investment projects, and lower free-riding risks in the event of firm liquidation—can benefit the client with a lower interest rate. Finally, regardless of the firm's riskiness, it seems that an exclusive and long-term banking relationship 'penalizes' the firm through higher personal collateral requirements. In a subsequent study, Hernández-Cánovas and Martínez-Solano (2010) demonstrate that having two banking relationships is sufficient to gain an advantage in terms of lower interest rates. Furthermore, consolidating the bank–firm relationship through trust improves access to financing and reduces financing costs, but increases the probability of providing collateral.

López-Espinosa et al. (2017) identify a non-linear relationship where interest rates initially increase with relationship duration but decrease after sufficient soft information is accumulated. Specifically, interest rates increase up to a certain point (about two years) and then start to decrease. As more information is gathered during the bank–firm relationship, the problem of informational asymmetry is reduced thanks to the acquisition of 'soft' information, and the bank can begin to reduce the interest rate applied to the firm.

Jiménez et al. (2024) demonstrate that during the pandemic, firms with pre-existing relationships were more likely to receive guaranteed loans. This effect is more pronounced for riskier firms and those in sectors most affected by the pandemic, and the benefits consist of an extension of existing loans and access to new loans. Peltoniemi (2007) and Peltoniemi and Vieru (2013) analyze Finnish data, showing that long-term relationships reduce credit costs and benefit riskier firms, especially in relationship-based lending contexts. In particular, Peltoniemi (2007) investigates the effects of relationship lending on the effective cost of credit in Finland, and the empirical evidence suggests a negative relationship between relationship lending and the cost of credit. Firms with a long-standing relationship with their main bank receive credit on more favourable terms. Furthermore, in the presence of consolidated and exclusive credit relationships, riskier firms tend to benefit from relatively more favourable contractual conditions than less risky ones. Although riskier firms generally pay higher interest rates, the interest rate applied to them decreases more rapidly with the duration of the relationship lending than it does for less risky firms. This result implies that riskier firms benefit from relationships with a single bank if and only if they establish a close, long-term relationship. The study also reveals that personal collateral requirements entail a higher interest rate and that riskier firms are more likely to offer personal collateral. Finally, further investigations suggest that longer and larger loans have a significant negative effect on the interest rate applied. The general conclusion is that, in this specific case, the benefits of relationship lending outweigh the costs, making it a desirable practice, especially for riskier and smaller firms. These results appear robust concerning the presence of collateral, the characteristics of the loan and the firm, and the macroeconomic trend of interest rates.

Peltoniemi and Vieru (2013), in a subsequent study, further examine the role of personal and collateral guarantees concerning two alternative lending strategies: transaction-based and relationship-based lending. The research results suggest that (1) personal guarantees are generally correlated with transaction-based lending technologies, and the use of personal guarantees increases the cost of credit; (2) analyzing separately firms characterized by relationship-based and transaction-based lending shows that the latter pay higher risk premiums when personal guarantees accompany the loan. These results are due to the fact that in a transaction-based relationship, the level of informational asymmetry is typically higher than in relationship-based relationships. Personal guarantees in transaction-based relationships are used to mitigate informational asymmetry problems and are associated with higher risk and, thus, higher credit costs. Conversely, in relationship-based relationships, personal guarantees are used to confirm the existing relationship between the bank and the client. Therefore, with personal guarantees, transaction-based loans are more expensive than relationship-based loans.

In France, Beatriz et al. (2022) find evidence of interest-rate smoothing, with higher rates during growth periods and lower rates during crises. However, this benefit does not extend to riskier or single-banked firms, which face higher rates due to hold-up effects. Competition and non-bank financing alternatives can mitigate these risks. The authors demonstrate the validity of the so-called interest-rate smoothing, but their results show that riskier and single-banked firms do not benefit from this insurance mechanism and are 'captured' by the bank, which applies a higher interest rate. Competition among local banks and openness to non-bank financing can alleviate the hold-up risk. Finally, they demonstrate that small, well-capitalized banks support the advantages of relationship lending through the provision of long-term and small-sized loans.

The literature on the bank–firm relationship in Italy has developed since the late 1990s along three lines of research. The first studies the effects of relationship lending on the contractual conditions applied to firms. Therein, Angelini et al. (1998) focus on the bank–firm relationship in the case of cooperative credit banks and member SMEs. In this case, relationship lending produces benefits in terms of more credit granted and more favourable interest rates. However, in the more general case where the same firms are considered but clients of banks other than cooperative credit banks, the result is reversed. As the duration of relationship lending increases, firms tend to pay higher interest rates; the same applies to cooperative credit banks in relation to non-member SMEs.

Additionally, only cooperative credit bank members enjoy easy access to credit, which does not hold for the same firms that are clients of other banks and for non-member clients of cooperative credit banks. This result, however, according to the authors, is due to the legal specificity of cooperative credit banks rather than the benefits of relationship lending. In a subsequent study, D'Auria et al. (1999) analyze the effects of relationship lending on interest rates and find that relationship lending facilitates the application of more favourable interest rates.

The second line of empirical investigations is directly related to the relationship between relationship lending and competitive conditions in the credit market. In a study on the Italian market, Tirri (2007) shows that firms located in less concentrated credit markets and multi-banked have a lower probability of being rationed. On the one hand, the neoclassical literature on market power suggests a direct link between market concentration and performance: this means that a high degree of banking market concentration is generally associated with non-competitive behaviour (higher interest rates and lower credit supply). On the other hand, considering the theory of informational asymmetries, an alternative approach develops in which competition in the credit market reduces banks' incentives to invest in soft information, thus weakening relationship lending. In a model that simultaneously considers both the competitive aspects of the credit market and the informational asymmetries between banks and firms, Tirri (2007) demonstrates, contrary to Petersen and Rajan (1995), that the risk of rationing increases with the degree of credit market concentration. In concentrated credit markets, multiple banking lending would, therefore, represent a strategy to reduce both the risk of rationing and the hold-up risk (see Sect. 4.1). It is also emphasized that the presence of multiple credit relationships does not necessarily exclude the presence of an intense and privileged relationship with a main bank, a condition that can benefit the firm. Presbitero and Zazzaro (2011) demonstrate that the relationship between relationship lending and market concentration depends on the organizational structure of the market. Specifically, the authors show that where relational lending technologies are already used in the market by a large group of small cooperative credit banks, increased competition can push banks to cultivate their extensive customer relationships further. The case is different in markets where large banks dominate. In this latter case, increased competition weakens the relationship lending.

The third line of investigation draws inspiration from the relationship between relationship lending and individual or systemic crises. Regarding a sample of 13,597 SMEs, Omiccioli and Carmignani (2007) verify the impact of a high degree of credit concentration at a single bank on the probability of financial distress for the firm. On the one hand, higher banking credit concentration reduces the probability of a firm experiencing a financial crisis and subsequently being liquidated. On the other hand, a higher concentration of credit lines implies greater liquidity risk for firms, making financial distress and subsequent liquidation more likely.

To face a systemic financial crisis like that of 2007–2008, it is essential to understand how relationship lending can mitigate credit rationing for borrowing firms. Specifically, Cotugno et al. (2013), using a proprietary dataset of over 5,000 credit positions, demonstrate that the exclusivity of the relationship facilitates SMEs' access to credit even during a crisis. The organizational structure can also facilitate credit access. The authors show that the shorter the 'hierarchical distance' between the firm and the person responsible for financing decisions, the easier it is to access credit, aligning with the idea that proximity facilitates the transmission of soft information and the firm's evaluation for financing purposes. Fiordelisi et al. (2014) demonstrate that during a crisis period like 2008–2010, increasing hierarchical distance increases non-performing loans and, in general, the probability of their downgrading. However, other factors of relationship lending, such as the high degree of creditor concentration and the duration of the banking relationship, reduce the incidence of firm defaults. This result is broadly consistent with the informational argument that a smaller number of investors increases the incentive to monitor (thanks to lower monitoring costs) and reduces informational asymmetries and adverse selection risks.

That hierarchical distance plays a role in influencing the quality of loans granted, and thus, the probability of default of the financed firm is confirmed by Calcagnini et al. (2018). The study shows that the probability of loan default increases when the approval decision is made at higher levels of the lending decision hierarchy.

The heterogeneity of the results obtained in the empirical literature analyzed in this section makes it difficult to identify an empirical regularity associated with the phenomenon of relationship lending. The dependence of the financial system's functioning on external factors, such as the institutional characteristics of markets and operators, implies different indications depending on the country or period analyzed. Reducing a complex model, such as the one describing the bank–firm relationship, to a reduced form likely means that the estimation results are unstable: this explains why seemingly established arguments about relationship lending can lead to contradictions when empirically tested with data from different countries and time horizons. These problems are further exacerbated by sampling difficulties and the structural heterogeneity of the data used in different studies. Beyond the individual empirical results discussed in the literature, relationship lending seems to offer SMEs an opportunity worth pursuing, especially in the current context where firms face significant challenges in terms of growth and retraining (see, among others, Gambini & Zazzaro, 2013; Murro et al., 2023).

Recent studies have continued to explore the implications of relationship lending, particularly in the context of financial crises and firm decision-making. Murro et al. (2023) examine how relationship lending affects employment decisions in firms during periods of financial distress. Their findings indicate that firms with strong banking relationships are more likely to retain employees during economic downturns, emphasizing the stabilizing role of relationship lending in mitigating credit constraints and preserving firm operations. This result aligns with earlier studies highlighting the benefits of strong bank–firm ties during financial crises (Dewally & Shao, 2014; Jiménez et al., 2024). Another pertinent study is Cao et al. (2025), who investigate how long-term bank–firm relationships affect the transmission of monetary policy to loan rates, particularly in low-interest-rate environments. The authors find that firms with prolonged banking relationships experience a diminished pass-through of policy rate cuts, implying that relationship lending can influence the effectiveness of monetary policy on contractual loan conditions. Additionally, Gambacorta et al. (2025) explore the intersection of technological advancements and relationship lending and provide evidence on how the adoption of AI in evaluating borrower creditworthiness impacts credit conditions, potentially altering traditional dynamics of relationship-based lending. These studies collectively enhance our understanding of how relationship lending influences contractual conditions, offering insights into interest rate dynamics, collateral requirements and the broader implications of technological integration in banking relationships.

4.4 Relationship *vs.* Transaction Lending and Corporate Banking

So far, we have seen that relationship lending, or relational credit, is characterized as a relationship between a bank and a business primarily based on confidential and non-codified information (so-called soft information), essential for evaluating the ability to repay clients characterized by informational opacity. Empirical investigations have generally highlighted that a relationship between banks and businesses developed on a relational logic is associated with better lending conditions: greater credit availability, lower interest rates and fewer collateral requirements. However, this model does not preclude the use of more standardized and impersonal forms of client relationships, such as transaction lending, which relies more on quantitative-objective information (hard information).

The mechanisms by which banks extend credit to businesses have significant implications for financial stability and economic growth. Relationship lending and transaction lending are two contrasting paradigms within this framework, each relying on different types of information and client relationship dynamics. Relationship lending is built upon the accumulation and use of soft information, which includes confidential, qualitative and non-codified data. This information is gathered through long-term, personalized interactions between the bank and the client. Such interactions allow the bank to develop a deep understanding of the client's business operations, management quality and long-term potential. This approach is particularly advantageous for SMEs that often lack extensive financial documentation and thus exhibit high informational opacity (Berger & Udell, 2006). For these firms, soft information can provide insights into their creditworthiness that are not captured by traditional financial metrics.

Empirical research underscores the benefits of relationship lending. It has been shown to be associated with more favourable lending conditions, such as increased credit availability, lower interest rates and fewer collateral requirements. For instance, Petersen and Rajan (1994) found that firms with stronger banking relationships received more credit at lower interest rates compared to those with weaker relationships. The personalized nature of relationship lending also helps in mitigating problems of adverse selection and moral hazard, as the bank's deep knowledge of the client reduces the risk of lending to less creditworthy borrowers.

Conversely, transaction lending relies on hard information, which includes quantitative, objective, and verifiable data such as financial statements, credit scores and collateral values. This method is more standardized and impersonal, focusing on easily measurable financial metrics to assess creditworthiness. Transaction lending is efficient and scalable, making it particularly suitable for larger firms with well-documented financial histories and for situations where rapid credit decisions are necessary (Boot & Thakor, 2000). Transaction lending's strength lies in its cost-effectiveness and speed. The reliance on standardized information allows for quicker credit assessments and decisions, which can be crucial in competitive and fast-moving markets. However, this approach may not fully capture the complexities of a borrower's ability to repay, especially for businesses with less transparent financials.

Recent literature has continued to explore the distinctions and implications of transaction lending versus relationship lending. A notable study by Holod et al. (2024) examines the value of relationship lending for community banks. Their research indicates that small commercial and industrial loans, which are often relationship-based, command a significant premium over their book values during bank acquisitions. This finding underscores the financial benefits of relationship lending for smaller banking institutions. Another study by Murro et al. (2023) investigates how relationship lending influences firms' employment decisions during economic downturns. The authors find that firms with strong banking relationships are more likely to retain employees during negative sales shocks, highlighting the stabilizing effect of relationship lending in challenging times.

Additionally, research by Bolton et al. (2016) explores how relationship and transaction lending vary over the business cycle. Their model suggests that while relationship banks have higher operating costs, they offer more favourable lending terms during crises due to their in-depth knowledge of borrowers. Empirical evidence from Italian banks during the 2007–2008 financial crisis supports this model, demonstrating that relationship banks provided more favourable continuation lending terms and experienced fewer defaults compared to transaction banks.

These studies collectively highlight the nuanced roles of transaction and relationship lending, particularly emphasizing the advantages of relationship lending in enhancing bank value and providing stability during economic downturns. The choice between relationship lending and transaction lending involves, therefore, a trade-off between the costs and benefits of gathering and processing different types of information. Relationship lending's strength in providing nuanced, client-specific insights comes at a higher resource cost. It requires significant time and effort to build and maintain these relationships. Conversely, while transaction lending is less resource-intensive, it may overlook important qualitative aspects of the borrower's business that could impact credit risk.

Theoretical analysis and empirical evidence suggest that the two models (relationship lending and transaction) are not mutually exclusive but complementary, forming what is known in the literature as the 'corporate banking' model. In other words, relationship lending does not disappear but evolves into the more comprehensive and articulated corporate banking model. More specifically, recent works on the subject refer to lending technologies characterized by various combinations of hard and soft information (Brighi et al., 2019; Udell, 2018).

The hybrid approach of the corporate banking model reflects a transition towards integrating both relationship and transaction lending; it leverages the strengths of both paradigms, utilizing a blend of hard and soft information to create a more comprehensive assessment of credit risk. Corporate banking aims to tailor financial services to meet the diverse needs of businesses, enhancing the accuracy and efficiency of credit evaluations (Udell, 2018). In the corporate banking model, banks develop sophisticated information systems and analytical tools to combine quantitative data with qualitative insights gained from long-term client relationships. This integration allows for more nuanced credit assessments, accommodating the complexities of larger and more diverse corporate clients. Recent studies underscore that this model does not signify the obsolescence of relationship lending but rather its evolution into a more complex and articulated framework (Brighi et al., 2019).

Technological advancements have further propelled this evolution, with innovations in data analytics, artificial intelligence, and machine learning enabling banks to process vast amounts of both structured and unstructured data (see Sect. 6.1). These technologies enhance the bank's ability to predict credit risk more accurately, identify potential default patterns and offer customized financial solutions. Consequently, the corporate banking model represents a sophisticated approach to lending, where relationship management and quantitative analysis coalesce to support robust financial decision-making.

In conclusion, the dichotomy between relationship lending and transaction lending highlights the diversity of approaches in credit allocation, each with its own set of advantages and limitations. Relationship lending, with its reliance on soft information, provides deep client-specific insights but is resource-intensive. Transaction lending, based on hard information, is efficient and scalable but may not capture the full spectrum of a borrower's creditworthiness. The evolution towards corporate banking signifies an integrative trend, combining the detailed, client-specific insights of relationship lending with the efficiency and scalability of transaction lending. This synthesis, augmented by technological innovations, promises a more comprehensive and adaptable framework for credit evaluation and financial decision-making, better equipped to meet the diverse and complex needs of contemporary businesses.

4.5 Bibliometric Analysis of Relationship Lending Literature

We performed a bibliometric analysis to see how the literature on relationship lending developed over the years. We selected from the database Web of Science (WOS) all the publications on the topic 'relationship lending' published from 1985 to 2024 (the widest data range available on WOS) by searching in the fields 'title', 'abstract' and 'author keywords', and as a result we found a total of 312 articles. Then, to refine the data, we applied two primary filters:

(i) The publication must fall within the research categories of Economics, Business Finance, Business, Management, Operations Research Management Science, International Relations, Development Studies, Agricultural Economics Policy, Law, Mathematics Interdisciplinary Applications, Political Science, and Social Sciences Mathematical Methods.
(ii) The publications must be written in English and in the form of regular articles, articles published as early access, proceedings papers, book chapters and reviews.

The final sample consists of 303 articles, the majority of which (see Fig. 4.2) are in the fields of Economics, Business Finance, Business, Management and Operations Research Management Science.

Table 4.4 provides an overview of the primary data structure utilized in this study. The publication data spans from 1995 to 2024 and encompasses 303 documents. These documents have been published in 136

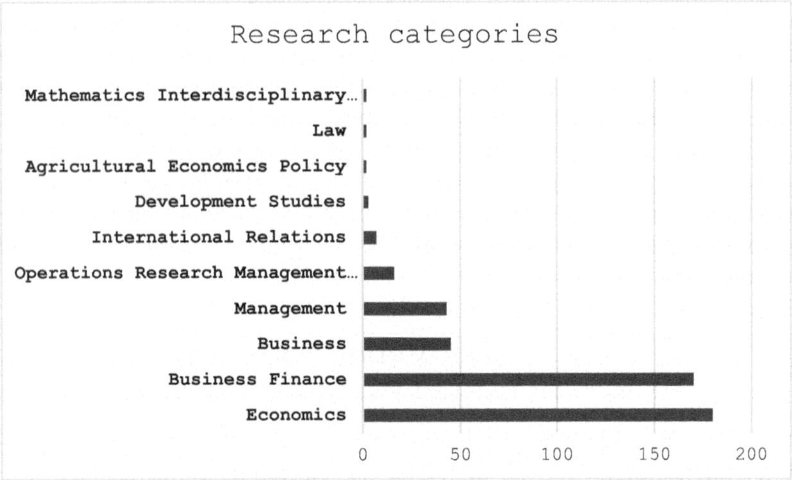

Fig. 4.2 Research categories (*Source* Web of Science Core Collection)

journals and authored by 618 researchers. Of the total articles, only 62 are attributed to single authors, indicating a prevailing trend of collaboration within the topic of credit rationing. The average citation level for these articles is approximately 41 citations per paper, which signals the growing impact and interest in this research field, as reflected by the substantial number of citations received (8,366).

Regarding keywords, the selected articles are associated with 716 author-suggested keywords (provided below the abstract of each article) and 515 database-generated keywords known as 'keywords plus'. As we will see in the remainder of this section, these keywords collectively contribute to a comprehensive understanding of the themes and topics explored within the credit rationing literature.

Table 4.4 Descriptive statistics

Description	*Results*
Main information about data	
Timespan	1995–2024
Sources (Journals, Books, etc.)	136
Documents	303
Annual growth rate %	11.07
Document average age	8.22
Average citations per Doc	41.34
References	8,366
Document contents	
Keywords Plus (ID)	515
Author's Keywords (DE)	716
Authors	
Authors	618
Authors of single-authored docs	62
Authors collaboration	
Single-authored docs	64
Co-authors per Doc	2.49
International co-authorships %	31.02
Document types	
Article	266
Article; book chapter	3
Article; early access	4
Article; proceedings paper	10
Editorial material; book chapter	1
Proceedings paper	18
Review	1

Source Web of Science Core Collection

Figure 4.3 depicts the research papers' temporal distributions and average citation levels over time. We observe that the research on this topic in the first period (1995–2006) started growing slowly, then grew at a fast pace in the second period (2007–2021) and finally slowed down in the last period (2022–2024). Regarding the citations, we observe a continuously growing path from the very beginning of the observed period until 2021. Both indicators signal a continuously growing interest in this topic in the academic arena.

Figure 4.4 presents prominent journals that publish research on credit rationing. Most published literature on relationship lending belongs to the journal categories of finance and economics.

Figure 4.5 presents a comprehensive overview of the most highly cited publications, considering their total citations. Within this index, called 'Most Global Cited Documents', Bibliometrix includes the total 'global citations'; that is, the citations that an article included in the sample has received from documents indexed on a bibliographic database (WoS, Scopus, etc.). So, global citations are those received by a selected article 'all over the world'.

The ranking of authors serves two primary purposes: firstly, to identify prominent contributors and the leading articles in the field of credit rationing, and secondly, to acknowledge their significant impact on the existing body of literature. The foremost authors in this ranking are Berger and Udell (1995), with 1,443 citations, which maintains by far the top position, followed by other two of their publications (2002, 2006) with 858 and 733 citations, Boot and Thakor (2000) with 610, Degryse and Van Cayseele (2000) with 377, and Wilner (2000) with 309 citations.

Figure 4.6 represents graphically the same picture of the most highly cited authors by a so-called 'references spectroscopy', which depicts the patterns, frequencies and characteristics of citations and references within our sample of publications. In particular, the black line represents the number of cited references, while the red line shows the deviation from the 5-year median. As we can see, there has been an increasing number of citations during the first period (1964–2000), with an important peak in 2000 due to the seminal works of Berger and Udell, followed by a decreasing path in the following years (2001–2024).

As we did previously (see Sect. 3.3), we now employ cartographic/keyword and trend analyses to provide a comprehensive depiction of the development and progression of the literature concerning relationship lending. Keyword analysis highlights the literary landscape within various

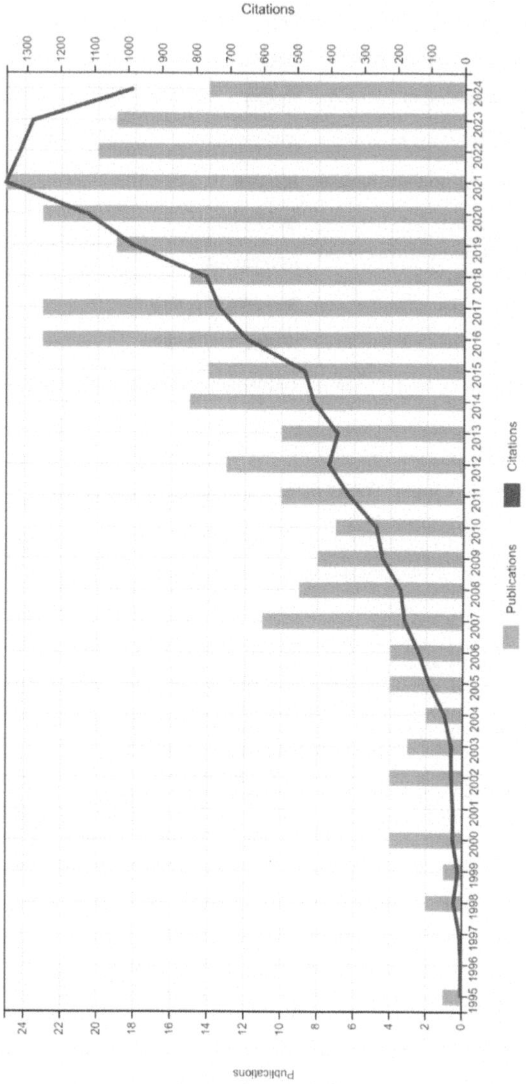

Fig. 4.3 Publication growth: number of publications and citations per year (*Source* Web of Science Core Collection)

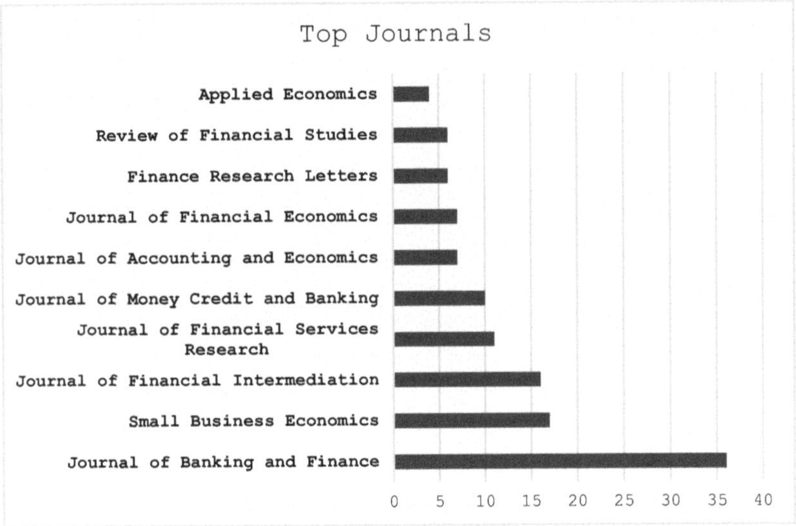

Fig. 4.4 Top journals (*Source* Web of Science Core Collection)

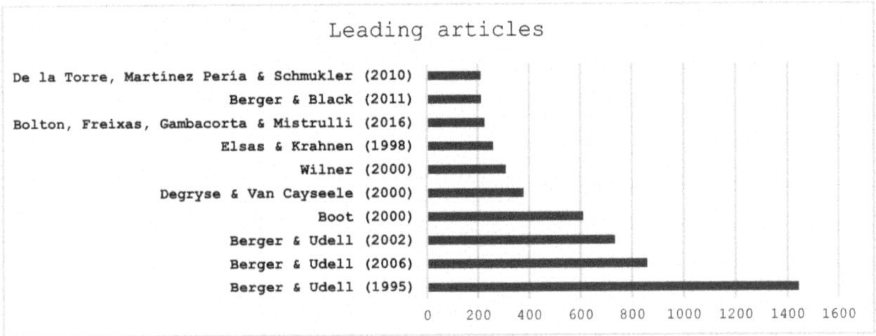

Fig. 4.5 Leading articles (*Source* Web of Science Core Collection)

clusters identified by different colours. Trend analysis, on the other hand, helps to understand the evolution of literature over different periods. To conduct these analyses, like we did previously, we establish a minimum inclusion threshold of five occurrences for a specific keyword.

Figure 4.7 shows that 'credit', 'information', 'competition' and 'lending relationships' are the most frequent keywords. The keyword

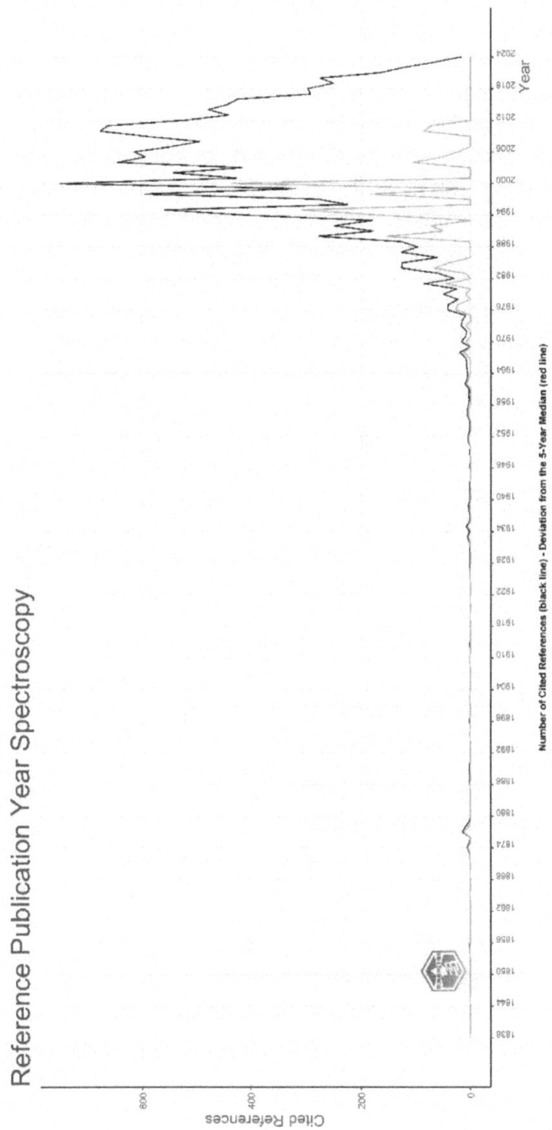

Fig. 4.6 References spectroscopy (*Source* Web of Science Core Collection)

analysis confirmed that the literature mainly centred on the role played by the information available and the competition in the development of relationship lending.

Figure 4.8 shows instead the co-occurrence between the different keywords, that is, the number of publications in which two keywords occur together and the corresponding clusters. We can see that the most important cluster (yellow colour), as expected, is represented by the group of keywords linked to 'relationship lending', then 'information' (purple colour) and 'credit' (blue colour), while the other clusters are those linked to the keywords 'lending relationship', 'competition' and 'asymmetric information'.

The last step of this bibliometric analysis consists of the so-called stream analysis, composed of a thematic map and a coupling map. As already seen in previous chapter (see Sect. 3.3) a thematic map is a visual representation used to illustrate the conceptual structure of a research field by highlighting the relationships between different topics, themes or keywords.

Figure 4.9 shows the clusters of themes, where each cluster represents a group of related themes or topics that frequently co-occur in the

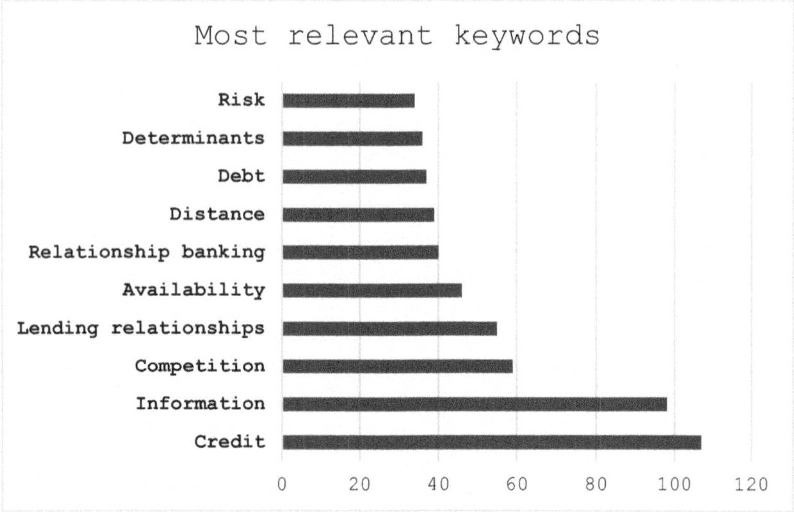

Fig. 4.7 Most relevant keywords (*Source* Web of Science Core Collection)

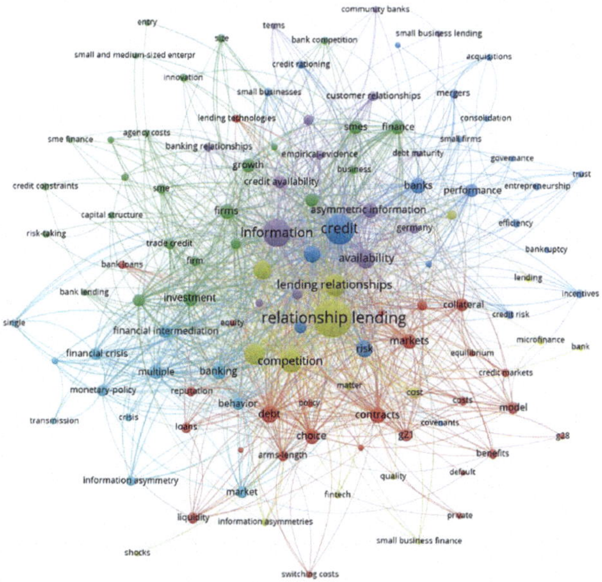

VOSviewer

Fig. 4.8 Keyword analysis (*Source* Web of Science Core Collection)

literature. The vertical axis represents the 'density', which refers to how closely related the themes within a cluster are to each other, while in the horizontal axis, it is represented the 'centrality', which refers to the importance of a theme in connecting different clusters or in the overall research field. In this way, we have a strategic diagram, which helps in identifying which themes are motor themes (high centrality and high density), basic themes (high centrality but low density), emerging or declining themes (low centrality and low density), and niche themes (low centrality but high density). As we can see, the motor themes are those of relationship lending, relationship banking, collateral, lending relationship, and asymmetric information, while the niche themes are those of credit rationing, lending technologies, and adverse selection. The soft information, fintech, information asymmetries cluster is highly coherent and gaining relevance, suggesting it's a promising area for future research and innovation.

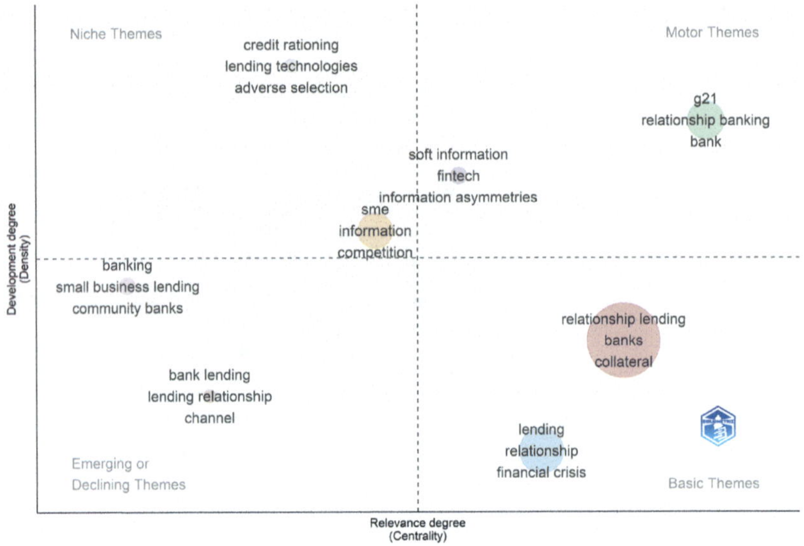

Fig. 4.9 Thematic map (*Source* Web of Science Core Collection)

Figure 4.10 shows the coupling map, where the primary objective is to elucidate the dimensions and trends of literature within a particular research field. Bibliographic coupling occurs when two documents cite the same references. The coupling map shows how closely related different documents are based on the number of shared references they have. Documents that are strongly coupled (i.e., share many references) tend to cluster together on the map.

The outcomes of our bibliographical coupling analysis show the two current main research streams in the literature about relationship lending. The most important stream in recent years links relationship lending, collateral and lending, while the stream which links the topics of relationship lending, lending and relationship, has become the second most important.

In summary, after the seminal work of Berger and Udell (1995), different theoretical models have addressed the challenges of relationship lending through various mechanisms.

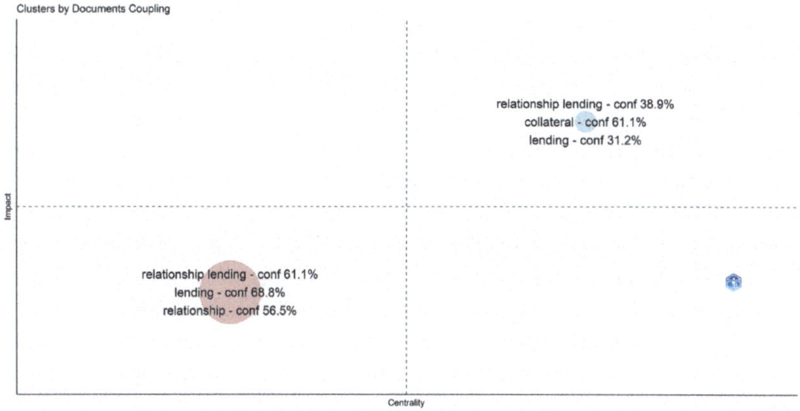

Fig. 4.10 Coupling map (*Source* Web of Science Core Collection)

4.6 Concluding Remarks

The financial landscape has undergone significant transformations over recent decades, evolving from simplistic models of perfect markets to more nuanced understandings that incorporate informational asymmetries and the complex dynamics of lending relationships. This evolution underscores the intricate interplay between relationship lending, transaction lending, corporate banking and multi-banking.

The presence of informational asymmetries and the resulting problem of credit rationing can be mitigated, at least in part, through a continuous and established relationship between the bank and the firm. This relationship, referred to in the literature as relationship lending, can also pose risks, such as the risk of customer capture by the bank (hold-up) or the risk of the bank becoming overly exposed to the firm, especially when the latter is experiencing a financial crisis (soft-budget constraint). The literature on this subject is extensive and sometimes inconsistent regarding the effects of relationship lending. Different institutional and regulatory contexts, as well as various temporal analyses, can justify divergent results on how a consolidated credit relationship impacts interest rates, collateral requirements and the amount of credit extended.

Relationship lending and transaction lending represent two distinct yet complementary approaches to credit allocation. Relationship lending, grounded in the collection of soft information through long-term interactions, offers a personalized assessment of a borrower's ability to repay. This method is particularly beneficial for SMEs and firms with high informational opacity (Berger & Udell, 2006). However, it carries risks such as potential hold-up problems and the possibility of banks extracting rents ex-post, which can distort the incentives for entrepreneurs (Padilla & Pagano, 1997). Transaction lending, on the other hand, relies on hard, quantitative data, making it efficient and scalable. This approach is suitable for larger firms with extensive financial histories and in contexts where rapid credit decisions are essential (Boot & Thakor, 2000). Despite its efficiency, transaction lending may overlook critical qualitative aspects of a borrower's creditworthiness, particularly for less transparent businesses.

The corporate banking model represents an evolution that integrates the strengths of both relationship and transaction lending. By combining qualitative insights from relationship lending with the quantitative rigour of transaction lending, corporate banking provides a comprehensive framework for credit assessment. This hybrid approach leverages advanced data analytics and technological tools to enhance the accuracy and efficiency of credit evaluations (Udell, 2018). Thus, corporate banking not only improves the precision of risk assessment, but also offers tailored financial solutions to meet the diverse needs of modern businesses.

Multi-banking emerges as a strategic response to mitigate risks associated with single banking relationships. Firms engage in multi-banking to diversify their sources of credit, thereby reducing the risk of being unable to refinance their projects if their primary bank faces a liquidity crisis (Detragiache et al., 2000). This diversification is particularly crucial in environments characterized by significant informational asymmetries and regulatory constraints. From the banks' perspective, multi-banking helps manage counterparty risk and achieve greater diversification in their loan portfolios. This strategy is especially relevant for smaller banks that might face high exposure relative to their size and for banks operating in markets with stringent capital requirements and high monitoring costs (Carletti et al., 2007). Moreover, multi-banking can serve as a mechanism to maintain competitive pressure among lenders, preventing any single bank from exploiting its informational advantage to extract rents (Bolton & Scharfstein, 1996; Hart, 1995).

The interconnections between these lending models have significant implications for financial stability. The evolution of corporate banking reflects a trend towards integrating diverse information sources and technological innovations to better address credit risks. However, the increasing reliance on multi-banking strategies highlights the need for robust regulatory frameworks to manage the potential systemic risks associated with interconnected banking relationships (Cappelletti & Mistrulli, 2023). In conclusion, the relationship between relationship lending, transaction lending, corporate banking and multi-banking illustrates the financial system's adaptability to changing economic conditions and technological advancements. Each model offers distinct benefits and addresses specific risks, and their interplay enhances the overall resilience and efficiency of the credit market. Future research and policy development should continue to explore these dynamics to ensure a stable and inclusive financial environment.

References

Alessandrini, P., Presbitero, A. F., & Zazzaro, A. (2009). Banks, distances and firms' financing constraints. *Review of Finance, 13*(2), 261–307.

Alessandrini, P., Presbitero, A. F., & Zazzaro, A. (2010). Bank size or distance: What hampers innovation adoption by SMEs? *Journal of Economic Geography, 10*(6), 845–881.

Angelini, P., Di Salvo, R., & Ferri, G. (1998). Availability and cost of credit for small business: Customer relationships and credit cooperatives. *Journal of Banking and Finance, 22*, 925–954.

Aoki, Y. (2023). Determinants of the intensity of bank–firm relationships: Evidence from Japan. *The Review of Corporate Finance Studies*, cfad017.

Beatriz, M., Coffinet, J., & Nicolas, T. (2022). Relationship lending and SMEs' funding costs over the cycle: Why diversification of borrowing matters. *Journal of Banking & Finance, 138*, Article 105471.

Beck, T. (2013). Bank financing for SMEs—Lessons from the literature. *National Institute Economic Review, 225*(1), R23–R38.

Berger, A. N., & Udell, G. F. (1995). Relationship lending and lines of credit in small firm finance. *Journal of Business, 68*(3), 351–382.

Berger, A. N., & Udell, G. F. (1996). Universal banking and the future of small business lending. In A. Saunders & I. Walter (Eds.), *Financial system design: The case for universal banking* (pp. 559–627). Irwin Publishing.

Berger, A. N., Klapper, L. F., & Udell, G. F. (2001). The ability of banks to lend to informationally opaque small businesses. *Journal of Banking & Finance, 25*(12), 2127–2167.

Berger, A. N., & Udell, G. F. (2002). Small business credit availability and relationship lending: The importance of bank organizational structure. *The Economic Journal, 112*(477), F32–F53.

Berger, A. N., Miller, N. H., Petersen, M. A., Rajan, R. G., & Stein, J. C. (2005). Does function follow organizational form? Evidence from the lending practices of large and small banks. *Journal of Financial Economics, 76*(2), 237–269.

Berger, A. N., & Black, L. K. (2011). Bank size, lending technologies, and small business finance. *Journal of Banking & Finance, 35*(3), 724–735.

Berger, A. N., Cowan, A. M., & Frame, W. S. (2011). The surprising use of credit scoring in small business lending by community banks and the attendant effects on credit availability, risk, and profitability. *Journal of Financial Services Research, 39*, 1–17.

Berger, A. N., Goulding, W., & Rice, T. (2014). Do small businesses still prefer community banks? *Journal of Banking & Finance, 44*, 264–278.

Berger, A. N., & Udell, G. F. (2006). A more complete conceptual framework for SME finance. *Journal of Banking & Finance, 30*(11), 2945–2966.

Berlin, M., & Mester, L. J. (1999). Deposits and relationship lending. *The Review of Financial Studies, 12*(3), 579–607.

Bernini, C., & Brighi, P. (2018). Bank branches expansion, efficiency and local economic growth. *Regional Studies, 52*(10), 1332–1345.

Bhattacharya, S., & Chiesa, G. (1995). Proprietary information, financial intermediation and research incentives. *Journal of Financial Intermediation, 4*, 328–357.

Bofondi, M., Carpinelli, L., & Sette, E. (2018). Credit supply during a sovereign debt crisis. *Journal of the European Economic Association, 16*(3), 696–729.

Bolton, P., Freixas, X., Gambacorta, L., & Mistrulli, P. E. (2016). Relationship and transaction lending in a crisis. *The Review of Financial Studies, 29*(10), 2643–2676.

Bolton, P., & Scharfstein, D. S. (1996). Optimal debt structure and the number of creditors. *The Journal of Political Economy, 104*(1), 1–25.

Boot, A. W. A. (2000). Relationship banking: What do we know? *Journal of Financial Intermediation, 9*(1), 7–25.

Boot, A. W. A., Greenbaum, S. I., & Thakor, A. V. (1993). Reputation and discretion in financial contracting. *American Economic Review, 83*, 1165–1183.

Boot, A. W. A., & Thakor, A. V. (1994). Moral hazard and secured lending in an infinitely repeated credit market game. *International Economic Review, 35*, 899–920.

Boot, A. W. A., & Thakor, A. V. (2000). Can relationship banking survive competition? *The Journal of Finance, 55*(2), 679–713.

Bornheim, S. P., & Herbeck, T. H. (1998). A research note on the theory of SME—Bank relationships. *Small Business Economics, 10*, 327–331.

Braggion, F., & Ongena, S. R. G. (2011). A century of firm–bank relationships: Why the transition to multiple banking? *SSRN Electronic Journal.*

Brick, I. E., & Palia, D. (2007). Evidence of jointness in the terms of relationship lending. *Journal of Financial Intermediation, 16*, 452–476.

Brighi, P., Lucarelli, C., & Venturelli, V. (2019). Predictive strength of lending technologies in funding SMEs. *Journal of Small Business Management, 57*(4), 1350–1377.

Brighi, P., & Venturelli, V. (2014). How do income diversification, firm size and capital ratio affect performance? Evidence for bank holding companies. *Applied Financial Economics, 24*(21), 1375–1392.

Brighi, P., & Venturelli, V. (2017). Demand and supply determinants of credit availability: Evidence from the current credit crisis for European SMEs. *Financial markets, SME financing, and emerging economies* (pp. 41–70). Palgrave Macmillan.

Calcagnini, G., Cole, R., Giombini, G., & Grandicelli, G. (2018). Hierarchy of bank loan approval and loan performance. *Economia Politica, 35*, 935–954.

Cao, M., Duan, K., & Ibrahim, H. (2025). Constraining effects of local government debt on bank loan growth. *Economic Analysis and Policy, 85*, 371–382.

Cappelletti, G., & Mistrulli, P. E. (2023). The role of credit lines and multiple lending in financial contagion and systemic events. *Journal of Financial Stability*, 101141.

Carletti, E., Cerasi, V., & Daltung, S. (2007). Multiple-bank lending: Diversification and free-riding in monitoring. *Journal of Financial Intermediation, 16*(3), 425–451.

Cole, R. A. (1998). The importance of relationships to the availability of credit. *Journal of Banking & Finance, 22*(6–8), 959–977.

Cotugno, M., Monferrà, S., & Sampagnaro, G. (2013). Relationship lending, hierarchical distance and credit tightening: Evidence from the financial crisis. *Journal of Banking & Finance, 37*(5), 1372–1385.

D'Auria, C., Foglia, A., & Reedtz, P. M. (1999). Bank interest rates and credit relationships in Italy. *Journal of Banking & Finance, 23*(7), 1067–1093.

De la Torre, A., Pería, M. S. M., & Schmukler, S. L. (2010). Bank involvement with SMEs: Beyond relationship lending. *Journal of Banking & Finance 34*(9), 2280–2293.

Degryse, H., Masschelein, N., & Mitchell, J. (2005). SMEs and bank lending relationships: The impact of mergers. In R. De Young, & D. Evanoff (Eds.), *Proceedings of the Federal Reserve Bank of Chicago Conference on Bank Structure and Competition* (pp. 148–165). Federal Reserve Bank of Chicago.

Degryse, H., Matthews, K., & Zhao, T. (2018). SMEs and access to bank credit: Evidence on the regional propagation of the financial crisis in the UK. *Journal of Financial Stability, 38*, 53–70.

Degryse, H., & Ongena, S. (2004). *The impact of competition on bank orientation and specialization* (CEPR Discussion Paper No. 4543).

Degryse, H., & Ongena, S. (2005). Distance, lending relationships, and competition. *The Journal of Finance, 60*(1), 231–266.

Degryse, H., & Van Cayseele, P. (2000). Relationship lending within a bank-based system: Evidence from European small business data. *Journal of Financial Intermediation, 9*(1), 90–109.

Detragiache, E., Garella, P. G., & Guiso, L. (2000). Multiple versus single banking relationships: Theory and evidence. *The Journal of Finance, 55*(3), 1133–1161.

Dewally, M., & Shao, Y. (2014). Liquidity crisis, relationship lending and corporate finance. *Journal of Banking & Finance, 39*, 223–239.

Dewatripont, M., & Maskin, E. (1995). Credit and efficiency in centralized and decentralized economies. *Review of Economic Studies, 62*, 541–555.

Diamond, D. W. (1984). Financial intermediation and delegated monitoring. *The Review of Economic Studies, 51*(3), 393–414.

Diamond, D. W. (1991). Monitoring and reputation: The choice between bank loans and directly placed debt. *Journal of Political Economy, 99*, 688–721.

Elsas, R., & Krahnen, J. P. (1998). Is relationship lending special? Evidence from credit-file data in Germany. *Journal of Banking and Finance, 22*, 1283–1316.

Elsas, R. (2005). Empirical determinants of relationship lending. *Journal of Financial Intermediation, 14*, 32–57.

Farinha, L. A., & Santos, J. A. C. (2002). Switching from single to multiple bank lending relationships: Determinants and implications. *Journal of Financial Intermediation, 11*(2), 124–151.

Felici, R., & Pagnini, M. (2008). Distance, bank heterogeneity and entry in local banking markets. *The Journal of Industrial Economics, 56*(3), 500–534.

Fiordelisi, F., Monferrà, S., & Sampagnaro, G. (2014). Relationship lending and credit quality. *Journal of Financial Services Research, 46*, 295–315.

Flögel, F. (2018). Distance and modern banks' lending to SMEs: Ethnographic insights from a comparison of regional and large banks in Germany. *Journal of Economic Geography, 18*(1), 35–57.

Fracasso, A., Peruzzi, V., & Tomasi, C. (2024). Multiple banking relationships: The role of firm connectedness. *Industrial and Corporate Change, 33*(5), 1231–1252.

Freixas, X. (2005). Deconstructing relationship banking. *Investigaciones Económicas, XXIX*(1), 3–31.

Gambacorta, L., & Mistrulli, P. E. (2014). Bank heterogeneity and interest rate setting: What lessons have we learned since Lehman Brothers? *Journal of Money, Credit and Banking, 46*(4), 753–778.

Gambacorta, L., Sabatini, F., & Schiaffi, S. (2025). *Artificial intelligence and relationship lending* (BIS Working Papers, 1244).

Gambini, A., & Zazzaro, A. (2013). Long-lasting bank relationships and growth of firms. *Small Business Economics, 40*, 977–1007.

Greenbaum, S. I., Kanatas, G., & Venezia, I. (1989). Equilibrium loan pricing under the bank-client relationship. *Journal of Banking and Finance, 13*, 221–235.

Greenbaum, S. I., & Thakor, A. V. (1995). *Contemporary financial intermediation*. Dryden Press.

Harhoff, D., & Körting, T. (1998). Lending relationships in Germany—Empirical evidence from survey data. *Journal of Banking & Finance, 22*(10–11), 1317–1353.

Hart, O. (1995). *Firms, contracts, and financial structure*. Oxford University Press.

Hauswald, R., & Marquez, R. (2003). Information technology and financial services competition. *The Review of Financial Studies, 16*(3), 921–948.

Hauswald, R., & Marquez, R. (2006). Competition and strategic information acquisition in credit markets. *The Review of Financial Studies, 19*(3), 967–1000.

Hernández-Cánovas, G., & Martínez-Solano, P. (2006). Banking relationships: Effects on debt terms for small Spanish firms. *Journal of Small Business Management, 44*(3), 315–333.

Hernández-Cánovas, G., & Martínez-Solano, P. (2010). Relationship lending and SME financing in the continental European bank-based system. *Small Business Economics, 34*, 465–482.

Hester, D. D. (1977). *Customer relationships and terms of loans: evidence from a pilot survey* (Federal Reserve Special Studies Paper, No. 102).

Hodgman, D. R. (1963). *Commercial bank loan and investment policy*. University of Illinois.

Holmstrom, B., & Tirole, J. (1997). Financial intermediation, loanable funds, and the real sector. *Quarterly Journal of Economics, CXII*(3), 663–691.

Holod, D., Peek, J., & Torna, G. (2024). *Relationship lending: That ship has not sailed for community banks* (Federal Reserve Bank of Boston Working Papers, No. 24–5).

Hotelling, H. (1929). Stability in competition. *The Economic Journal, 39*(153), 41–57.

Ioannidou, V., & Ongena, S. (2010). Time for a change: Loan conditions and bank behaviour when firms switch banks. *The Journal of Finance, 65*(5), 1847–1877.

James, C., Lu, J., & Sun, Y. (2021). Time is money: Real effects of relationship lending in a crisis. *Journal of Banking & Finance, 133*, 106283.

Jiménez, G., Laeven, L., Martinez-Miera, D., & Peydró, J. L. (2024). Public guarantees, private banks' incentives, and corporate outcomes: evidence from the COVID-19 crisis (No. 2913). ECB Working Paper.

Kang, E., Zardkoohi, A., Paetzold, R. L., & Fraser, D. (2013). Relationship banking and escalating commitments to bad loans. *Small Business Economics, 40*, 899–910.

Lehmann, E., & Neuberger, D. (2001). Do lending relationships matter? Evidence from bank survey data in Germany. *Journal of Economic Behavior & Organization, 45*(4), 339–359.

Lim, I., & Nguyen, D. D. (2021). Hometown lending. *Journal of Financial and Quantitative Analysis, 56*(8), 2894–2933.

López-Espinosa, G., Mayordomo, S., & Moreno, A. (2017). When does relationship lending start to pay? *Journal of Financial Intermediation, 31*, 16–29.

Memmel, C., Schmieder, C., & Stein, I. (2008). *When do companies choose a relationship lender? When do they switch?* (Unpublished manuscript), Deutsche Bundesbank.

Mian, A. R. (2006). Distance constraints: The limits of foreign lending in poor economies. *Journal of Finance, 61*, 1465–1505.

Mkhaiber, A., & Werner, R. A. (2021). The relationship between bank size and the propensity to lend to small firms: New empirical evidence from a large sample. *Journal of International Money and Finance, 110*, Article 102281.

Mocetti, S., Pagnini, M., & Sette, E. (2017). Information technology and banking organization. *Journal of Financial Services Research, 51*, 313–338.

Murro, P., Oliviero, T., & Zazzaro, A. (2023). Relationship lending and employment decisions in firms' bad times. *Journal of Financial and Quantitative Analysis, 58*(6), 2657–2691.

Omiccioli, M., & Carmignani, A. (2007). Costs and benefits of creditor concentration: An empirical approach. *Temi di Discussione (Working Paper)*, No. 645. Bank of Italy.

Ongena, S., & Smith, D. C. (2001). The duration of bank relationships. *Journal of Financial Economics, 61*(3), 449–475.

Ongena, S., Tümer-Alkan, G., & Westernhagen, N. V. (2012). Creditor concentration: An empirical investigation. *European Economic Review, 56*(4), 830–847.

Ornelas, J. R. H., Da Silva, M. S., & Van Doornik, B. F. N. (2022). Informational switching costs, bank competition, and the cost of finance. *Journal of Banking & Finance, 138*, 106408.

Padilla, A. J., & Pagano, M. (1997). Endogenous communication among lenders and entrepreneurial incentives. *The Review of Financial Studies, 10*(1), 205–236.

Peltoniemi, J. (2007). The benefits of relationship banking: Evidence from small business financing in Finland. *Journal of Financial Services Research, 31*, 153–171.

Peltoniemi, J., & Vieru, M. (2013). Personal guarantees, loan pricing, and lending structure in Finnish small business loans. *Journal of Small Business Management, 51*(2), 235–255.

Petersen, M. A., & Rajan, R. G. (1994). The benefits of lending relationships: Evidence from small business data. *The Journal of Finance, 49*(1), 3–37.

Petersen, M. A., & Rajan, R. G. (1995). The effect of credit market competition on lending relationships. *Quarterly Journal of Economics, 110*(2), 407–443.

Petersen, M. A., & Rajan, R. G. (2002). Does distance still matter? The information revolution in small business lending. *Journal of Finance, 57*(6), 2533–2570.

Presbitero, A. F., & Zazzaro, A. (2011). Competition and relationship lending: Friends or foes? *Journal of Financial Intermediation, 20*(3), 387–413.

Presbitero, A. F., Udell, G. F., & Zazzaro, A. (2014). The home bias and the credit crunch: A regional perspective. *Journal of Money, Credit and Banking, 46*(s1), 53–85.

Rajan, R. G. (1992). Insiders and outsiders: The choice between informed and arm's-length debt. *Journal of Finance, 47*, 1367–1400.

Refait-Alexandre, C., & Serve, S. (2020). Multiple banking relationships: Do SMEs mistrust their banks? *Research in International Business and Finance, 51*, Article 100908.

Salop, S. C. (1979). Monopolistic competition with outside goods. *The Bell Journal of Economics*, 141–156.

Santikian, L. (2014). The ties that bind: Bank relationships and small business lending. *Journal of Financial Intermediation, 23*(2), 177–213.

Sharpe, S. (1990). Asymmetric information, bank lending, and implicit contracts: A stylized model of customer relationships. *The Journal of Finance, 45*, 1069–1087.

Stein, J. C. (2002). Information production and capital allocation: Decentralized versus hierarchical firms. *The Journal of Finance, 57*(5), 1891–1921.

Stein, I. (2015). The price impact of lending relationships. *German Economic Review, 16*(3), 367–389.

Stiglitz, J. E. (1990). Peer monitoring and credit markets. *World Bank Economic Review, 4*, 351–366.

Thakor, A. V. (1996). Capital requirements, monetary policy, and aggregate bank lending: Theory and empirical evidence. *The Journal of Finance, 51*(1), 279–324.

Tirri, V. (2007). *Multiple banking relationships and credit market competition: What benefits the firm?* Paper presented at the EFA 2007 Annual Meeting, Ljubljana.

Udell, G. F. (2018). SME access to intermediated credit: What do we know and what don't we know? *Journal of Financial Intermediation, 32*, 34–49.

Varian, H. R. (1990). Monitoring agents with other agents. *Journal of Institutional and Theoretical Economics, CXLVI*, 153–174.

Vesala, T. (2007). Switching costs and relationship profits in bank lending. *Journal of Banking and Finance, 31*, 477–493.

Von Thadden, E. L. (1992). *The commitment of finance, duplicated monitoring and the investment horizon* (CEPR Discussion Paper, No. 27).

Von Thadden, E. L. (1995). Long-term contracts, short-term investments and monitoring. *The Review of Economic Studies, 62*(4), 557–575.

Von Thadden, E.-L. (2004). Asymmetric information, bank lending and implicit contracts: The winner's curse. *Finance Research Letters, 1*(1), 11–23.

Wilner, B. S. (2000). The exploitation of relationships in financial distress: The case of trade credit. *The Journal of Finance, 55*(1), 153–178.

CHAPTER 5

Financial Risks and the Role of Banking Regulation

5.1 The Role of Banking Regulation

Banking regulation helps mitigate the adverse effects of asymmetric information in several key ways. First of all, regulations often mandate that banks and financial institutions disclose comprehensive and accurate information on their financial status, lending practices and the creditworthiness of borrowers. This transparency reduces the information gap between banks and potential lenders or investors, making it easier for market participants to make informed decisions. Examples of enhanced transparency and disclosure requirements are financial statements, quarterly reports and disclosures about loan portfolios help mitigate the information asymmetry between the bank and external stakeholders, such as investors and regulators.

Regulations standardize the processes and criteria for credit evaluation and risk management. By adhering to common standards, banks reduce the variability and uncertainty associated with credit assessments, which helps to minimize adverse selection. Examples of standardization of practices include the Basel Accords, which set standards for capital requirements, stress testing and risk management practices that banks must follow. This uniformity helps ensure that all banks operate under the same risk assessment framework.

P. Brighi and M. Mussoni, *The Bank-Business Relationship*,
https://doi.org/10.1007/978-3-031-91068-5_5

Regulatory bodies actively monitor and supervise banking activities to ensure compliance with laws and regulations. This oversight helps detect and prevent fraudulent or risky behaviour that could arise from asymmetric information. Examples of monitoring and supervision include regulatory audits and examinations by bodies like the Federal Reserve or the European Central Bank (ECB) to ensure that banks adhere to sound practices and maintain adequate risk management procedures.

Regulations often include provisions to protect savers from unfair practices due to information asymmetry. These protections can increase trust in the banking system and promote fair treatment. These safeguards help enhance trust in the banking system and ensure fair treatment of depositors. For example, regulations such as deposit insurance schemes or transparency requirements aim to clearly disclose the terms and risks associated with savings products, enabling savers to make informed decisions about where to place their funds.

Regulatory frameworks impose specific risk management requirements, such as maintaining minimum capital adequacy ratios and creating provisions for bad loans. These requirements help ensure that banks remain solvent and resilient to financial losses, thereby mitigating the negative effects of information asymmetry. A key example of such risk management measures is the Basel III framework, which mandates that banks maintain a minimum percentage of their risk-weighted assets as Tier 1 capital. This capital serves as a buffer to absorb potential losses, particularly those arising from credit risk.

Regulations often mandate the establishment of central credit registers that collect and share information on borrowers' credit exposures. This collective data pool helps banks assess the creditworthiness of potential borrowers more accurately, reducing the risks associated with lending. Important examples are the Central Credit Registers managed by central banks, which collect data on the credit exposures of households and businesses, which banks can use to assess credit risk more effectively.

Regulatory environments support the establishment and functioning of credit-scoring and rating agencies that provide independent assessments of borrowers' risk profiles. These scores and ratings help mitigate information asymmetry by providing reliable and standardized information on borrowers. Examples of consumer credit-scoring and rating agencies are agencies like Standard & Poor's, Moody's and Fitch, which provide credit ratings for borrowers, which banks use to make more informed lending decisions.

Regulations often include mechanisms to mitigate moral hazard by aligning the interests of banks and their borrowers or stakeholders. For instance, regulations may enforce penalties for risky behaviour or incentivize sound financial practices. One example of mitigation of moral hazard is the deposit insurance schemes, which protect depositors, reducing the likelihood of bank runs. However, they are coupled with strict supervision to prevent banks from taking excessive risks with insured deposits. By implementing these regulatory measures, the adverse effects of asymmetric information, such as adverse selection and moral hazard, are significantly mitigated, leading to a more stable and efficient banking system.

5.2 Loan Origination and Monitoring (LOM) Guidelines

The lending function plays a key role in the operations of banking institutions. In previous chapters, this function has been examined through the lens of information asymmetry theory, which, beginning in the 1970s, reshaped the theoretical frameworks of financial intermediation (see Tirole, 1994; Thakor, 1995). Information asymmetries underlie credit risk in the lender–borrower relationship, occurring ex-ante (during the credit granting phase) as an adverse selection risk and ex-post (after the loan has been issued) as a moral hazard. According to theory, screening serves to reduce ex-ante risk, while monitoring mitigates ex-post moral hazard. Similarly, regulators have developed rules governing credit activities both ex-ante and ex-post, as outlined in the guidelines on Loan Origination and Monitoring (LOM).

On May 29, 2020, the European Banking Authority (EBA) issued the final version of these guidelines (EBA, 2020) that, according to the principle of proportionality, are applicable to all Significant and Less

Significant Banks[1] at both individual and consolidated levels. The effective date was set for June 30, 2021, for new financing, with a transitional period for other credits. Specifically, the application to existing loans subject to renegotiation or contractual modification was set for June 30, 2022, while the alignment of monitoring frameworks/infrastructure is permitted until June 30, 2024.

The goal of the LOM guidelines is to instil a proactive approach to 'credit quality monitoring, identifying deteriorating credit early and managing overall credit quality and the associated risk profile of the portfolio, including through new credit origination activities'.[2] Credit policies should adopt a forward-looking approach to credit management, with a recommendation to evaluate, as part of credit risk analysis, 'the current and future capacity of the client to meet obligations arising from the loan agreement'.[3] Accordingly, banks in their credit assessments should prioritize 'a realistic and sustainable estimate of the client's income and future cash flow rather than available collateral'. This shift reflects a greater focus on assessing overall creditworthiness and a broader analysis of risk. The LOM guidelines, therefore, encourage banking intermediaries to view collateral as a supplementary element in loan assessment rather than as the primary factor, emphasizing that 'collateral should be considered the second exit option for the institution in case of default or significant deterioration of the risk profile and not the primary source of repayment'.[4] In other words, this approach departs from a backward-looking or reactive

[1] A bank is classified as a Significant Institution (SI), and therefore subject to direct supervision by the European Central Bank (ECB) if it meets at least one of the following criteria: (a) the total value of its assets exceeds €30 billion or, unless the total asset value is below €5 billion, exceeds 20% of the national GDP; (b) it is one of the three most significant banks located in a member country, due to its economic importance for the country itself or for the economy of the European Union as a whole; (c) the total asset value exceeds €5 billion, and the ratio of cross-border assets in more than one other participating Member State to total assets is over 20%, or the ratio of cross-border liabilities in more than one other participating Member State to total liabilities is over 20%; (d) it has requested or received funding under the European Stability Mechanism (ESM) or the European Financial Stability Facility. Less Significant Institutions (LSIs) are small and medium-sized banks supervised directly by National Competent Authorities under the oversight of the ECB (see Bank of Italy Glossary).

[2] Paragraph 35 of LOM guidelines.

[3] Paragraph 118 of LOM guidelines.

[4] Paragraph 120 of LOM guidelines.

model where collateral was assessed only once the underlying credit was already in an anomalous phase.

The LOM guidelines provide banks with recommendations and best practices in credit origination and monitoring to ensure the adoption of solid and prudent standards for assuming, managing and monitoring credit risk, thereby ensuring that newly originated loans maintain high credit quality over their lifecycle. The LOM guidelines are structured into five sections covering the following thematic areas:

1. Internal governance for credit granting and monitoring.
2. Loan origination procedures.
3. Pricing framework.
4. Valuation of immovable and movable property.
5. Monitoring framework.

Regarding 'Internal governance for credit granting and monitoring', the guidelines particularly focus on three main areas: (i) defining and approving the credit risk strategy; (ii) credit granting; and (iii) credit risk controls. First, in relation to the credit risk strategy, the guidelines suggest that banks define credit risk appetite in alignment with the risk appetite framework (RAF),[5] supported by specific metrics and indicators. In this respect, banks must cultivate and disseminate a 'credit risk culture at all levels of the organization, ensuring that all personnel involved in credit risk assumption, management and monitoring are fully aware of and accountable for their actions'.[6] Furthermore, regarding the credit granting process, the guidelines stipulate that 'the structure of credit decision-makers should be aligned with and integrated into the credit risk appetite and [...] the institution's business model'.[7] Credit granting powers and limits should consider credit portfolio diversification across client segments, geographic areas, economic sectors and asset classes. In line with internal governance policies, credit decisions should be impartial

[5] Banks establish a Risk Appetite Framework (RAF) to define, ex-ante, the risk/return objectives the institution aims to achieve and the resulting operational limits (Circular 285/2013).

[6] Paragraphs 27 and 28 of LOM guidelines.

[7] Paragraph 64 of LOM guidelines.

and objective, free from conflicts of interest. The guidelines also call for strengthened first-line controls on automated decision-making engines.

For credit risk control processes, banks should define roles and responsibilities across business lines, functions and internal structures supported by a transparent and periodic reporting mechanism. Clear delineation of responsibilities across business lines, functions and internal structures, alongside transparent, periodic reporting mechanisms, is essential for internal controls.

The 'Loan origination procedures' are grounded in the assessment of creditworthiness, which requires sufficient, accurate and up-to-date information and data on the borrower and any guarantors relative to their connected customer group. Credit assessment criteria differ based on whether the client is retail or corporate and the purpose of the financing (e.g., real estate, project finance or shipping). In line with the forward-looking principle underpinning the guidelines' goals, credit assessment must consider prospective cash flow and the bank's sensitivity analyses.

When conducting a sensitivity analysis on a client's repayment capacity under adverse future conditions, institutions should consider the following events, which are particularly relevant to the client's specific circumstances and business model (EBA, 2020, paragraph 158):

- Idiosyncratic Events

  (a) Significant yet plausible decline in a client's revenues or profit margins.
  (b) Severe but plausible operational loss event.
  (c) The occurrence of serious but plausible management issues.
  (d) The failure of a key business partner, client or supplier.
  (e) Significant yet plausible reputational damage.
  (f) Severe but plausible outflow of liquidity, changes in funding or an increase in a client's leverage.
  (g) Adverse fluctuations in the prices of goods to which the client is predominantly exposed (e.g., commodities or finished products) and in exchange rates.

- Market Events

  (h) Significant yet plausible macroeconomic downturn.
  (i) Severe but plausible contraction in the economic sectors in which the client and its customers operate.

(j) Substantial shift in political, regulatory and geographical risk.
(k) Significant yet plausible increase in the cost of financing, such as a 200 basis point rise in interest rates across all of the client's credit lines.

Regarding the 'Pricing framework', the LOM guidelines suggest cost and risk components that should be factored into pricing decisions; however, they do not prescribe a specific pricing strategy, which remains solely at the bank's discretion. Pricing should reflect: (i) the bank's risk appetite; (ii) competition and market conditions; (iii) the characteristics (e.g., retail, micro-enterprise, or corporate) and quality of the client; (iv) costs, including the cost of capital, funding costs, and operating and administrative expenses; and (v) credit risk costs.

The LOM guidelines stipulate that 'valuation of immovable and movable property' should be conducted accurately at the time of financing. For real estate collateral in particular, banks should rely on appraisals by independent evaluators, supplemented, where possible, by advanced statistical models. In real estate valuations, banks should account for Environmental, Social, and Governance (ESG) factors that influence the collateral's value, such as the energy efficiency of buildings and the physical risk of the property's location. A proactive credit evaluation approach requires monitoring of collateral as well, with banks establishing policies and procedures specifying the approach and frequency of this monitoring.

Finally, the 'Monitoring framework' introduced by the LOM guidelines mandates alignment with banks' credit risk strategies and continuous monitoring of credit exposures, both at an aggregate (i.e., portfolio) and individual level. Institutions must maintain a 'robust and effective monitoring framework, supported by an adequate data infrastructure [...] relevant and up to date'.[8] Banks should develop a data infrastructure enabling automatic collection and subsequent analysis/processing of data without undue delays. Additionally, integrating quantitative data with external data sources and incorporating Key Risk Indicators (KRIs) for credit monitoring is recommended.

Regarding monitoring, banks must verify whether the client and the collateral align with the repayment obligations established in the contract, as well as the credit risk policies and conditions set at the time of credit

[8] Paragraph 240 of LOM guidelines.

origination. Concerning the review process, the LOM guidelines mandate 'regular reviews of clients' creditworthiness [...] aimed at identifying any changes in their risk profile, financial standing, or credit quality [...] and reviewing and updating any internal ratings/credit scoring'.[9] Moreover, banks are encouraged not to overlook qualitative information (e.g., management quality, turnover, market positioning) that could significantly impact loan repayment. This integrated client assessment approach aligns with the latest literature on relationship lending (see Chapter 4) as well as with the rating model frameworks introduced under the Basel Accords.

Credit monitoring is completed through the activation of Early Warning Indicators (EWI) at both the individual exposure and portfolio levels, as well as through forward-looking stress tests. In cases where early warning limits are exceeded, or adverse results arise from stress tests, banks must be prepared to initiate immediate corrective actions and follow up on outcomes. The early warning system is designed as a proactive alert mechanism that identifies deterioration in the credit quality of an exposure or debtor by employing EWI to categorize a credit position on a watch list or as performing (*bonis*) or default.

In conclusion, it is important to emphasize that the LOM guidelines fit within a broader regulatory context, which includes oversight from the European Central Bank (ECB) as a supervisory authority. This framework encompasses a series of guidelines and best practices aimed at managing credit risk, considering also emerging risks, such as ESG, Information and Communication Technology (ICT) risks, and security risks (see Chapter 6).

5.3 Overview of Financial Risks: Traditional and Emerging Risks

In previous chapters, we addressed informational asymmetries as drivers of adverse selection and moral hazard risks within credit contracts. In financial markets, one party often lacks sufficient knowledge of the other party to make well-informed decisions in a transaction. This imbalance is known as informational asymmetry. Informational asymmetry can lead to inefficiencies and even market failure, which necessitates mechanisms such

[9] Paragraph 265 of LOM guidelines.

as regulation, information transparency, well-structured contracts, and appropriate incentives to ensure desired behaviours from parties involved in economic transactions (see Thakor, 1995; Tirole, 1994).

In this chapter, we focus more specifically on financial risks, which are those risks associated with decision-making under conditions of uncertainty, which is when full knowledge is unavailable or future outcomes are difficult to predict with certainty. Investors in financial instruments are aware of their exposure to risks and understand that investment outcomes may be lower than anticipated. The debtor's default, fluctuations in exchange rates for foreign currency securities, interest rate changes and shifts in the macroeconomic environment can all adversely affect the value of financial assets.

In modern financial theory, risk is understood as the possibility of obtaining returns that deviate from expected outcomes, whether lower or higher. This concept is broader than the common view that links risk solely with the possibility of negative returns. Financial theory assumes that an investor can estimate the possible outcomes of an investment and the respective probabilities of occurrence. With this information, both expected return and risk can be quantified.

The expected return, denoted as $E(r)$, is the mean of the n possible end-of-period results r_i, each weighted by its probability of occurrence p_i. This can be expressed as:

$$E(r_i) = \sum_{i=1}^{n} p_i \times r_i \tag{5.1}$$

In each possible scenario, the expected return is calculated by relating the cash flows received during the period to the purchase price or beginning-of-period price. These cash flows consist of periodic cash flows generated by the investment (such as coupons or dividends) and the difference between the purchase (or start-period) and sale (or end-period) price. The risk is measured by the dispersion of outcomes around the expected return, more specifically by the variance (or standard deviation, which is the square root of the variance) of the return probability distribution:

$$\sigma_i^2 = \sum_{i=1}^{n} p_i \times [r_i - E(r_i)]^2 \tag{5.2}$$

The standard deviation σ_i has the advantage of being expressed in the same unit as the expected return. The notions of risk and return introduced here refer to a single financial asset. When extending the analysis to a portfolio of multiple financial assets, portfolio theory suggests that diversification can provide benefits by achieving specific return objectives while reducing risk. Portfolio risk consists of two components:

(i) Specific risk (also known as diversifiable or idiosyncratic risk) is inherent to each asset.
(ii) Systematic risk (also known as non-diversifiable risk) is independent of the individual debtor and arises from the general economic system.

Formally, the variance of a portfolio P is represented as:

$$\sigma_P^2 = \sum_{i=1}^{N} x_i^2\sigma_i^2 + \sum_{i=1}^{N} \sum_{\substack{j=1 \\ j \neq i}}^{N} x_i x_j \sigma_{i,j} \tag{5.3}$$

where x_i represents the portion of the portfolio invested in asset i and $\sigma_{i,j}$ denotes the covariance between the returns of assets i and j.

As the number of securities in a portfolio increases, the variance of its return decreases, converging towards the average covariance value (specific risk diminishes until it is eliminated, while the significance of covariance grows). In other words, diversification achieved by randomly increasing the number of securities in a portfolio reduces the specific risk to zero. However, this approach may have minimal impact on covariance, which requires selecting securities with low or negative correlation according to Markowitz's portfolio theory.[10]

Beyond variance and standard deviation, several advanced techniques are utilized in financial risk measurement. Among them, Value at Risk (VaR) is one of the most widely used metrics. VaR quantifies the maximum potential loss in value of a portfolio over a given period, under normal market conditions, with a given confidence level. It is defined as:

$$P(r_P \leq -\text{VaR}) = (1 - \alpha) \tag{5.4}$$

[10] For further insights into portfolio theory, refer to Hillier et al. (2020).

which represents the probability that the portfolio return r_P will fall below the negative VaR threshold, where VaR represents the maximum expected loss over a given time horizon at the confidence level α (e.g., 95% or 99%), and $(1 - \alpha)$ represents the probability of an extreme loss beyond the VaR threshold. We will see in the next Sect. 5.4 that VaR is used for estimating the unexpected loss, i.e., the most likely loss on a given credit exposure (and thus to measure the credit risk).

Essentially, the equation states that there is a probability of $(1 - \alpha)$ that the portfolio's return will be worse than the estimated VaR. Three primary methods exist for calculating VaR:

1. Parametric (variance-covariance) VaR, which assumes returns are normally distributed, and estimates risk using mean and standard deviation.
2. Historical simulation, which uses past data to simulate future potential losses.
3. Monte Carlo simulation, which generates thousands of random return scenarios to estimate the loss distribution.

While VaR is useful, it has limitations, such as its failure to capture tail risk. This is addressed by measures like Conditional Value at Risk (CVaR), which evaluates expected losses beyond the VaR threshold. CVaR, also known as Expected Shortfall (ES), measures the expected loss in the worst $1 - \alpha\%$ of cases:

$$\mathrm{CVaR}_\alpha = E[r \mid r \leq -\mathrm{VaR}_\alpha] \tag{5.5}$$

CVaR is considered a superior risk measure because it accounts for extreme losses in the tail of the distribution, making it more reliable for stress testing. Other advanced risk measures are the following:

1. Maximum Drawdown (MDD), which measures the maximum observed loss from peak to trough over a specified period.
2. Sharpe Ratio, which evaluates risk-adjusted return by comparing excess return to volatility:

$$\mathrm{SR} = \frac{E(r_P) - r_f}{\sigma_P} \tag{5.6}$$

where r_f is the risk-free rate.

3. Sortino Ratio, which is a modification of the Sharpe Ratio that considers downside risk only.
4. Beta (β) Coefficient, which measures systematic risk relative to the market:

$$\beta_i = \frac{\text{Cov}(r_i, r_M)}{\text{Var}(r_M)} \tag{5.7}$$

where r_M is the return of the market.
5. Stress Testing and Scenario Analysis, which simulates extreme market conditions to evaluate portfolio resilience.

Risk measurement is, therefore, a cornerstone of modern financial analysis, influencing investment decisions and regulatory frameworks. While variance and standard deviation remain fundamental, advanced methods such as VaR, CVaR and stress testing provide a more comprehensive view of potential losses. The choice of risk measures depends on the context, investment horizon and risk tolerance of the investor or institution. Ongoing research continues to refine these models, incorporating non-normal distributions and behavioural aspects of risk perception.

The taxonomy of financial risks is a widely recognized concept used to classify and catalogue the risks that financial institutions may encounter in their operations. The primary distinction is between traditional risks, which have long been identified and managed, and emerging risks related in particular to Environmental, Social and Governance (ESG) factors and Information and Communication Technology (ICT) risks.

The *traditional risks* can be classified by various criteria, such as whether they originate from within or outside the bank, their degree of predictability or the extent of their impact. Based on the last criterion, we can categorize risks as follows.

1. *Macroeconomic risks*, due to the potential threats represented by the broad economic factors, may adversely impact the financial and operational conditions of banks. These risks are often linked to events or shifts at national or global levels that can significantly affect the economy, making them non-diversifiable. Included in this category is systemic risk, typically associated with the payment system, where a bank's inability to meet its obligations within clearing systems could trigger a domino effect or cascade of defaults among other

banks. More broadly, systemic risk can be described as a process that escalates a localized crisis into widespread challenges for the entire financial system.[11]

2. *Microeconomic risks*, due to specific sectors, geographic areas or institutional entities; that is, to the specific threats stemming from the financial and operational conditions of individual businesses or loans within a bank's portfolio. These risks are intrinsic to direct relationships between banks and their clients or counterparties and are further divided into (i) *internal (or management) risks*, which are tied to strategic and managerial choices and the conduct of operations, including risk appetite, investment and financing decisions, production processes and human resources; (ii) *external (or relational) risks*, which arise from the bank's continuous and systematic interactions with various counterparties, such as supervisory authorities, lenders, borrowers, capital markets and securities transaction counterparties.

A list with descriptions of individual risks is provided in Table 5.1.

Over time, the classification of traditional financial risks has been defined with increasing specificity by regulatory authorities. In particular, the Basel Committee distinguishes, within the scope of capital computation to cover risks, between: (i) credit risk; (ii) market risk; (iii) operational risk; and has since added: (iv) liquidity risk.

- *Credit risk* refers to the possibility that a debtor may fail (fully or partially) to meet repayment obligations, resulting in a financial loss for the financial intermediary. This is one of the most traditional risks borne by financial intermediaries in their lending function, as it represents the risk of losses due to the borrower default in repaying a loan and accrued interest or other forms of credit.
- *Market risk* is the risk that the value of an investment decreases due to fluctuations in market variables, including equity risk, interest rate risk and exchange rate risk. This involves fluctuations in the prices of financial instruments, such as stocks, bonds, currencies

[11] Among macroeconomic risks, we can also include climate risk, which represents one aspect of ESG risks. For a more detailed discussion, see Chapter 6.

Table 5.1 Taxonomy of financial risks

Macroeconomic risks	*Microeconomic risks*	
	Internal risks	*External risks*
• The **economic recession risk** is associated with a significant contraction in economic activity, which may lead to a decline in loan demand, an increase in default rates, and reduced bank revenues	• The **operational risk** refers to the possibility that a bank may incur financial or reputational losses due to human error, process inefficiencies, technological issues, fraud, unforeseen external events or other non-financial causes	• The **counterparty risk** is further divided into **credit risk** and **settlement risk**. Credit risk refers to the possibility that a counterparty may be unable to fulfil its payment obligations or repay loans, while settlement risk refers to the possibility of default or non-performance in the settlement of financial transactions
• The **financial instability risk** arises from events such as financial crises, market shocks, speculative bubbles or sector-specific crashes that can cause turbulence in financial markets	• The **technological risk** concerns threats associated with the use and management of technology. This may include system failures or disruptions, cybersecurity breaches, data loss or corruption, as well as the inability to adapt to new technologies or market developments	• The **funding risk** (or **supply risk**) is linked to the institution's ability to continuously secure necessary financial resources from various counterparties (such as customer deposits, bonds, interbank deposits, or equity from shareholders) in quantities and at prices (interest rates) that align with growth objectives, asset composition choices and investment returns
• The **interest rate risk** stems from changes in market interest rates that can affect banks' profitability	• The **strategic risk** arises from inadequate planning, implementation or adaptation of business strategies	• The **market risk**, i.e., the risk that fluctuations in financial instrument prices, interest rates, exchange rates, or other market factors may negatively impact the value of assets or the outcome of a bank's operations

(continued)

Table 5.1 (continued)

Macroeconomic risks	*Microeconomic risks*	
	Internal risks	*External risks*
• The **exchange rate risk** refers to the risk of fluctuations in currency values	• The **reputational risk** is related to actions, behaviours, or events that undermine the trust of clients, investors or the general public. This risk may stem from poor management, unethical behaviour, financial scandals, data security breaches or other events that damage the bank's image and public trust	• The **liquidity risk**, i.e., the risk that a bank may be unable to meet its payment obligations as they fall due or access sufficient liquidity to support operational needs
• The **Government policy risk** includes changes in fiscal, regulatory or monetary policies		• The **regulatory risk** refers to the potential negative impacts on banks due to new regulations or changes to existing regulatory frameworks
• The **sovereign default risk** pertains to the possibility that a government may be unable to meet its debt obligations		

Source Elaboration by the authors

and commodities, which may negatively impact the value of an investment portfolio. Market risk is divided into three subcategories:

- *Interest rate risk* refers to the possibility that changes in interest rates may adversely affect the value of an investment or financial position, stemming from uncertainty about fluctuations in benchmark interest rates, such as market interest rates or central bank rates. This risk is particularly relevant for investors or financial institutions holding fixed-rate instruments, such as bonds, loans or fixed-rate mortgages; as interest rates rise, the value of fixed-rate securities tends to decline because investors demand higher yields. Conversely, as interest rates fall, the value of fixed-rate securities tends to rise. Therefore, managing interest rate risk requires careful strategies, including hedging techniques like the use of derivative instruments or adopting variable-rate instruments to mitigate the impact of interest rate fluctuations on investment values or financial positions.

- *Equity risk* arises from the variability and uncertainty of returns on equity investments, reflecting the potential for significant fluctuations in the value of equity investments, either up or down. Equity risk is influenced by several factors, including market volatility, economic, political, and social factors, and the financial performance of issuing companies. Managing equity risk includes portfolio diversification strategies, fundamental analysis of companies, close monitoring of financial markets, and risk management measures to balance potential rewards with the risks associated with equity investments.
- *Currency risk* refers to the possibility that fluctuations in the exchange rate between different currencies could negatively impact the value of an investment or an international transaction. It is influenced by the uncertainty of future exchange rate movements between two currencies, which economic, political and financial factors may affect. Currency risk can significantly affect international investments, as exchange rate fluctuations can impact cash flows, profits and losses. Effective currency risk management requires hedging strategies, such as using derivative instruments, and an accurate assessment of currency exposure to mitigate the impact of exchange rate fluctuations and preserve the value of investments or international transactions.

• *Operational risk* is associated with internal or external events that can cause financial losses due to inefficiencies, errors, fraud or disruptions in operations. It represents the risk arising from the execution of an enterprise's business functions and encompasses a broad range of risks, including fraud, legal, physical or environmental risks etc. According to the Bank of Italy's online glossary, operational risk is defined as 'the risk arising from inadequacy or dysfunction in procedures, human resources, and internal systems, or from exogenous events; risk of losses due to errors or damages caused by people, systems, or processes'. Losses associated with this risk can vary in magnitude, from minor losses in basic commercial activities such as retail banking and wealth management to more significant losses related to sales and trading. Examples of losses due to human error include internal fraud within institutions or errors made during transactions. On a larger scale, fraud may occur through breaches of a bank's cybersecurity (see security risk or cyber risk), where hackers steal customer information and extort large sums of money. In such cases, the capital loss is compounded by reputational damage, which may negatively impact the bank's future ability to attract capital.

- *Liquidity risk* refers to the financial intermediary's ability to meet payment obligations promptly without causing interruptions or difficulties in operations. It also pertains to uncertainty about banks' capacity to maintain sufficient funds to meet clients' loan demands.

The evolving economic and financial environment necessitates an update to the mapping of traditional risks alongside technological advancements and regulatory frameworks in which banks operate. The *new risks* identified by the Single Supervisory Mechanism (SSM)[12] in recent years as sources of vulnerability for banking activities that have shaped supervisory priorities include the following.

- *Innovation risk* refers to the possibility that the adoption of new technologies and business models may introduce unforeseen or unknown risks to financial institutions. Examples include risks associated with implementing new digital payment systems or using artificial intelligence for financial data analysis, that is, technologies that offer significant benefits but also present major challenges in terms of security, data privacy and regulatory compliance.
- *Cybersecurity* or *cyber risk* arises from cyber threats and attacks that can compromise the security of financial information and harm the reputation of financial institutions. This risk has emerged as a significant threat in the digital age and with the growth of the internet, as financial institutions manage vast amounts of sensitive data and conduct online financial transactions, making them prime targets for cyber-attacks. Cybersecurity breaches can compromise customer data confidentiality, damage reputation and lead to financial losses. Financial institutions must, therefore, invest in robust technological infrastructures, implement stringent security policies and adopt preventive measures to protect sensitive information.

[12] The Single Supervisory Mechanism (SSM) is the European banking supervision system that includes the ECB and the national supervisory authorities of participating countries.

- *Sustainability* or *ESG risk* refers to the financial risks arising from current or potential impacts of Environmental, Social, or Governance (ESG) factors, which may affect the financial performance or solvency of clients or the assets in which a bank invests. In June 2022, the Basel Committee on Banking Supervision (BCBS) issued the 'Principles for the Effective Management and Supervision of Climate-Related Financial Risks',[13] addressing the financial risks banks face due to exposure to counterparties that may influence or be influenced by climate change. For these risks, the banks must preliminarily identify the transmission channels[14] within the traditional risk categories. Thus, these risks are not a standalone category in taxonomic terms, but banks should consider them for their potential financial impact on all traditional risks. Therefore, they should be included in 'materiality analysis', which focuses on a company's performance. The term 'materiality' emphasizes the significance, concreteness and measurability of the factors considered, which must align with corporate objectives. Material aspects are those that are relevant because they can influence the evaluations and decisions of stakeholders—such as citizens, employees, local entities, organizations, associations, financial partners, suppliers and clients—or because they have importance regarding the economic, social, and environmental impacts generated across the entire value chain (see Chapter 6).

Understanding and managing both traditional and new financial risks is essential for promoting financial stability and maintaining investor and market confidence. Through its annually published supervisory priorities (see Sect. 6.1),[15] the SSM urges supervised entities to develop appropriate strategies and tools to identify, assess and mitigate these risks, adapting to changes in the financial environment and stakeholder requirements.

[13] BCBS, Principles for the Effective Management and Supervision of Climate-Related Financial Risks, June 2022.

[14] BCBS, Climate-Related Risk Drivers and Their Transmission Channels, April 2021.

[15] www.bankingsupervision.europa.eu/framework/priorities/html/ssm.supervisory_priorities202312~a15d5d36ab.en.html.

5.4 Credit Risk Management: The Role of NPLs and NPEs

The primary risk associated with the lending function of banks is credit risk, which pertains to all active transactions undertaken by an intermediary with its clients (on-balance-sheet loans and securities as well as off-balance-sheet items, such as guarantees, securities transactions, currency exchanges or pending derivative settlements). This risk arises from the possibility that within a given time frame, certain clients may become partially or entirely unable to meet their contractual obligations. Credit risk is thus the risk that the bank may incur a loss due to a counterparty defaulting on credit exposure, resulting in an inability to repay some or all of the debt (principal and/or interest) according to the contractual terms.

Credit risk can be defined broadly as the possibility that an unexpected change in a counterparty's ability to repay results in a corresponding unexpected change in the current value of the associated credit exposure. This definition encompasses at least three general characteristics.

- Credit risk is linked to both a counterparty's insolvency and a mere deterioration in its credit quality (downgrading), meaning a migration to a lower credit category. Thus, it represents a risk not only of default but also of an increased probability of future default.
- The risk is contingent on unexpected events related to changes in creditworthiness that were unforeseen by the bank at the time of lending and pricing decisions.
- The risk is associated with 'credit exposures', which include not only traditional bank loans (on-balance-sheet exposures) but also derivatives, securities transactions, currency exchanges, and guarantees (so-called 'off-balance-sheet exposures').

Credit risk is primarily associated with the *banking book*; i.e., the credits granted to customers, arising from financing activities like credit provision or securities subscription (direct channel). It pertains to the possibility that the debtor may fail to fulfil payment obligations or reduce reliability in honouring commitments, such as interest payments and principal repayment.

Credit risk also encompasses *counterparty risk*, defined as 'the risk that the counterparty to a transaction default before the final settlement of the financial flows'.[16] Counterparty risk is associated with the *trading book*; i.e., it is the insolvency risk of a contractual counterparty obligated to deliver a certain amount of money in exchange for specific financial instruments or vice versa. As regulated by the Capital Requirements Regulation,[17] counterparty risk is a specific form of credit risk and pertains only to certain types of transactions with specific characteristics: (i) they generate exposure equal to their positive fair value, (ii) they have a market value that changes over time based on underlying market variables, and (iii) they involve payment exchanges or the exchange of financial instruments or goods for payments. The transactions include:

- Derivative contracts, as outlined in Capital Requirement Regulation (CRR) Annex II.
- Securities Financial Transactions (SFTs), such as repos and securities lending.
- Medium- and long-term settlement transactions.

Counterparty risk refers to potential counterparty default before contract maturity, commonly called replacement risk, where 'the market value of the position becomes positive, and if the counterparty defaults, the solvent party must replace the position on the market, incurring a loss'.[18] A loss is incurred if the transactions with a specific counterparty hold a positive value at the time of default. Unlike credit risk from a loan, where the risk of loss is unilateral as it lies solely with the lending bank, counterparty risk generally creates bilateral loss potential, as the transaction's market value may be positive or negative for both parties.

If derivative exchanges occur on organized markets, a clearinghouse acts as a counterparty to contracts, autonomously managing risk by offsetting debit and credit positions, thereby reducing or eliminating counterparty risk. However, since the 1980s, volumes of derivatives traded on non-organized markets (OTC markets) have grown significantly, where no clearing system exists, prompting supervisory authorities to issue recent recommendations and general principles for measuring and managing counterparty risk associated with OTC derivatives trading.

[16] Supervisory Provisions for Banks, Circular No. 285, 2013, Annex A.

[17] CRR, EU Regulation No. 575/2013 and subsequent amendments.

[18] Basel III, Pillar III, Public Disclosure as of December 31, 2022.

Given the various causes that may trigger credit risk, it can be divided into several types of risks.

- *Default risk* occurs when the counterparty cannot meet payment obligations or defaults, resulting in a potential loss equal to the product of Exposure at Default (EAD) and the Loss Given Default (LGD).
- *Migration or downgrading risk* occurs when there is a deterioration in the debtor's credit quality; 'rating transition matrices' are used to measure this risk, as the counterparty's credit quality may improve or deteriorate, with the latter implying a higher probability of default.
- *Spread risk* is linked to a general increase in the risk premium (spread) demanded by markets from borrowers, signalling heightened risk aversion among investors and reducing the current value of the exposure without a deterioration in the borrower's credit quality.
- *Recovery risk* is the risk that the amount actually recovered from an insolvent counterparty is lower than initially expected due to longer recovery times or lower-than-anticipated collateral realization values. Under the EBA's Loan and Monitoring Guidelines (LOM), the collateral role in credit evaluation has diminished, prioritizing an overall assessment of the financed project's quality.
- *Exposure risk* is the risk that exposure increases as default approaches (e.g., in the case of overdraft facilities, where financially distressed firms tend to utilize the facility fully), resulting in exposure greater than initially estimated in the event of default.
- *Pre-settlement* or *replacement risk* is associated with the possibility of counterparty default in OTC derivative contracts before contract maturity, potentially requiring replacement in the market with a new contract.
- *Settlement risk* is the risk of counterparty default in OTC derivative contracts at contract maturity or settlement; this risk is present only within the brief period between the two transactions (a few hours) and may be mitigated in organized markets with centralized clearinghouses.
- *Country risk* is the risk that the default probability of a non-resident counterparty increases due to political or legislative events beyond its control.
- *Portfolio* or *concentration risk* is linked to the overall characteristics of the financial intermediary's loan portfolio rather than individual

credit exposures and stems from exposure to counterparties within the same economic sector, performing the same activities, or operating in the same geographic region. This risk must be considered in assessing the intermediary's overall credit risk and can be managed or reduced through appropriate credit portfolio segmentation and diversification techniques (by size, economic sector, type, geographic area and client type).

In order to quantify credit risk, it is essential to measure ex-ante; i.e., at the time of credit issuance, the potential loss a bank might incur in the event of a counterparty's default or a deterioration in their ability to repay. This assessment involves distinguishing between the following two possible loss components.

- *Expected Loss* (EL): the ex-ante estimate of the most likely loss over one year, defined as the average amount expected to be lost on each financing operation within a given timeframe. As an 'expected' loss, it is not strictly considered a risk since it can be incorporated into the loan's interest rate (pricing) by adding an appropriate risk premium (spread), much like other cost elements such as operating expenses. If accurately estimated, the expected loss represents the minimum spread the bank should apply to ensure sufficient remuneration to cover the assumed risk.
- *Unexpected Loss* (UL): the variability of the expected loss around its mean value, which is characterized by the maximum potential loss within a certain confidence interval (e.g., with a 99% confidence interval, only 1% of cases would exceed the estimated unexpected loss). UL represents the true credit risk, that is, the risk that the actual loss exceeds the ex-ante estimate ex-post. At the portfolio level, the total amount of UL can be reduced through appropriate credit diversification, while EL cannot be mitigated by diversifying the loan portfolio.

Estimating the expected loss depends on the evaluation of several other variables, which are described below.

- *Probability of Default* (PD): the likelihood that a debtor will default within a year and thus be unable to fulfil their obligations. PD varies based on the counterparty's specific characteristics and is calculated through historical analysis of their rating class.

- *Exposure at Default* (EAD): the expected value of the credit amount at the time of the debtor's default, influenced by the credit facility's structure (e.g., partial repayment may have already occurred in the case of a loan or an overdraft may only be partially drawn).
- *Loss Given Default* (LGD): the proportion of the exposure the bank expects to lose, net of recoveries, representing the complement to the recovery rate (RR) and determined by the collateral backing the credit. LGD is the expected loss percentage after recovery procedures against the defaulting counterparty, influenced by loan terms, collateral, recovery procedures and costs.
- *Maturity* (M): the remaining economic life of exposure, and is based on the duration of the financing operation.

Analytically, the expected loss can be calculated as:

$$\mathrm{EL} = \mathrm{PD} \cdot \mathrm{LGD} \cdot \mathrm{EAD} \cdot \mathrm{M} \tag{5.8}$$

For estimating the unexpected loss, the model currently adopted by banking regulatory bodies is the Value at Risk (VaR) model, which we presented in the previous section (see Sect. 5.3). This model estimates the maximum potential loss on a given credit exposure over a specified time frame (e.g., one year) with a predefined probability (e.g., 99%). Statistically, the unexpected loss measures the difference between the maximum potential loss (VaR) and the expected loss, treating VaR as a measure of statistical dispersion (see Fig. 5.1).

As discussed later regarding the Basel Accords (see Sect. 5.6), for calculating capital requirements and thus the unexpected loss, the four risk component estimates (PD, LGD, EAD, and M)—provided by banks or supervisory authorities, which project potential future losses on loan—are incorporated into a 'risk-weighting function' determined by supervisory authorities. This function translates these risk components into *Risk-Weighted Assets* (RWA) and, thus, into capital requirements.

The aim of quantifying and measuring credit risk by separating expected and unexpected loss components is to identify optimal risk management strategies. Quantifying the expected loss allows for estimating the annual write-down on credit (an expense recorded in the

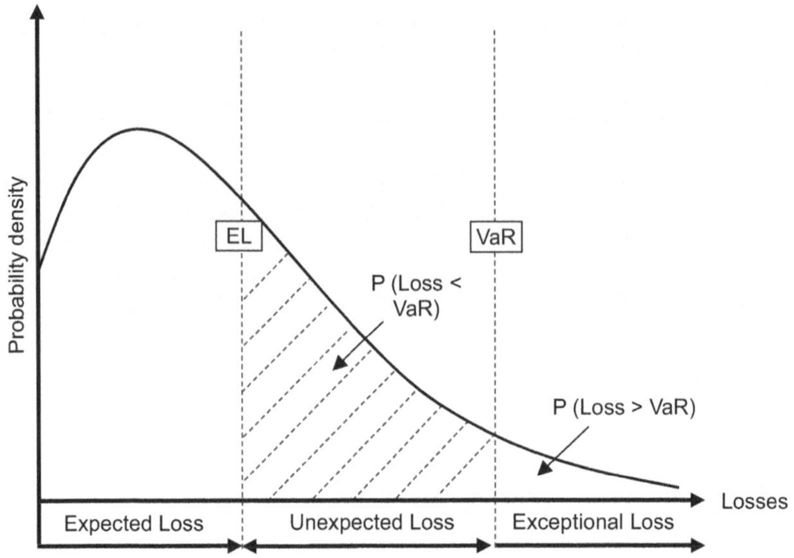

Fig. 5.1 Credit risk loss components (*Source* Elaboration by the authors)

income statement), enabling a corresponding reserve allocation specifically in Expected Credit Loss Allowance for expected credit losses. Estimating unexpected loss, on the other hand, requires an assessment of the proprietary capital needed to cover it, termed *Economic Capital* (EC), calculated as:

$$EC = VaR - EL \tag{5.9}$$

thus, ensuring that the bank's capital adequately covers the unexpected loss.

Estimating expected and unexpected losses is also critical for a bank when determining the ex-ante interest rate to be applied to clients (pricing), accounting for both provisions for expected losses and the capital cost necessary to address unexpected losses. Post-event, the economic implications are those related to the financial impact of losses due to a counterparty's partial or total default, while a mere credit quality deterioration leads to negative effects from the reduced value of assets held in the portfolio. A downgrade in a counterparty's credit quality, for example, increases the risk associated with its exposure. Consequently, future cash flows from that debtor will need to be discounted at higher rates, reducing their present value and, thus, the bank's assets.

Credit risk is, therefore, associated with the financed party's conditions and their variability over time (conditions that may deteriorate up to the extreme case of default), generating adverse economic effects on the intermediary's income statement and balance sheet. From an accounting perspective, expected and unexpected losses are treated as follows.

- The expected loss represents a statistically certain cost component and should thus be explicitly factored into the credit price (interest rate) via a risk premium (spread). If the loss materializes, the bank's current profit remains unaffected, as the risk is already 'expensed' through suitable provisions in the income statement during the lending period. Expected loss is thus covered through provisions and adjustments, recording the credit at its net realizable value (nominal value minus expected loss) in the balance sheet.
- The unexpected loss is covered by the bank's capital, representing a prudential buffer used to absorb unexpected losses (or recover the excess, in the opposite case).

Non-Performing Loans (NPL) are exposures to clients who are unable to fulfil their contractual obligations, either in whole or in part, due to a deterioration in their economic and financial situation. While credit risk relates to the probability that a borrower may fail to meet contractual obligations, NPLs serve as a concrete manifestation of this risk, signalling that the borrower is encountering difficulties in paying interest or repaying the principal loan amount. Thus, NPLs indicate that credit risk is materializing and provide insight into the extent to which this is occurring, acting as evidence that the ex-ante assessments on the probability of borrower default are proving accurate.

Generally, the presence of NPLs can have a significant impact on banks, leading to issues such as profit reductions, liquidity constraints and elevated risk levels. NPLs reflect the effectiveness of a bank's credit risk management practices, as an increase in NPLs may suggest inefficiencies in credit risk assessment and management. High levels of NPLs can also erode a bank's financial stability, as they do not generate expected income flows and may require appropriate write-downs. Furthermore, potential losses arising from NPLs affect a bank's ability to absorb losses, potentially exacerbating its credit risk and creating a feedback loop. The presence of NPLs may also prompt banks to create provisions (reserves) to cover potential losses on these loans, reflecting the bank's expectations regarding the credit risk associated with its loan portfolio. In essence, NPLs are both an indicator and an amplifier of credit risk, making effective monitoring and management crucial for banks to control and mitigate their overall credit risk.

Alongside the percentage of NPLs relative to a bank's total loans, there is now another metric used to manage credit risk: the Non-Performing Exposure (NPE) ratio. This ratio indicates the percentage of all deteriorated exposures within a bank's entire credit portfolio, encompassing all credit exposures regardless of form, including both on-balance-sheet loans and other off-balance-sheet instruments. The NPE ratio has become increasingly important for banks as a tool for assessing their credit risk exposure and implementing appropriate risk management measures. It is also valuable for investors and financial analysts, as it provides an overview of a bank's financial health and its exposure to non-performing loans, enabling investors to evaluate the bank's financial soundness and make informed investment decisions.

To monitor and manage the NPLs and NPEs indicators, banks use risk control tools such as credit portfolio analysis, regular monitoring of overdue or distressed loans, and the implementation of loss prevention policies. Effective management of NPLs and NPEs enables banks to promptly identify risks and take actions to minimize adverse effects on their financial stability. Both NPLs and NPEs indicators are, therefore, essential in the banking and financial sectors, particularly during periods of economic downturn or financial instability, as they provide an assessment of the banking system's efficiency and its exposure to potential loan losses, which is crucial for the stability and prosperity of banks.

The term non-performing loans generally refers to all loans and credits no longer repaid under original conditions, often due to missed or delayed payments. However, NPLs are classified into different categories based on the severity of non-compliance with contractual obligations (e.g., bad loans, overdue or late payments). Since 2014, European regulation has introduced a harmonized definition (CRR, Article 47 bis) as well as guidelines for classifying and quantifying risk on non-performing exposures (CRR, Article 178). In line with these, the Bank of Italy, similar to other financial supervisory authorities, employs its classification for statistical reporting of non-performing loans[19] based on international guidelines, particularly those set by the European Banking Authority (EBA 2016) and the European Commission's Implementing Technical Standards (ITS, Regulation 2021/451).

The Bank of Italy's classification defines the following three primary categories of non-performing loans based on their level of criticality.

- *Bad Loans*: exposures to counterparts in a state of insolvency (even if not legally recognized) or comparable situations, irrespective of the bank's potential loss projections (excluding any collateral securing the exposure).
- *Unlikely to Pay* (UTP): exposures where, in the bank's judgement, it is unlikely the borrower will fully meet contractual obligations without recovery actions (e.g., collateral enforcement). Exposures may fall into this category even in the absence of payment defaults, provided some elements suggest the risk of non-compliance. There is a difference in classification between European harmonized rules and Bank of Italy guidance: while the former specifies that exposures overdue for less than 90 days fall into UTP (over 90 days into past-due exposures), the latter includes all 'risky' exposures under UTP, whether overdue (less than 90 days) or not.
- *Past-Due Exposures*: distressed exposures that, as of the reporting date, have been overdue or beyond credit limits for over 90 days. The harmonized European guidelines state that past-due exposures should be overdue between 91 and 180 days.

Furthermore, the *forbearance* category is also foreseen, which includes exposures that have been restructured or refinanced for borrowers facing or likely to face financial difficulties, excluding restructurings for purely commercial reasons. The term 'forbearance' refers to both contractual modifications granted to the debtor and the issuance of new financing to enable the fulfilment of a pre-existing obligation. In general, forbearance encompasses any contractual adjustments freely requested by a debtor within an existing agreement, but only in cases where the bank determines that there are grounds to consider the debtor as being in financial

[19] Circular No. 272 of 30 July 2008, 'Credit Quality' section.

difficulty (embedded forbearance clauses). However, forbearance exposures, as outlined in the Implementing Technical Standards (ITS), do not constitute a standalone category of non-performing loans; rather, they fall within one of the three categories mentioned above, effectively representing a subset of those classifications.

It is important to note that the classification of individual non-performing loans may change over time, depending on the evolution of credit conditions and the bank's recovery actions. Banks must adhere to their central bank guidelines to classify NPL accurately and monitor credit portfolio quality. In particular, the specific non-performing loans must continue to be reported in their respective categories throughout the three months stipulated by the EBA Guidelines.[20]

The classification of non-performing exposures is essential for banks in managing the associated credit risk, involving the estimation of loss based on homogeneous categories (identified by risk level, risk duration and exposure materiality) and the application of valuation adjustments for each position. Depending on the severity, banks may also adopt various strategies, including: (i) restructuring loans to facilitate repayment, (ii) selling non-performing loans to third parties, such as special-purpose entities handling bad debt, or (iii) engaging debt collection agencies. Each strategy has its advantages and disadvantages, and banks must carefully assess the best option based on their needs and the broader economic context.

5.5 New Credit Risk Financial Reporting Standards (IFRS 9)

The 2007–2008 financial crisis exposed the limitations of International Accounting Standard (IAS) No. 39, the predecessor to the current International Financial Reporting Standard (IFRS) No. 9. In fact, the IAS 39 approach, typical of the pre-crisis period, was based on an incurred loss model, allowing banks to estimate expected losses only when there was objective evidence of credit impairment as of the balance sheet date. This backward-looking approach, lacking a forward-looking perspective, prevented banks from factoring potential future adverse events into their loss estimates. The consequences of this approach became

[20] EBA 2016, paragraph 71(a).

apparent between 2012 and 2014, as significant write-downs of credit were reported by banks only after the crisis had already unfolded. This delay in accounting recognition amplified procyclical effects, resulting in capital shortfalls and banking crises occurring simultaneously with borrower defaults, thus undermining investor confidence, as they relied on banks' financial statements until the last moment.

To address these issues, IFRS 9 was introduced and came into effect in 2018. This standard adopted an Expected Credit Loss (ECL) approach, shifting away from *incurred loss* to a model based on *anticipated losses*. The ECL model considers not only past and present events, but also reasonably foreseeable future events and possible macroeconomic scenarios to ensure more relevant and timely accounting information.

A key aspect of IFRS 9 is that each balance sheet must include an impairment test for credit exposures to determine if there is evidence suggesting their carrying amount may not be fully recoverable. In order to estimate and record potential impairments, a 'three-bucket' procedure is implemented, classifying credit exposures into three levels or stages: (i) Stage 1, for low-risk positions without evidence of significant credit risk deterioration (from initial recognition to balance sheet date); (ii) Stage 2, for performing positions that have shown a significant increase in risk since initial recognition; and (iii) Stage 3, for non-performing or impaired positions with evidence of value loss, which are subsequently classified within the three NPL categories (bad loans, unlikely-to-pay and past-due exposures).

The arrival of the COVID-19 pandemic in 2020, however, posed a significant challenge for applying IFRS 9. From early 2020, unintended effects emerged following the automatic application of the ECL principle, countering IFRS 9's objectives. Recognizing that a rigid application of the standard could itself create procyclical effects and threaten government support measures addressing the pandemic crisis, supervisory authorities intervened to mitigate its adverse impacts. In Europe, supervisory bodies such as the EBA, ECB, ESMA and Bank of Italy adopted measures to ensure flexibility in applying IFRS 9 criteria, defining the pandemic context as an extraordinary event to avoid negatively affecting government support measures for businesses in early 2021. International accounting bodies, including the IFRS Foundation and Basel Committee, also provided guidelines on how banks should consider the pandemic's impact when assessing Significant Increases in Credit Risk (SICR) and estimating expected losses. Specifically, they stated that moratoriums or public support measures should not automatically shift expected loss measurement from 12 months to a lifetime.

Additionally, the Bank of Italy introduced amendments to its circular on bank financial statements (Circular 272/2008), requiring additional information on COVID-19 impacts, including effects on financial instruments and support measures. These amendments aim to ensure that the accounting information provided by banks adequately reflects the pandemic's impact and is useful for financial market participants and supervisory authorities. During the COVID-19 pandemic, adapting and supplementing existing accounting standards was necessary to address the extraordinary challenges and consequences caused by the crisis. IFRS 9 served as a fundamental reference during this period, while supervisory authorities and accounting bodies worked to provide guidance and flexibility in applying the related principles to ensure an accurate representation of COVID-19 effects in bank financial statements and disclosures.

In general, capturing signals of deterioration and/or recovery within credit risk evaluation systems during an economic phase marked by continuous structural adjustments due to financial management measures is highly challenging. In such cases, credit assessment models, being relatively inflexible, require modification and approval processes by supervisory authorities, which can be time-intensive. This is why, over time, efforts have aimed to develop a more forward-looking approach capable of anticipating adverse events. Despite the forward-looking perspective of the new IFRS 9 accounting standard, the question remains whether the expected loss philosophy is more or less procyclical compared to the incurred loss model. In this regard, the COVID-19 pandemic has shown how the automatic application of the expected loss approach can lead to unintended procyclical risks. Therefore, it is essential that forward-looking mechanisms embedded in banks' provisions can detect economic recovery signals and differentiate between clients likely to overcome the crisis and those likely to remain affected. Determining whether IFRS 9 will prove more or less procyclical than previous accounting approaches in the future remains an open question, with answers expected to emerge once the COVID-19 crisis has passed, allowing for an assessment of IFRS 9's effectiveness and adaptability.

5.6 Regulatory Pillars and Basel Accords (Basel I–IV)

The Basel Committee on Banking Supervision is an international organization established by the central bank governors of the ten most industrialized countries (G10) in late 1974, operating under the auspices of the Bank for International Settlements. Its purpose was to promote cooperation among central banks and equivalent agencies to pursue monetary and financial stability. The Committee coordinates the allocation of supervisory responsibilities among national authorities to oversee banking activities worldwide. Its headquarters are in Basel, and it meets four times a year. The first Basel Accords (Basel I) were introduced in 1988, then reformed in 2004 as Basel II and following the 2007–2008 financial crisis, were further reformed and strengthened with Basel III in 2010. A final update, known as Basel III.5, was introduced in 2019.

The context in which the Basel Accords emerged in 1988 reflected a shift, discussed since the 1980s, from a *structural* banking regulation—impacting the morphology of the banking-financial system (operational prohibitions, activity entry requirements, growth limits, etc.)—to a *prudential* regulation that linked operational scope and risk-taking to adequate capital resources and appropriate organizational, control and risk management safeguards. With the Basel Accords, in addition to the traditional stability objective of financial regulation (in both micro-stability for individual financial intermediaries and macro-stability for the system as a whole), efficiency and competition objectives were also introduced. Moreover, in terms of protecting vulnerable contracting parties, the focus expanded from the traditional protection of depositors to the broader safeguarding of investors, incorporating regulations on transparency and fairness.

Before the Basel Accords, banking systems were regulated differently in each country, typically through 'light' regulation, which set minimum balance sheet requirements for capital adequacy, particularly for covering credit risk, primarily based on a simple capital-to-total-assets ratio, with definitions of capital and indicator values differing across countries. One consequence was that international banks' exposures to emerging markets raised concerns over these banks' capital adequacy. Additionally, the 1980s saw the emergence of off-balance-sheet transactions in derivatives that did not impact total bank assets, thereby avoiding any effect on the capital a bank was required to hold. It became evident that total assets were not a reliable indicator of a bank's overall risk exposure, necessitating a more accurate calculation of a bank's risk exposure to determine a more appropriate risk coverage measure.

To address this situation, in 1988, banking supervisory authorities from 27 countries, regularly meeting in Basel, Switzerland, within the BCBS, decided to sign an agreement on minimum bank capital, titled the 'International Convergence of Capital Measurement and Capital Standards', also known as 'The 1988 BIS Accord' or 'Basel I Accords'. The Basel I Accords introduced the first risk-sensitive capital ratio, known as the solvency ratio or Cooke Ratio, specifying a minimum capital level below which banks could not operate. These were the first minimum capital requirements for credit risk coverage, applicable to all internationally active banking groups. The significance of this agreement is reflected in its adoption by over 100 countries within a few years. In the European Union, Basel I was implemented through Directive 647/1989.

In the Basel I Accords, the minimum capital requirement (solvency ratio) was aimed solely at covering credit risk: banks were required to hold capital equal to at least 8% of their risk-weighted assets for credit risk.

$$\frac{\text{PTV}}{\sum(A_i \times \text{RW}_i)} \geq 8\% \tag{5.10}$$

The underlying assumption was that each on-balance-sheet activity would be assigned a 'risk weight' reflecting the risk of the corresponding asset category, thereby requiring a proportional capital reserve for precautionary purposes. This approach established a 'mandatory regulatory capital' (referred to as supervisory capital, or PTV) that needed to exceed a minimum requirement based on risk-weighted banking activities, specifically loans. The risk-weighting process utilized various criteria, such as the debtor's nature (government, corporations, individuals, etc.), country of residence, and asset liquidity (see Table 5.2).

In 1996, an amendment to the Basel I Accords was issued to incorporate market risk, in addition to credit risk, into the calculation of the minimum capital requirement. Specifically, a requirement for market risk coverage was added to the capital ratio calculation.

$$\frac{\text{PTV}}{\sum(A_i \times RW_i) + 12.5 \times \text{PTV}_{\text{mkt}}} \geq 8\% \tag{5.11}$$

Table 5.2 Risk weights for calculating the solvency ratio (Basel I)

Risk weight (%)	*Asset category*
0	Sovereign (loans to OECD governments)
20	Public entities and banks (loans to OECD banks)
50	Private mortgages (loans secured by property)
100	Corporates (other loans)

Source Elaboration by the authors

However, under Basel I, the minimum capital amount was linked solely to the size of assets rather than their quality, assigning different weights to assets based on the attributes and characteristics of the borrower, but without a thorough risk analysis. As a result, risk itself had only a marginal influence. While the Basel I Accords helped increase the capitalization of banking systems, emphasized capital as a core element for risk coverage, and initiated regulatory harmonization (the so-called 'level playing field' process), they had several limitations:

- They addressed only credit and market risk (the latter included only from 1996).
- They exhibited low-risk sensitivity by applying the same weighting to similar counterparties, disregarding the varied creditworthiness of individual companies and, consequently, disadvantaging loans to more reliable firms.
- They lacked incentives for banks to improve risk measurement and management systems, as they did not recognize the relationship between maturity and credit risk, the benefits of supervisory capital diversification, or risk mitigation instruments (which were only partially acknowledged).
- They did not differentiate between expected and unexpected losses.

With the 2004 Basel II Accords, which came into effect in 2007, a comprehensive revision of the previous rules was conducted, beginning with the introduction of the *three Basel Pillars*.

(1) The *First Pillar* establishes new *minimum capital requirements* and a new set of rules for measuring the minimum capital requirement to address the three main risks: credit, market and operational

risk. Basel II details criteria and introduces new risk measurement methods, precisely defining the methodology for determining absorbed capital to enhance risk measurement and management capabilities.

(2) The *Second Pillar* introduces the *supervisory review* which comprises new rules for prudential supervision by regulatory authorities to assess a financial intermediary's capital adequacy in light of its operational specifics through a process called the *Supervisory Review and Evaluation Process* (SREP), which grants supervisory authorities greater powers.

(3) The *Third Pillar* regulates *market discipline*, which introduces disclosure and transparency obligations, enabling the market to assess the financial intermediary's capital adequacy. These transparency and communication rules aim to increase 'market discipline', requiring banks to disclose information on capital allocation techniques and risk management and control processes, including tools, methodologies and implemented processes.

Another significant innovation in Basel II was the subdivision of Regulatory Capital (RC), which differs from balance sheet capital into several components (Tiers) that reflect varying capacities for loss absorption and, hence, different qualities of capital positions. The various components of regulatory capital, which must collectively equal at least 8% of *Risk-Weighted Assets* (RWA), establish the following hierarchy based on the quality of these capital positions.

- *Tier 1* (core capital or *going concern capital*) must absorb losses in a going concern situation; it must represent at least 4% of RWA and consists of two components:
  - CET1 (Common Equity Tier 1 or Core Equity Tier 1), at least 2% of RWA, high-quality capital including paid-in equity net of specific deductions, share premium reserves, retained earnings, revaluation reserves and other disclosed reserves.
  - AT1 (Additional Tier 1), at least 2% of RWA, comprising additional core capital instruments not included in CET1 but with full loss of absorption capacity in a going concern (e.g., convertible bonds).

- *Tier 2* (supplementary capital or *gone concern capital*), at least 4% of RWA, is intended to cover losses in liquidation, composed of revaluation reserves and innovative hybrid capital instruments (e.g., subordinated bonds).
- *Tier 3* (third-level subordinated loans) is a capital component solely for market risk, which was later eliminated in the Basel III Accords.

As a result of introducing these various components of regulatory capital, whereas Basel I had a single minimum capital ratio (the solvency ratio or *Cooke Ratio*), Basel II introduced three different capital ratios below which banks could not fall, reflecting the different components of Regulatory Capital: *Tier 1* ratio, *CET1* ratio, and *Total Capital* ratio (see Table 5.3).

The Basel II Accords undoubtedly made capital ratio systems more flexible and sensitive to credit risk, particularly by introducing a progressive approach that encourages banks to move from simpler to more sophisticated risk measurement methods. Through the three-pillar framework, Basel II not only reformed capital requirements but also extended the role and responsibilities of supervisory authorities and the market, with a strong emphasis on the organizational and operational aspects of banks.

However, almost concurrently with the implementation of Basel II, the 2007–2008 global financial crisis struck, followed by the sovereign debt and real economy crisis in 2010–2011. These crises clearly showed that even the new accords were insufficient to ensure the full stability of the

Table 5.3 Basel II capital requirements

Regulatory capital component	*Capital ratio*	*Basel I RWA: credit risk only until 1996, then credit and market risk (%)*	*Basel II RWA: credit, market and operational risk (%)*
CET1	CET1 ratio		2
Tier1	Tier1 ratio		4
Total regulatory capital	Total capital ratio	8	8

Source Elaboration by the authors

financial system. The main limitations of Basel II that emerged included the following.

- The standardized approach to credit risk assessment featured only minimally differentiated risk weights across rating bands, resulting in limited credit risk sensitivity.
- The methods for measuring credit risk concentration and correlation in the internal ratings approach proved rigid.
- The measures required by the accord were objectively complex to implement.
- The framework had an inherent procyclicality.

Thus, starting in 2009, a new reform process to further strengthen the Basel II Accords began, leading to the introduction of Basel III in 2013, with subsequent updates in 2019 as Basel III.5. The Basel III framework aimed to strengthen capital requirements further, introduce new tools for managing liquidity risk, mitigate procyclicality and consider the unique aspects of institutions with high systemic risk by introducing additional capital buffers. Specifically, within the three pillars, Basel III introduced the following innovations.

(1) Regarding the *First Pillar*, the entire framework for capital ratios and risk safeguards was revised, strengthened and expanded, confirming that capital adequacy rules are the primary means to influence banks' risk-taking incentives and determine their loss absorption capacity. Procyclicality was reduced by introducing countercyclical buffers, regulatory capital was clearly defined, and capital requirements were raised (both in terms of capital quality and quantity). Additional safeguards were introduced for specific risks (including market risk), and rules were established to limit leverage (leverage ratio).
(2) Within the *Second Pillar*, the SREP (Supervisory Review and Evaluation Process) was strengthened, enhancing the interactive process between banks and supervisory authorities.
(3) Regarding the *Third Pillar*, the disclosure rules were reinforced to improve transparency, requiring banks to disclose information that enables the market to evaluate their capital adequacy. These disclosure requirements aim to increase 'market discipline', obliging

banks to publicly report on capital allocation techniques, risk control and management processes, and the tools, methodologies and processes they have implemented.

Additionally, Basel III introduced new measures to manage short- and long-term liquidity control, effectively establishing a sort of 'fourth pillar' in the form of binding minimum liquidity standards. These minimum standards are based on two new liquidity ratios: the *Liquidity Coverage Ratio* (LCR), which measures short-term liquidity, and the *Net Stable Funding Ratio* (NSFR), which assesses long-term funding stability by comparing it to both the bank's assets and off-balance sheet operations.

In the European Union, Basel II and Basel III were implemented through the Capital Requirement Regulation (CRR, Regulation 2013/575) and the corresponding Capital Requirement Directive IV (CRD IV, Directive 2013/36), both approved in 2013 and effective from 2014. Subsequent updates to the capital requirement calculation methodologies were introduced through three additional provisions: Capital Requirement Regulation II (CRR II, Regulation 2019/876), effective from June 28, 2021, with some articles effective earlier; Capital Requirement Directive V (CRD V, Directive 2019/878), with provisions taking effect on different dates (December 29, 2020; June 28, 2021; and January 1, 2022); and Directive 2019/879, amending the Bank Recovery and Resolution Directive (BRRD, Directive 2014/59).

The outlined framework is still evolving rapidly. The European Banking Authority (EBA) is expected to provide further guidance to the European Commission on the first pillar (prudential capital requirements) by 2023. Moreover, the Basel IV framework, formally recognized as the finalization of Basel III, has introduced significant changes aimed at reinforcing the global banking sector's resilience and stability. These updates stem from ongoing efforts by the BCBS to address vulnerabilities exposed during the 2007–2008 financial crisis and subsequent economic downturns. Basel IV was introduced in December 2017, with a staggered implementation schedule starting from January 1, 2023, and extending through January 1, 2028, allowing banks sufficient time to adjust to the new regulatory demands. The Basel IV Accords (see Sect. 5.6.4) also introduced new sustainability requirements to cover ESG risks, which will be incorporated into the regulatory framework for banks as part of the European objective of climate neutrality. This, in turn, will lead to new ESG standards for a broader segment of the European economy.

5.6.1 *First Pillar: Capital Requirements*

The First Pillar outlines the risk-weighting criteria and introduces, with the Basel II agreements, new methods for measuring and weighting risks to calculate capital requirements in terms of minimum capital levels that banks must adhere to. The innovations introduced by Basel II primarily involve expanding the range of risks that must be considered for capital reserves, adding operational risk in addition to credit and market risks. Supervisory capital must always be at least 8% of risk-weighted assets, but now three types of risk need to be considered: credit risk, market risk and operational risk.

$$\frac{\text{PTV}}{\sum(A_i \times \text{RW}_i) + 12.5 \times \text{PTV}_{\text{mkt}} + \text{PTV}_{\text{op}}} \geq 8\% \tag{5.12}$$

One of the main novelties introduced by Basel II is the requirement to cover operational risk, which encompasses the risk of losses arising from failures in procedures, personnel, and internal systems or from exogenous events, including legal risk but excluding strategic and reputational risk. For this risk, several possible evaluation and measurement methodologies are introduced, differentiated based on the sophistication and complexity of the financial intermediaries considered: (i) Basic Indicator Approach, (ii) Standardized Approach, and (iii) Advanced Measurement Approach (AMA).

For credit risk, asset-weighting methodologies are introduced that consider the varying creditworthiness of individual enterprises, taking into account the specific conditions of the funded entity and the potential variability of these conditions over time (which may improve or deteriorate, potentially leading to default). In this regard, Basel II addresses one of the main limitations of Basel I, namely the need to link minimum required capital to asset quality. Considering the quality of clients involves more accurate asset weighting, resulting in various methods for measuring regulatory capital based on a more precise assessment of credit risk: the Standardized Approach or two different internal rating-based (IRB) models, one 'Foundation' (IRB Foundation Approach) and one 'Advanced' (IRB Advanced Approach).

The new internal rating methods supporting the determination of minimum capital requirements imply that, as client risk increases, with all else equal, a greater amount of supervisory capital must be allocated.

This approach overcomes one of the limitations in Basel I, where individual client ratings were not considered. With the introduction of Basel II, if a company's rating improves, the bank benefits from reduced capital reserves, allowing it to offer lower interest rates to more reliable clients.

An additional limitation of Basel I addressed in Basel II is the distinction between expected and unexpected loss. A more accurate assessment of credit risk requires, as previously discussed (see Sect. 5.3), measuring both expected loss (EL)—calculated as the product of the counterparty's probability of default (PD), exposure at default (EAD), loss given default (LGD), and remaining loan maturity (M)—and unexpected loss (UL), which represents the difference between value-at-risk (VaR); i.e., the maximum probable loss (at a given confidence level) over a specified time horizon, and the expected loss.

These two components have significantly different implications for a bank's management strategy: expected loss is pre-emptively covered through an annual estimation of credit impairment (the 'adjustments' item on the income statement), with the net amount recorded on the balance sheet after applying this adjustment. For unexpected loss coverage, however, 'economic capital' (EC), representing the bank's capital required to absorb the unexpected component of credit losses, must be estimated.

The three methodologies available for calculating the capital requirement against credit risk function as follows, based on these foundational elements: (i) the *Standard method* utilizes, if available, ratings provided by external agencies (External Credit Assessment Institutions—ECAIs, such as Moody's and S&P); (ii) the *Foundation IRB* approach (basic) uses the bank's internal ratings to calculate only the probability of default (PD); (iii) the *Advanced IRB* approach relies on the intermediary's internal data to estimate all four components that determine expected loss (EL).

The Standard approach is not significantly different from the minimum capital requirement method against credit risk established in Basel I, as it does not explicitly distinguish between expected loss (EL) and unexpected loss (UL). The main difference compared to Basel I is that this method links credit weightings for businesses to the ratings of external agencies recognized by regulators (ECAIs). For retail customers, a 75% weighting is applied. The capital requirement is still the capital coefficient of 8% of risk-weighted assets (RWA, as per prescribed weightings); however, to avoid 'duplications', provisions are made to account for general and specific provisions. In the standard approach:

- General provisions are included in supplementary capital (Tier 2), up to 1.25% of RWA (otherwise, 'risk funds' excluded from supervisory capital would be funded by provisions affecting the income statement while simultaneously absorbing capital for the same risks).
- Specific provisions are deducted from credit risk exposures before applying the relevant weightings (otherwise, capital would be absorbed by portions of exposures already covered and expensed in the income statement).

Compared to Basel I, Basel II prescribes a reduction in the risk weight for loans secured by real estate (non-commercial), gold, cash and eligible securities; a 25% reduction in the risk weight for retail loans; and a risk-based classification of clients for larger companies with external ratings, while a 100% weighting, as in Basel I, is retained for most unrated companies.

For internal rating-based (IRB) systems, intermediaries must be authorized by supervisory authorities, and they base the calculation of capital requirements on their estimations of risk components (PD, LGD, EAD, M). The two IRB approaches differ from the standard method in that they rely on distinct estimates for expected losses (EL) and unexpected losses (UL). EL and UL are treated separately because EL is 'covered' by provisions/impairment adjustments and does not absorb capital, whereas UL does.

The fundamental principle is that banks authorized to adopt one of the IRB approaches base (in whole or part) the calculation of capital requirements on their risk component estimates rather than relying on external agency ratings: in the IRB Foundation approach, only the probability of default (PD) is estimated internally, while regulatory authorities fix LGD, EAD, and M; in the IRB Advanced approach, all four risk components are estimated by the bank. This creates a link between default probability and client rating, as these are two measures of the same phenomenon (rating systems must provide PD alongside the rating). As client quality declines, default probability rises, leading to increased risk and greater capital reserves.

For each asset class identified in the IRB approach, the following key elements are present:

- Risk components: risk parameter estimates provided by banks or regulatory authorities that determine potential future loan losses (PD, LGD, EAD, M).
- Risk-weighting functions, which transform risk components into risk-weighted assets (RWA) and thus capital requirements, with RWA calculated as follows: RWA = capital requirement × 12.5.

After estimating the expected loss, banks must compare the amount of provisions/impairment adjustments (A) with expected loss (B), as defined by the Basel Committee, and act accordingly:

- If B > A (shortfall), the bank must deduct the difference from the capital.
- If A > B (excess), the difference is considered Tier 2 capital up to 0.6% of RWA.

To estimate unexpected loss and calculate the corresponding minimum capital requirement, banks must input PD, LGD, EAD, and M estimates for each loan into a 'weighting function' determined by the authorities. For instance, for a €1,000 loan to a company with a 1% default probability and revenue exceeding €50 million, with LGD at 45%, the minimum regulatory capital required would be €73.86. In other words, Basel II's portfolio model suggests that, in 99.9% of cases, €73.86 of capital would be necessary to cover unexpected losses on this loan.

Following the 2007–2008 financial crisis, a significant limitation of this capital requirement calculation mechanism in Basel II was identified: it exacerbated financial conditions during downturns (economic cycles) by producing procyclical effects. The bank's capital contraction due to deteriorating credit quality during periods of economic downturn led to a reduction in its loan portfolio, resulting in less credit extended to households for consumption and businesses for production. This reduction in bank loans further worsened corporate performance, leading to further credit quality declines, which, in turn, would cause further capital contractions for the bank.

The subsequent Basel III agreement introduced countercyclical measures to encourage banks to build up capital reserves during favourable phases of the economic cycle, when risk accumulates on their balance sheets, so they can utilize these reserves when economic conditions worsen and the risk materializes, thereby avoiding undesirable (procyclical) effects on credit supply during economic downturns (economic crises).

The measures introduced by Basel III to mitigate the pro-cyclicality of regulations and move towards an anti-cyclical system aimed at enhancing capital quality involve requiring additional capital reserves (buffers) beyond the previous 8% level, particularly by increasing CET1 capital. Specifically, the measures introduced are as follows.

- New models that adjust bank-estimated ratings through risk measures less influenced by economic conditions, notably by transforming the PD from a point-in-time to a through-the-cycle measure.
- A new capital coefficient, the Capital Conservation Buffer (CCB), an additional 'buffer' of capital above the regulatory minimum for all banks, is to be maintained during economic expansion phases. This measure prevents distribution policies adopted in growth phases from subsequently reducing the capital base during potential economic downturns. Specifically: (i) banks must maintain a capital buffer above the minimum at 2.5% of CET1 capital relative to risk-weighted assets (RWA); (ii) limitations are placed on dividend distributions and bonus payments if the CCB is not met.
- A macroprudential tool, the Countercyclical Capital Buffer (CCyB), which national authorities activate in situations of economic overheating, using a semi-automatic criterion to accumulate capital during credit growth phases relative to GDP. Specifically: (i) banks must maintain a capital buffer above the minimum, ranging from 0 to 2.5% of CET1 capital and other high-quality instruments, relative to RWA; (ii) activation of the CCyB is decided by national authorities (in Italy, the CCyB was zero in Q1 2022).

Additionally, two systemic buffers have been introduced, applicable only to larger banks known as globally systemically important banks, further classified into two categories, Global Systemically Important Institutions (G-SIIs) and Other Systemically Important Institutions (O-SIIs), based on the principle that 'systemically important banks should have a loss-absorbency capacity beyond the announced standards' (Basel Committee on Banking Supervision, 2017). These two new buffers (the

G-SIIs buffer and the O-SIIs buffer) thus represent additional capital requirements deemed necessary for institutions that, due to their systemic relevance globally or domestically, pose greater risks to the financial system (systemic risk), where a crisis involving these entities could impact taxpayers worldwide:

- The G-SIIs buffer comprises an additional CET1 capital requirement ranging from 0% to 3.5%, depending on the systemic importance of the bank. The Financial Stability Board (FSB) annually identifies the G-SIIs globally. In November 2024, the G-SII list included 29 global systemically relevant banks/groups, 8 in the US, 7 in the EU, 5 in China, 3 in the UK, 3 in Japan, 2 in Canada and 1 in Switzerland.[21]
- The O-SIIs buffer consists of an additional CET1 capital reserve ranging from 0 to 2%, which national central banks may impose on each O-SII. National authorities identify O-SIIs.

If a bank or banking group is subject—at a consolidated level—to both the G-SII and O-SII buffers, the higher capital reserve must be applied. In addition to setting more demanding capital requirements (in terms of both quality and quantity), Basel III also introduced changes in the composition of regulatory capital, the most notable of which are:

- Preference is given to 'core' capital instruments, i.e., the highest quality component of capital, introducing a new restrictive definition of CET1 (Core Equity Tier 1), which primarily comprises common shares and retained earnings.
- Stricter criteria for the inclusion of capital instruments in CET1, excluding preference shares.
- The exclusion of certain capital instruments (legacy instruments), for which a gradual exclusion clause ('grandfathering clause') is provided to transition to the new standards.
- Stricter rules for the eligibility of subordinated debt instruments within supplementary capital.

[21] https://www.fsb.org/2024/11/2024-list-of-global-systemically-important-banks-g-sibs/#g-sibs-2012-2024.

- A simplified definition of regulatory capital with the elimination of lower-quality elements (Tier 3).

Under Basel III, regulatory capital is thus divided into the following components.

1. Tier 1, which must be at least 6% of RWA, is further subdivided into CET1, at a minimum of 4.5% of RWA, and AT1, at a minimum of 1.5% of RWA.
2. Tier 2, which must be at least 2% of RWA.
3. Tier 3 has been eliminated.

The new capital requirements and corresponding capital ratios introduced by Basel III are detailed in Table 5.4.

Finally, other measures introduced by Basel III under the first pillar include enhanced controls for certain risks (such as market risk, through the introduction of the Stressed VaR model), the implementation of the leverage ratio to limit financial leverage and the addition of two

Table 5.4 Basel III capital requirements

Regulatory capital component	*Capital ratio*	*Basel I RWA: credit and market risk (%)*	*Basel II RWA: credit, market and operational risk (%)*	*Basel III RWA: credit, market and operational risk (%)*	
CET1	CET1 ratio		2	4.5	
Tier1	Tier1 ratio		4	6	
Total regulatory capital	Total capital ratio	8	8	8	
				2.5	CCB buffer
				0–2.5	CCyB buffer
				0–3.5	G-SIIs buffer
				0–2	O-SIIs buffer

Source Elaboration by the authors

liquidity ratios: the LCR (Liquidity Coverage Ratio) and NSFR (Net Stable Funding Ratio). The introduction of the minimum liquidity standards LCR and NSFR, which are almost a fourth pillar due to their importance, was driven by the fact that, prior to the 2007–2008 financial crisis, the potential scope of liquidity risk was significantly underestimated by both banks and supervisory authorities. This underestimation assumed that well-developed and integrated interbank markets would enable banks to meet liquidity needs. An international regulatory system for liquidity management was essentially absent, while national regulations varied significantly both qualitatively and quantitatively. The only reference to liquidity risk could be found in the second pillar of Basel II, alongside other risks that required management.

The crisis revealed a systemic liquidity shortfall, prompting the Basel Committee to establish certain objectives for introducing quantitative rules to prevent future liquidity management imbalances from jeopardizing both individual institutions and potentially impacting other operators. The new rules introduced by Basel III are essentially of two types:

- Banks are required to hold buffers of liquid assets in compliance with the Liquidity Coverage Ratio (LCR) indicator to ensure short-term financial balance (protecting against short-term liquidity risk). The LCR is designed to ensure the maintenance of sufficient liquidity to withstand a 30-day stress period, ensuring resources are available to cover expected cash outflows over a 30-day horizon under severe stress conditions without requiring market access or central bank refinancing.
- Banks must also comply with the Net Stable Funding Ratio (NSFR) indicator, aiming to prevent long-term imbalances (over more than one year) by adopting a sustainable asset-liability maturity structure in stress periods. This involves controlling potential maturity mismatches to avoid structural imbalances in the composition of asset and liability maturities, thus limiting excessive reliance on the short-term interbank market.

5.6.2 *Second Pillar: Prudential Supervision and SREP*

The Second Pillar introduced by the Basel II agreements on supervisory review establishes an interactive process between banks and supervisory authorities aimed at monitoring the adequacy of banks' capital levels relative to the risks they assume, as well as the coherence of management processes (internal systems, tools, organizational structures) implemented by banks to comply with regulatory ratios. This process, known as the Supervisory Review and Evaluation Process (SREP), falls under the responsibility of the European Central Bank (ECB) and the Bank of Italy (Circular No. 285/2013, Title III) and consists of two integrated processes: the first concerns the self-assessment phase for banks, while the second involves the activities supervisory authorities must conduct for reviewing and evaluating intermediaries.

The Second Pillar, through the SREP, is founded on the strengthening of risk-based supervision, with the following objectives: (i) to enhance supervisory authorities' capacity to understand the development of markets and products; (ii) to frame these phenomena and associated risks within an integrated logic to evaluate interconnections during stress periods; iii) to enable more proactive supervisory action when necessary.

The first issue to clarify concerns the supervisory authorities responsible for implementing the SREP process, a non-trivial aspect following the establishment of the first pillar of the European Banking Union (EBU) in 2012, prompted by the 2009–2010 sovereign debt crisis. Prior to the introduction of the Single Supervisory Mechanism (SSM) by the EBU, which grants the ECB a primary supervisory role over EU banks, national central banks were solely responsible for implementing SREP. Since the introduction of the SSM in 2014, the following two distinct cases have been defined.

- *Significant Institutions* (SIs), or larger banks, are under the direct supervision of the ECB, with standardized methodology and timing. At the end of 2024, SIs were 114.
- *Less Significant Institutions* (LSIs), or smaller banks, are under the direct supervision of national central banks, which retain responsibility for SREP according to ECB guidelines, following the principle of proportionality. At the end of 2024, LSIs were 2.204.

The proportionality principle guiding national central banks in SREP application for LSIs entails grouping banks into homogeneous categories and managing supervisory interventions proportionate to the specific characteristics of each supervised institution, with measures and sanctions tailored to the gravity of different situations. Generally, the intensity and focus of supervision depend on each bank's risk profile and size, categorizing institutions based on size, organizational structure, territorial reach, operational complexity and systemic risk.

In early 2015, the ECB issued its initial SREP decisions, still grounded in national approaches, incorporating results from its 2014 Comprehensive Assessment. By the second SREP decision cycle at the end of 2015, a common approach was applied across the euro area, marking a significant step towards equal conditions in the European banking sector. Ensuring a level playing field requires applying consistent standards to all banks, and in this regard, SREP provides supervisory authorities with a harmonized toolkit to assess banks' risk profiles.

Additionally, the ECB is tasked with 'mapping risks' and defining the supervisory priorities for inclusion in SREP based on an evaluation of primary risks and vulnerabilities that supervised entities face in the current economic, regulatory and prudential context. Each year, the ECB determines the main areas of intervention for banking supervision in the upcoming years, though supervisory priorities may be reassessed if risk developments necessitate revision (see Sect. 6.1). Furthermore, SREP methodology may continue evolving to fulfil better the ultimate goal of adequately monitoring banks' activities and risks, increasingly with a forward-looking perspective.

In recent years, several new risks that increasingly affect banks have been identified and defined, including:

- *ICT risk*: 'the risk of incurring economic, reputational, and market share losses related to the use of information and communication technology' (Bank of Italy Circular No. 285/2013), covering a wide range of events from IT system malfunctions to 'cybersecurity incidents', which include cyber risk.
- *Cyber risk*: 'the risk of unauthorized access to ICT systems and data from within or outside the institution' (EBA Guidelines, EBA 2017); the risk of incurring economic, reputational and market share losses following operational disruptions or unauthorized data access resulting from cyber events.

- *Environmental risk* and *ESG risks* (see Chapter 6): the risk of negative financial impacts arising, directly or indirectly, from environmental, social and governance factors. ESG risks are transversal to other risk types, materializing indirectly when ESG factors negatively impact the performance or solvency of a bank's counterparties and can be transmitted through channels such as physical risk, transition risk and legal risk.

To implement the SREP, several regulatory and legal instruments have been adopted by the competent authorities, particularly in Europe, where the legal basis is contained in CRD IV, Article 97, alongside additional regulatory technical standards (RTS) and implementation technical standards (ITS), as well as guidelines from the European Banking Authority (EBA). Here is a tentative list:

- Implementation Technical Standards (ITS) on prudential requirements.
- Regulatory Technical Standards (RTS) on the functioning of supervisory authorities.
- Guidelines on common procedures and methodologies for SREP (issued in 2014 and updated first in 2018 and then in 2022).[22]
- Guidelines on Internal Capital Adequacy Assessment Process (ICAAP) and Internal Liquidity Adequacy Assessment Process (ILAAP) information collected for SREP (issued in 2016 and last updated in 2022).[23]

[22] The EBA has issued several guidelines to harmonize the SREP across the European Union. The most recent guidelines are: (1) Guidelines on Common Procedures and Methodologies for the SREP and Supervisory Stress Testing (published on March 18, 2022), which focus on key SREP elements, including business model analysis, internal governance, assessment of risks to capital, and liquidity and funding assessments; (2) Guidelines on Common Procedures and Methodologies for the SREP under the Investment Firms Directive (released on July 21, 2022), which provide a framework for assessing investment firms.

[23] The EBA has updated related guidelines, such as the Guidelines on Common Procedures and Methodologies for the SREP and Supervisory Stress Testing, which were revised on March 18, 2022. These revisions may have implications for ICAAP and ILAAP assessments within the broader SREP framework.

- Guidelines on Information and Communication Technology (ICT) and security risk management (issued in 2025 and replacing previous Guidelines on ICT Risk Assessment under SREP of 2017).[24]

The ECB also adopted two methodological regulatory tools: (i) the SREP Methodology Booklet; (ii) the SSM Supervisory Manual—European banking supervision: functioning of the SSM and supervisory approach.

As previously noted, the SREP is divided into two phases. The first phase involves banks' self-assessment process, where they must conduct a current and forward-looking self-assessment in four areas: (1) business model assessment, evaluating the feasibility and sustainability of their business model; (2) risks to capital assessment through the ICAAP, assessing their capital adequacy to cover potential risks beyond those of the first pillar; (3) risks to liquidity and funding assessment via the ILAAP, covering short-term liquidity risk, funding sustainability and related factors; (4) governance and risk management assessment, evaluating the adequacy of their governance and risk management frameworks. All four areas must follow a common logic to achieve a robust overall risk assessment.

Within this first phase, intermediaries must consider both first-pillar risks (credit, market and operational risks) and additional risks, such as concentration, sovereign, residual, IRRBB, securitization, reputational and strategic risks. Financial intermediaries must independently conduct stress tests to assess their vulnerability to exceptional but plausible events, using both sensitivity analyses (evaluating potential impacts of specific events) and scenarios simulating joint movements of economic-financial variables (adverse scenarios). This allows banks to quantify the internal

[24] On February 11, 2025, the EBA published amendments to the existing Guidelines on ICT and Security Risk Management (EBA/GL/2019/04). These amendments were made in response to the application of the Digital Operational Resilience Act (DORA), which came into effect on January 17, 2025 (see Sect. 6.2.1). The primary change involves narrowing the scope of the existing guidelines due to the harmonized ICT risk management requirements introduced by DORA. In additions to these guidelines, the EBA, in collaboration with other European Supervisory Authorities, has developed Regulatory Technical Standards (RTS) on the ICT risk management framework. These RTS identify further elements related to ICT risk management to harmonize tools, methods, processes, and policies across financial sectors.

capital needed to cover various risks and verify the accuracy of their models.

Through this self-assessment process, banks conduct an in-depth analysis of their risk profile, and the synthesized results provide a basis for necessary actions. The first SREP phase thus focuses on the intermediary's situation regarding capital and risk management requirements, applying consistent parameters across banks to ensure a level playing field and equipping supervisors with harmonized tools for evaluating each bank's risk profile from a comprehensive perspective.

The second SREP phase involves supervisory authorities' review and evaluation of the outcomes from banks' self-assessments. In this phase, supervisory authorities conduct an overall assessment using a holistic, forward-looking approach, forming a comprehensive opinion on the bank's economic sustainability based on both quantitative and qualitative factors, taking its specific characteristics into account. Banks are then assigned a score (1–4, with 1 indicating no risk detected and 4 indicating high risk) with appropriate rationale and primary conclusions, which may include necessary corrective actions if warranted. Through SREP, authorities thus ensure that banks maintain appropriate capital, organizational, and liquidity management buffers relative to the risks assumed, even under stress scenarios, to ensure the overall stability of the bank's management.

This review and evaluation phase involves three steps: (1) data collection, primarily of reporting (Common Reporting on Capital Adequacy, COREP) and financial (Financial Reporting, FINREP) data; (2) the assignment of an 'anchor' score through an automatic procedure; (3) the supervisory judgement, a 'binding judgement' that can adjust the anchor score by one level higher or up to two levels lower to account for each bank's specificity and complexity, with possible requests for additional actions and corrections.

The bank's score is based on two dimensions evaluated across the four areas: i) risk level (RL), the amount of risk undertaken by the bank for each risk declared; ii) risk control (RC), the effectiveness of governance and control functions in managing these risks. The sum of the scores for RL and RC provides the overall combined score assigned by the supervisory authority (ECB or national central bank) and ranges from 1 to 4, where 1 is assigned to the most deserving bank and 4 to the least, with a scale of: 1 = no risk detected, 2 = low risk, 3 = medium risk, 4 = high risk. The final SREP supervisory judgement may, therefore, involve the assignment of the score with related rationale and corrective measures, such as quantitative capital measures, liquidity measures and other supervisory actions.

The SREP process spans the entire year, as the submission of relevant documentation for SREP evaluation (ICAAP, ILAAP, etc.) typically occurs within the first four months. In the subsequent four to five months, an in-depth 'dialogue' between the bank and the supervisory authority is established, during which the authority may request supplementary information or clarifications on the submitted documents. The final evaluation is then conducted over the last three to four months of the year by the supervisory Joint Supervisory Team (JST), and the outcome is formalized in the SREP Letter, signed by the Chair of the Supervisory Board.

Upon completion of the SREP cycle, supervisory authorities may impose additional (add-on) measures on banks in three areas: (1) additional capital requirements (second-pillar requirements, known as *Pillar 2 Requirement* and *Pillar 2 Guidance*); (2) bank-specific additional liquidity requirements (such as liquidity coverage ratio [LCR] above the regulatory minimum); and (3) other qualitative supervisory measures (requirements and/or restrictions). Specifically, the second-pillar capital add-ons are always expressed in terms of Common Equity Tier 1 (CET1) capital, vary across banks according to the SREP assessment, and may be of two types:

- *Pillar 2 Requirement* (P2R), which is a mandatory capital add-on imposed as an obligation.
- *Pillar 2 Guidance* (P2G), which is an additional capital expectation, not obligatory but expected by authorities; non-compliance may lead to supervisory actions, such as restrictions on dividend distributions.

Based on the SREP supervisory assessment and the resulting score, additional capital adjustments under the second pillar may be required, supplementing the first-pillar capital requirements. The P2R is a specific capital requirement for individual banks, applied when the minimum capital requirement under the first pillar underestimates or does not cover certain risks. The P2R established within the SREP framework is legally binding, and non-compliance may subject entities to further supervisory measures, including sanctions. However, the P2R does not include excessive leverage risk, which is instead addressed by the Pillar 2 leverage ratio requirement, known as P2R-LR. In addition to complying with the mandatory P2R, supervisory authorities expect banks to adhere to the P2G, which indicates the capital level a bank should maintain to withstand financial stress. Unlike P2R, the P2G is not legally binding, as it reflects the supervisory expectations rather than enforceable requirements.

SREP thus becomes a pivotal framework for redefining the entirety of capital requirements that banks must meet. While Basel I primarily centred on an 8% risk-weighted asset ratio, the combined application of the first and second pillars (introduced by Basel II and updated by Basel III) now demands that banks not only hold significantly more capital but also structure their regulatory capital following a well-defined sequence of building blocks (see Fig. 5.2).

(1) First, there is the *Total SREP Capital Requirement* (TSCR), which consists of the minimum Pillar 1 Requirement (P1R) without buffers plus the additional second-pillar P2R requirement.
(2) Next, the *Overall Capital Requirement* (OCR) builds upon the TSCR by including the Combined Buffer Requirements additional buffers mandated by Basel III (and adopted by CRD IV, Title VII, Chapter IV), which must all be met with CET1 capital:

- *Capital Conservation Buffer* (CCB), a capital reserve for expansion phases of the economic cycle, is set at 2.5% of CET1 for all banks.

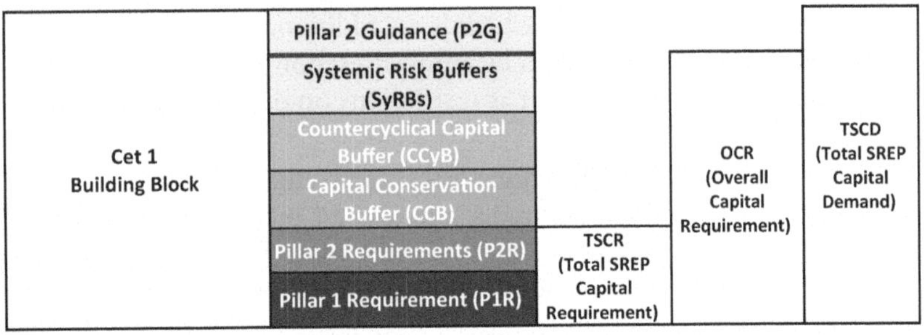

Fig. 5.2 Capital adequacy: a comprehensive overview of capital requirements: Pillar 1 and Pillar 2 requirements (*Source* European Central Bank, SREP Methodology for LSI 2020)

- *Countercyclical Capital Buffer* (CCyB), an anti-cyclical reserve ranging from 0 to 2.5% of CET1, is determined at the discretion of national authorities.
- *Systemic Risk Buffer* (SyRB), additional capital reserves for systemically important institutions: 0–3.5% of CET1 for Global Systemically Important Institutions (G-SIIs), as defined by the Financial Stability Board (FSB), and 0–2% of CET1 for Other Systemically Important Institutions (O-SIIs), designated by national discretion.

(3) Finally, there is the *Total SREP Capital Demand* (TSCD), which comprises the OCR plus second-pillar capital guidance, the P2G.

The threshold above which a bank may distribute dividends, known as the Maximum Distributable Amount (MDA), is determined by the OCR (see the red line in Fig. 5.2); however, the practice is to distribute dividends only after meeting and covering the P2G as well. Some of these capital requirements are uniform for all banks (such as the Pillar 1 Requirement and the CCB), while others vary across banks based on SREP outcomes (P2R and P2G), systemic importance (SyRB), or, on a national basis, through the application of countercyclical buffers (CCyB).

During the economic crisis triggered by the COVID-19 pandemic in March 2020, this system proved inadequate, prompting the ECB to implement specific supervisory measures to manage the crisis, primarily in the form of the following qualitative recommendations rather than strict supervisory measures.

- A pragmatic approach was taken in conducting the primary annual activities, maintaining stable P2R and P2G without updating SREP scores, unless modifications were warranted by exceptional circumstances affecting individual banks.
- Adjustments were introduced in the composition of regulatory capital for meeting P2R requirements, allowing partial use of non-CET1 resources (i.e., AT1 or T2), thus anticipating the implementation of CRD V (originally set for January 1, 2021).
- Certain operational flexibilities were granted for bank-specific supervisory measures, including the suspension and rescheduling of on-site inspections (OSI), extensions for remedial actions and

internal model reviews, and flexibility regarding non-performing loans (NPL).
- Additional supervisory measures were adopted, such as expansive non-standard monetary policy interventions and relaxation of automatic accounting mechanisms as prescribed by IFRS9.

The first element assessed in the SREP process is the ***bank's business model***, providing specific insights into the nature of risks faced by the bank. This analysis evaluates the bank's business model across the following three key dimensions.

- *Viability* is the feasibility of the business model or the ability to generate 'acceptable' profits over a one-year timeframe.
- *Sustainability* is the long-term sustainability of the business model or the ability to generate 'acceptable' profits over three years.
- *Economic Cycle Sustainability* is the capacity to produce 'acceptable' profits across the economic cycle, extending beyond three years.

The viability assessment involves verifying, for instance, if the business model (BM) generates returns exceeding costs, whether the projected funding composition aligns with the BM and investment strategy, or if the BM relies on a risk appetite significantly higher than that of competitors. The sustainability assessment, on the other hand, evaluates whether strategic assumptions and performance projections are plausible, the impact of economic conditions (macroeconomic factors, competition, market trends) on expected financial performance, and the risks of the strategy relative to success probabilities. Over time, primary business models have emerged among banks: depository banks, investment banks, diversified banks, retail banks, small-scale universal banks, specialized banks, universal banks, etc.

The business model analysis also involves identifying key business areas, operating context, corporate strategy and business plan, as well as primary vulnerabilities. Corporate strategies such as diversification, scaling/growth, internationalization, risk-taking, etc., lead to defining strategic business areas (SBA), including product differentiation, customer segmentation, process efficiency or risk management. Based on SBAs, the bank defines its business model, comprising the business mix (activity, liability, and revenue structure) and business strategies (revenue management, cost efficiency, risks, etc.).

The ultimate goal is to assess business and strategic risks and identify vulnerabilities with a high probability of significantly impacting the bank. Examples of vulnerabilities include projected poor financial performance, excessive risk-taking, profit concentration or an unsatisfactory financial structure.

The second element assessed in the SREP process is the *Internal Capital Adequacy Assessment Process* (ICAAP), which assesses all risk factors concerning a bank's capital and its adequacy. Authorities conduct this evaluation to assess the adequacy of the bank's funds by examining the bank's risks and control systems, also through stress testing. This evaluation ascertains the availability of an adequate safety net to absorb potential losses from various risk factors. The assessment must be conducted from three perspectives—supervisory, institutional and forward-looking—to evaluate the reliability of the bank's procedures in governance, capital planning, scenario definition, stress testing, internal controls, independent reviews, documentation, data infrastructure, risk identification, measurement and aggregation.

The ICAAP aims to determine whether the bank's funds provide adequate coverage against actual and potential risks, including those arising from excessive leverage of own funds. The adequacy of own funds and the associated stress impact are crucial for ensuring the bank's economic viability. Additional capital requirements are evaluated in terms of both quantity (amount) and quality (composition), ensuring that capital adequacy is assessed against all potential risks, not only those of the first pillar. Consequently, additional capital requirements may also be required to address risks related to the business model, controls, governance and other deficiencies identified.

The third element assessed in the SREP process is the *Internal Liquidity Adequacy Assessment Process* (ILAAP), which assesses inherent risks and controls over liquidity and funding. This involves evaluating the adequacy of liquidity resources to support business financing beyond the short term. This process verifies the bank's capability to meet specific, systemic and idiosyncratic liquidity needs. Similar to ICAAP, the ILAAP assessment must also consider supervisory, institutional and forward-looking perspectives to evaluate the reliability of the bank's procedures in governance, funding strategy and planning, liquidity measurement and monitoring, stress testing, contingency funding plans, internal controls, independent reviews, data infrastructure, and risk identification, measurement, and aggregation.

ILAAP's objective is to determine whether the bank's liquidity is sufficient to cover liquidity and funding risks. Key factors affecting the bank's economic viability are liquidity reserves, funding profile, and mechanisms for measuring and managing liquidity and funding risks. ILAAP may also result in requests for specific and additional liquidity requirements.

The fourth element assessed by authorities is the quality of a bank's *internal governance and risk management*, with particular attention to control functions (risk management, internal audit, compliance, anti-money laundering), as well as the bank's 'risk culture', data management infrastructure, reporting, and remuneration system. An analysis of the bank's organizational structure is conducted to evaluate potential risks arising from inadequacies in governance, organizational and control arrangements. Specific areas evaluated include the following ones.

- Overall corporate governance structure (ownership arrangements, strategic supervision, management and control bodies).
- Organizational structure.
- Control functions (internal audit, risk management, compliance, anti-money laundering).
- Risk culture.
- Data management infrastructure.
- Reporting.
- Remuneration policies.

Examples of vulnerabilities in this dimension include instances where a compliance officer lacks hierarchical and functional independence from other corporate bodies, weak control functions due to inadequate quantitative/qualitative resources or insufficient engagement, lack of managerial mechanisms for timely risk exposure mitigation, inadequate management of conflicts of interest among corporate officials, board composition (few independent members, lack of experience, excessive shareholder influence), or insufficient diversity among board members (age, gender, geographic origin, education, professional background). Upon completing this assessment, the score assigned to this element is based primarily on the bank's risk control capability.

5.6.3 *Third Pillar: Market Discipline*

The third pillar introduces regulations related to so-called market discipline, which aims to enhance transparency and disclosure by banks, allowing markets (in addition to supervisory authorities, as in the second pillar) to assess the bank's effectiveness in risk management and capital adequacy, with the broader goal of promoting global financial stability.

Basel II agreements introduced requirements for banks to publicly disclose a range of information on their risk profile, financial position and risk control and management practices. This information must be included in banks' annual reports, enabling markets to evaluate their financial soundness and risk management capacity. In this way, clients, investors and all bank stakeholders have access to the necessary information to make informed decisions, thereby contributing to a more stable financial system.

The third pillar, therefore, requires banks to meet the following three main requirements.

- *Disclosure requirement*: banks must systematically disclose extensive information concerning their exposure to various risk categories, such as credit, market, operational and liquidity risks, as well as details on their capital structure and adequacy. These disclosures typically appear in annual reports and publicly accessible financial statements (Hull, 2018).
- *Evaluation requirement*: with detailed and transparent disclosures, market participants can effectively assess the financial stability and risk management effectiveness of banking institutions. Academic research has demonstrated that improved disclosures significantly enhance the market's ability to price risk correctly, contributing to financial stability by reducing uncertainty and promoting prudent risk-taking behaviours (Acharya et al., 2014).
- *Monitoring requirement*: continuous and rigorous market monitoring acts as an additional check on banks, incentivizing them to maintain robust risk management practices. Effective market monitoring has been linked to better bank performance, improved resilience during economic downturns, and the reduced likelihood of banking crises (Beck et al., 2006).

Basel III then further strengthened the third pillar by enhancing disclosure requirements and promoting greater transparency. These enhancements include:

- More granular disclosures: banks are required to provide more detailed information on their risk exposures, including credit risk, market risk and operational risk.
- Improved risk measurement: Basel III introduced more sophisticated risk measurement methodologies, leading to more accurate and comparable disclosures.
- Increased frequency of disclosures: banks are required to disclose information more frequently, allowing for more timely monitoring by market participants.

These enhancements aim to improve the quality and comparability of information available to market participants, further strengthening market discipline and promoting financial stability. Market discipline plays a crucial role in complementing regulatory oversight. By providing detailed and timely information, banks enable market participants to assess their risk profile and financial health. This scrutiny incentivizes banks to adopt sound risk management practices and maintain adequate capital levels, as market participants can react by adjusting their investment decisions or pricing of bank liabilities.

Recent empirical studies support the efficacy of market discipline mechanisms. For example, research examining bank disclosures during the global financial crisis has indicated that institutions with higher-quality disclosures exhibited greater resilience and experienced fewer adverse outcomes compared to banks with less transparent reporting practices (Berger et al., 2016; Matos et al., 2024). Overall, the third pillar reinforces the essential role of transparency and market discipline in safeguarding financial stability.

5.6.4 *Basel IV: Main Updates and Implications*

The Basel IV update seeks to strengthen prudential regulation and risk management, addressing weaknesses exposed by the 2007–2008 financial crisis and whose implementation was delayed by the COVID-19 pandemic. Key measures include enhanced supervisory powers and a revised prudential framework. The framework introduces a standardized approach for risk assessment, with an 'output floor' for internal models to ensure that capital requirements do not fall below 72.5% of the requirements determined using standardized methods. Basel IV's phased implementation timeline, with major requirements starting in 2023 and extending through 2028, provides banks with a phased implementation period to facilitate operational adjustments. The EU's timeline involves a phased approach too, with deadlines around 2025 for many elements, and full implementation by 2029.[25]

The primary innovations of the Basel IV framework are as follows. Basel IV introduces an output floor that sets a minimum capital level for banks using internal models, in order to foster greater comparability and transparency across institutions. Starting from 2023, this floor ensures that capital requirements calculated through internal risk models cannot fall below 72.5% of requirements determined using standardized approaches. The output floor is designed to reduce inconsistencies in capital levels across institutions, enhancing comparability and transparency by providing a standardized baseline for capital requirements. This measure will be gradually phased in to provide banks with a phased implementation period to facilitate operational adjustments.

Basel IV revises the standardized approach for credit risk assessment by introducing a more granular framework, improving risk sensitivity. These changes aim to enhance the accuracy of credit risk assessments, particularly for institutions that do not use internal models, by offering a more detailed breakdown of risk weights across asset classes. Effective in 2023, this enhanced approach allows for better risk alignment and promotes consistency across the sector by providing a clear, standardized basis for calculating credit exposures.

Basel IV replaces previous methods for operational risk management with a standardized approach, focusing on simplicity and comparability. Under the new rules, which began to take effect in 2023, capital requirements are determined based on financial performance indicators and other

[25] In the EU, the Basel IV framework has been adopted through: (i) Regulation 2024/1623 of 31 May 2024 (CRR III), amending Regulation No. 575/2013 with respect to credit risk, credit valuation adjustment risk, operational risk, market risk, and the output floor; and (ii) Directive 2024/1619 of 31 May 2024 (CRD VI), amending Directive No. 2013/36 as regards supervisory powers, sanctions, third-country branches, and environmental, social and governance (ESG) risks.

objective criteria rather than highly variable internal models. This change aims to reduce complexity and improve transparency, making it easier for supervisory authorities to evaluate operational risk across institutions consistently.

Recognizing the complexities inherent in trading activities, Basel IV updates the market risk framework to capture these risks more effectively. By refining calculation methodologies, the framework ensures that market risks are assessed more accurately. Set to be fully implemented by 2028, these revisions address prior weaknesses in risk weighting for trading activities, ensuring that market risk capital requirements better reflect actual exposures and mitigate potential vulnerabilities in banks' trading books.

Finally, Basel IV also acknowledges the growing importance of Environmental, Social, and Governance (ESG) risks, encouraging banks to consider these factors in their risk management and capital planning processes. Although specific regulatory measures for ESG risks are not mandated in Basel IV, this inclusion marks a shift towards sustainable finance and reflects broader global trends emphasizing climate and social risk management. Banks are encouraged to incorporate ESG considerations into risk assessments, aligning with global efforts towards sustainability, such as the European Union's goal for climate neutrality by 2050.

These innovations collectively aim to strengthen the banking sector's resilience against future financial shocks, enhance risk transparency, and promote a more sustainable and stable financial environment. Through higher and more consistent capital requirements, a refined approach to risk assessment, and recognition of ESG factors, Basel IV establishes a comprehensive regulatory framework that supports the stability, transparency and adaptability of the global banking system.

5.7 The ECB Guide on Governance and Risk Culture

The European Central Bank (ECB) is deeply committed to fostering a robust and resilient banking sector within the Eurozone. Central to this commitment is the emphasis on strong governance frameworks and a sound risk culture within supervised institutions. The ECB recognizes that these elements are fundamental, not just for complying with regulatory requirements but for ensuring prudent management and sustainable growth in the long term. This focus is evident in the ECB's supervisory practices, its publications and its ongoing engagement with banks across the Eurozone.

The ECB's supervisory expectations regarding governance and risk culture are set out in the 2024 ECB 'Draft Guide on Governance and Risk Culture' (European Central Bank, 2024b). This guide builds on the 2016 'SSM supervisory statement on governance and risk appetite', which it supersedes as of its publication date, and incorporates additional insights gathered through supervisory activities. This comprehensive guide provides detailed insights into the ECB's expectations for banks' organizational structure, decision-making processes, risk management frameworks and overall risk culture. The guide stresses the importance of clear roles and responsibilities within the bank, effective communication channels and a culture of accountability. It also highlights the crucial role of the board of directors in setting the tone for the risk culture and ensuring that risk management is integrated into all levels of the organization.

Governance and risk culture in the banking sector are considered fundamental for the stability and proper functioning of the European financial system and are strongly interconnected. In fact, a strong *governance* framework is essential for banks to make sound decisions and manage risks effectively (Enria, 2023). On the other hand, *risk culture* is defined as the shared norms, attitudes and behaviours related to risk awareness, risk-taking, and risk management within a bank, and it is intrinsically linked to governance. The ECB Guide on governance and risk culture outlines supervisory expectations and good practices; in particular, it emphasizes the importance of a clear organizational structure, well-defined responsibilities and transparent reporting lines. It also highlights the role of the management body in setting the tone from the top and ensuring a culture of constructive challenge and accountability. Strong risk management and governance are fundamental to a well-functioning bank. Effective boards actively engage with management, ask challenging questions and promote a sound risk culture. They are expected to foster transparency and ensure that the bank's risk profile remains aligned with its defined risk appetite. This includes providing robust oversight and challenge not only to executive management but also to control functions such as risk management and compliance. To carry out this role effectively, boards must comprise a suitable mix of skills, experience and perspectives, including gender diversity. While individual members are not expected to master every area, the board collectively must be equipped to oversee all aspects of the bank's operations, risks and internal controls. Governance is the unifying element across these responsibilities, and strong governance is the foundation upon which well-run banks are built, and the reason why they do not fail (Enria, 2023).

A strong 'three lines of defence' model is considered a key element of a bank's internal governance framework. This model consists of:

- First line: business lines, responsible for taking and managing risks.
- Second line: risk management and compliance functions, providing oversight and control.
- Third line: internal audit function, providing independent assurance.

The management body is responsible for defining, overseeing, and ensuring the implementation of the governance arrangements, and it must demonstrate a capacity for constructive challenges and strong oversight of the management function and internal control functions. The management body should have access to quality data in a timely manner to make appropriate decisions. The internal control functions, including risk management, compliance and internal audit, must be independent, have sufficient authority and have access to the management body. Their opinions on the bank's business and activities should be duly considered.

A well-developed Risk Appetite Framework (RAF), articulated through a risk appetite statement, is essential for a sound governance framework. The RAF should be integrated into the bank's decision-making process, including strategic decisions, budget processes and remuneration policies. The ECB will then assess governance and risk culture using various tools, including off-site and on-site supervision; these assessments can include reviews of documentation, interviews, participation in meetings and thematic reviews. The ECB will also perform targeted analysis related to internal governance following its supervisory priorities (see Sect. 6.1).

The comparative analysis between the 2016 'SSM Supervisory Statement on Governance and Risk Appetite' and the 2024 'Draft Guide on Governance and Risk Culture' highlights a significant evolution in the regulatory approach within the banking sector. The Draft Guide considerably expands the perspective on governance and risk, introducing the concept of 'risk culture', understood as a set of shared values, attitudes and behaviours within an organization. Furthermore, it provides an in-depth examination of the role of internal control functions and emphasizes the interconnectedness between corporate values, behaviours and organizational structures. The ECB expects financial institutions to actively define and monitor their risk culture, values, and codes of conduct, integrating them into corporate governance. The Guide provides clear and detailed guidance on:

- The composition and functioning of management bodies and committees, to outline supervisory expectations.
- The roles and responsibilities of internal control functions, to ensure effective risk management.
- The Risk Appetite Framework (RAF), to offer banks a roadmap for establishing and implementing a more informed and consistent risk management approach.

The regulatory advancements introduced by the Draft Guide bring multiple benefits, including:

- Strengthening the regulatory framework, ensuring greater clarity and consistency in supervisory activities.
- Enhancing risk management effectiveness through the integration of risk culture into corporate governance.
- Providing banks with an operational framework, offering concrete guidelines for implementing the new regulatory requirements.

A key element of a strong risk culture is effective communication; that is, the ability of all staff to communicate effectively, challenge decisions and report mistakes. The management body is expected to facilitate a culture of open debate and ensure diversity of views. The remuneration framework should also be designed to encourage desired behaviours aligned with the long-term interests and risk profile of the bank, and incentives should be linked to both performance and risk management, and there should be consequences for misconduct.

The implementation of these new provisions presents a complex challenge for banks, requiring a profound cultural and organizational transformation. This process will necessitate substantial investments in human, technological and financial resources to comply with the new requirements. The ability of banks to adapt to this transformation will be crucial in determining their capacity to manage risks effectively and contribute to the overall stability of the financial system. In this context, the active role of supervisory authorities will be essential in monitoring the implementation of the Draft Guide and promoting the convergence of governance and risk culture practices across different banking institutions. Supervisory measures will define the specific actions that supervised entities must undertake to address identified deficiencies, with Joint Supervisory Teams (JSTs) responsible for ensuring their timely and effective implementation. From this point of view, governance and risk culture will remain critical factors for the long-term survival and prosperity of European banks, so the Draft Guide on Governance and Risk Culture will serve as a key resource, clarifying supervisory expectations and promoting best practices within banking institutions.

Over the past decade, European banking regulation on governance and risk culture has made substantial advancements, driven by new regulatory frameworks and institutional efforts. However, the banking sector continues to face complex challenges shaped by evolving economic conditions and emerging risks. To ensure the stability of the financial system and promote sustainable growth, further reinforcement of governance and risk culture within banks is essential. The ECB's banking supervision will, therefore, continue to refine its supervisory approach to address emerging risks, requiring constant adaptation to economic and regulatory developments. As a result, the expectations outlined in the Draft Guide will be periodically updated to align with regulatory developments and evolving industry practices within the supervisory community (European Central Bank, 2024b).

The ECB's emphasis on governance and risk culture is not merely a reaction to past crises, but also a proactive approach to building a more resilient and sustainable banking sector. The ECB recognizes that strong governance and sound risk culture are essential for navigating the complexities of the financial landscape, managing emerging risks and ensuring that banks can continue to support the economy in the long term. By promoting these principles, the ECB aims to foster a banking sector that is not only compliant with regulations but also capable of adapting to change, managing risks effectively and contributing to the stability and growth of the Eurozone economy.

Over the past decade, the governance of banks under European supervision has made substantial progress. When the new European banking supervision was introduced, many institutions exhibited severe deficiencies in both governance and risk culture. In some cases, board meetings were reduced to mere formalities, lacking critical discussion or in-depth debate. Additionally, about one-third of banks lacked a structured framework for defining their risk appetite, a key tool in determining the levels of risk an institution is willing to assume (Elderson, 2024). Before the 2007–2008 financial crisis, public finance monitoring and fiscal reserves in some Member States were inadequate. Furthermore, the absence of an effective supranational supervisory system contributed to regulatory fragmentation and the risk of a vicious cycle between banks and sovereign debt (European Court of Auditors, 2020).

Today, the situation has changed significantly because almost all banks conduct an annual internal assessment of their organizational structure, governance effectiveness and the collective suitability of their boards and committees. Moreover, all banks under European supervision have adopted an RAF, marking a substantial step towards more responsible and informed risk management. These developments demonstrate a strengthened regulatory environment and an enhanced commitment to sound governance and risk culture, reinforcing the resilience and stability of the European banking sector.

Despite the recent significant progress, certain structural weaknesses persist, particularly concerning the effectiveness of management bodies and the quality of supervision (European Central Bank, 2023). The global financial crisis and the sovereign debt crisis highlighted how deficiencies in internal governance and an inadequate risk culture can lead to severe problems for banking institutions. While institutional measures and regulatory frameworks introduced in the euro area—such as the Banking Union and new ECB intervention tools—have contributed to stabilizing the banking sector, several critical issues remain, including low profitability levels, high sovereign debt exposures, and a substantial volume of NPLs (European Court of Auditors, 2020).

Additionally, market dynamics and changes in financial intermediaries' operational models are becoming increasingly complex, making bank assessment a significant challenge for both market participants and supervisory authorities. Inadequate strategic decisions can compromise both risk management capabilities and the operational resilience of banks. Moving forward, it will be crucial to strengthen credit risk management to navigate an increasingly volatile and uncertain landscape, with a particular focus on liquidity and funding risks. Supervisory authorities will need to enhance bank monitoring efforts and implement corrective measures where necessary, and promoting a stronger risk culture within banks will be essential, encouraging greater risk awareness and accountability at all levels (European Central Bank, 2023). Although significant progress has been made, banks must continue to strengthen governance standards; meanwhile, the ECB will intensify its oversight efforts, intervening swiftly to ensure tangible improvements in banking governance and risk culture, and when necessary, it will employ all available supervisory tools to address any outstanding weaknesses in oversight and risk management (European Central Bank, 2024c).

References

Acharya, V. V., Engle, R. F., & Pierret, D. (2014). Testing macroprudential stress tests: The risk of regulatory risk weights. *Journal of Monetary Economics, 65*, 36–53.

Bank for International Settlements. (2006). International convergence of capital measurement and capital standards: A revised framework—Comprehensive version.

Bank for International Settlements. (2011). Basel III: A global regulatory framework for more resilient banks and banking systems.

Basel Committee on Banking Supervision. (2017). Basel III: finalising post-crisis reforms.

Beck, T., Demirgüç-Kunt, A., & Levine, R. (2006). Bank supervision and corruption in lending. *Journal of Monetary Economics, 53*(8), 2131–2163.

Berger, A. N., Imbierowicz, B., & Rauch, C. (2016). The roles of corporate governance in bank failures during the recent financial crisis. *Journal of Money, Credit and Banking, 48*, 729–770.

Elderson, F. (2024). Banks' governance and risk culture a decade on: progress and shortcomings. The Supervision Blog. European Central Bank.

Enria, A. (2023). *Well-run banks don't fail—Why governance is an enduring theme in banking crises.* https://www.bankingsupervision.europa.eu/press/speeches/date/2023/html/ssm.sp230601~0d92d89e8c.en.html

European Banking Authority (EBA). (2006). Guidelines on the Application of the Supervisory Review Process (SREP) under Pillar 2 (CP03 revised).

European Banking Authority (EBA). (2016). Guidelines on the application of the definition of default under Article 178 of Regulation (EU) No 575/2013 (EBA/GL/2016/07).

European Banking Authority (EBA). (2017). Guidelines on ICT Risk Assessment under the Supervisory Review and Evaluation process-SREP (EBA/GL/2017/05).

European Banking Authority (EBA). (2020). Guidelines on loan origination and monitoring-LOM (EBA/GL/2020/06).
European Central Bank (ECB). (2023). ECB banking supervision: SSM supervisory priorities for 2024–2026.
European Central Bank (ECB). (2024a). Guide on effective risk data aggregation and risk reporting.
European Central Bank (ECB). (2024b). Draft guide on governance and risk culture.
European Central Bank (ECB). (2024c). Public consultation on the guide on governance and risk culture.
European Central Bank (ECB). (2024d). Supervisory priorities 2025–27.
European Court of Auditors. (2020). How the EU took account of lessons learned from the 2008–2012 financial and sovereign debt crises.
Financial Stability Board. (2017). Framework for post-implementation evaluation of the effects of the Basel III regulatory reforms.
Hillier, D., Ross, S. A., Westerfield, R. W., & Jaffe, J. F. (2020). *Corporate finance*. McGraw Hill.
Hull, J. C. (2018). *Risk management and financial institutions* (5th ed.). Wiley.
Matos, T. F., Teixeira, J. C., & Dutra, T. M. (2024). The role of market discipline and macroprudential policies in achieving bank stability. *International Journal of Finance & Economics* (pp. 1–23).
Thakor, A. V. (1995). Financial intermediation and the market for credit. *Handbooks in Operations Research and Management Science, 9*, 1073–1103.
Tirole, J. (1994). On banking and intermediation. *European Economic Review, 38*(3–4), 469–487.

CHAPTER 6

The Digital and Green Twin Transition: Data Governance and Risk Management

6.1 Financial Implications of Digitalization and Sustainability: The ECB Supervisory Priorities

The banking sector is currently undergoing a dual transformation: the rapid digitalization of financial services and the growing emphasis on sustainability. In this context, banks are increasingly required to integrate environmental, social and governance (ESG) factors into their risk assessment and management processes in line with evolving regulatory expectations. The two 'transitions' are not mutually exclusive; rather, they intersect and influence each other, creating both challenges and opportunities with significant financial implications for banks, which will strongly affect the banking landscape.

Digitalization, through the adoption of advanced technologies such as cloud computing, artificial intelligence and blockchain, is fundamentally transforming the operational landscape of banks. Effective data collection and reorganization are essential for improving operational efficiency and ensuring the transparent flow of information, both of which are critical for enabling informed, data-driven decision-making within financial institutions. In this context, digitalization plays a dual role: (i) internally, it enhances the ability to manage, analyze and interpret data, thereby becoming a powerful tool for risk monitoring and compliance, including frameworks such as RDARR (Risk Data Aggregation and Risk Reporting; see Sect. 6.1.2); (ii) externally, it provides banks with the tools to design

P. Brighi and M. Mussoni, *The Bank-Business Relationship*,
https://doi.org/10.1007/978-3-031-91068-5_6

and deliver innovative financial products and services, tailored to evolving client needs.

As highlighted in information asymmetry theory (see Chapter 2), the core function of the financial system, and particularly the banking sector, is to reduce informational asymmetries between borrowers and lenders. Robust data collection mechanisms are therefore central to the banking system's ability to mitigate asymmetric information, as well as to resolve a range of agency problems and conflicts of interest: between shareholders and management, between shareholders and bondholders, and among other stakeholders involved in the banking business.

Beyond internal gains in efficiency and improved risk control, digitalization is enabling the emergence of entirely new business models. These include personalized customer journeys, predictive analytics and real-time decision-making developments with significant financial implications. On the one hand, the initial investment required for digital transformation—including infrastructure upgrades, cybersecurity and talent acquisition—is substantial. It involves significant capital expenditure and often requires a deep organizational shift in culture and structure (Vives, 2019). On the other hand, the long-term benefits include cost reductions through automation, process optimization, and rationalization of physical branches (Bonfim et al., 2021). These efficiencies can significantly enhance profitability and competitive positioning.

Furthermore, digitalization opens the door to new revenue streams. By enabling the creation of innovative financial services, banks can reach untapped customer segments and increase market share. The rise of fintech has further accelerated this transformation, pushing traditional banks to invest heavily in technology and adopt more customer-centric digital strategies in order to remain competitive (Degryse et al., 2025).

The sustainability transition, driven by growing environmental concerns and regulatory pressures, necessitates the incorporation of ESG factors into banks' strategic planning and risk assessment processes. This goes beyond simply offering 'green' financial products; it requires a fundamental shift in risk management, lending practices and investment strategies. Digitalization plays a crucial role in enabling this transition. Advanced data analytics and machine learning algorithms can be used to assess climate-related risks, measure the environmental impact of loan portfolios, and identify opportunities for sustainable finance (Weber, 2021). Digital platforms can facilitate the development and distribution of green financial products, such as green bonds and sustainability-linked loans, making it easier for investors to participate in the transition to a low-carbon economy. Furthermore, digitalization can improve transparency and traceability in supply chains, enabling banks to better manage environmental and social risks associated with their lending activities.

The intersection of these twin transitions creates synergistic opportunities. For example, digital platforms can be used to develop innovative financial products and services that cater to the growing demand for sustainable investments, such as digital green bonds or personalized ESG investment portfolios. Blockchain technology can enhance the transparency and security of green finance transactions, which would reduce the risk of greenwashing, and thereby build trust among investors. Furthermore, digital tools can streamline the process of ESG reporting and disclosure, making it easier for banks to demonstrate their commitment to sustainability and attract responsible investors.

However, the convergence of digitalization and sustainability also presents significant challenges. The so-called Information and Communication Technologies (ICT) risks are strongly amplified in the digital age, requiring banks to invest heavily in robust security measures to protect sensitive financial data and prevent cyberattacks. The increasing reliance on third-party technology providers also creates new risks related to data privacy, vendor management and operational resilience. Furthermore, ensuring that digitalization contributes to sustainability goals requires careful consideration of the environmental impact of technology itself, including the energy consumption of data centres and the management of electronic waste. Banks need to adopt a holistic approach to digitalization, ensuring that their digital transformation efforts are aligned with their sustainability goals.

Another critical challenge lies in addressing the potential for digital exclusion. As banking services become increasingly digital, there is a risk that vulnerable populations who lack access to technology or digital literacy skills may be excluded from the financial system. Banks have a responsibility to ensure that their services remain accessible to all customers, regardless of their digital capabilities. This requires a multifaceted approach, including providing digital literacy training, offering alternative channels for accessing banking services, and ensuring that digital products and services are designed to be inclusive and user-friendly (Weber et al., 2024).

The twin transition remains a focal point in the European Central Bank's (ECB) supervisory framework, as demonstrated by the explicit reference to climate and digitalization issues in its supervisory priorities since 2020. In the latest supervisory priorities for 2025–2027, the ECB expands its focus to include not only the oversight of business strategies and risk management in relation to climate-related and environmental risks, but also the strengthening of digital resilience and the management of risks associated with new technologies. Notably, a new supervisory priority has been introduced to address deficiencies in RDARR, reflecting the critical role of accurate and timely data in supporting both climate and digital transitions, as well as ensuring sound risk management and regulatory compliance. The latest ECB Supervisory Priorities thus provide for a comprehensive evaluation of data collection to control not only the traditional banking risks, but also emerging risks and the regulatory mechanisms designed to mitigate them.

The ECB acknowledges that while the European banking sector has demonstrated resilience amidst economic fluctuations, heightened geopolitical tensions pose significant uncertainties. As a result, the ECB emphasizes the necessity for banks to strengthen credit risk management frameworks. Specifically, banks must:

- Enhance early identification mechanisms for deteriorating asset quality.
- Maintain prudent provisioning levels, ensuring robust capital buffers.
- Develop scenario analyses to assess the impact of severe geopolitical disruptions on their operations.

The interconnected nature of financial markets necessitates a proactive stance in mitigating exposure to external shocks. In this regard, stress-testing methodologies have been reinforced, requiring banks to incorporate geopolitical risk factors into their internal risk assessments. The ECB's review of past supervisory cycles highlights persistent deficiencies in business strategies, climate-related risk governance and risk data aggregation. To address these issues, the ECB mandates banks to:

- Ensure full compliance with climate-related risk management expectations, particularly within the framework of the EU's sustainable finance agenda.

- Strengthen Risk Data Aggregation and Reporting (RDARR) capabilities to support more effective decision-making and strategic steering (see Sect. 6.1.2).
- Implement remedial actions in a timely manner, with escalation measures applied where progress remains insufficient.

Given the increasing materiality of climate-related and environmental (C&E) risks, the ECB has introduced more stringent requirements to integrate these risks into banks' capital adequacy assessments and stress-testing models. Digitalization and the adoption of emerging technologies, such as artificial intelligence (AI) and cloud computing, present both opportunities and risks. The ECB has prioritized the assessment of banks' digital strategies to ensure they align with regulatory expectations. Key supervisory expectations include:

- Implementing comprehensive frameworks to manage risks associated with digital transformation, particularly in cybersecurity and IT resilience.
- Ensuring compliance with the Digital Operational Resilience Act (DORA), which establishes new standards for ICT risk management and incident reporting (see Sect. 6.2.1).
- Conducting targeted reviews of outsourcing arrangements to mitigate concentration risks associated with third-party service providers.

Recent supervisory assessments indicate that while progress has been made in enhancing banks' operational resilience, gaps remain in cybersecurity defences and IT outsourcing risk management. The ECB will continue to monitor these vulnerabilities, utilizing targeted on-site inspections (OSIs) and thematic reviews. The evolving risk landscape necessitates a dynamic supervisory approach. The ECB has reaffirmed its commitment to:

- Regularly reassess supervisory priorities based on macroeconomic and geopolitical developments.
- Engage in forward-looking risk identification, leveraging advanced analytics and stress-testing methodologies.

- Implement proportionate supervision for less significant institutions while maintaining a level playing field across the European banking sector.

Moreover, transparency in supervisory expectations remains a cornerstone of the ECB's strategy, ensuring that banks are adequately prepared to address emerging challenges. The ECB's supervisory priorities for 2025–2027 reflect a *strategic shift from risk identification to risk remediation*. By integrating robust credit risk management, enhancing digital resilience and addressing climate-related risks, the ECB aims to fortify the stability of the European banking sector. The effectiveness of these priorities will largely depend on banks' commitment to implementing corrective measures and adapting to the evolving regulatory landscape. As supervisory expectations become more stringent, banks must proactively align their frameworks with best practices to ensure long-term resilience and compliance with the ECB's supervisory agenda.

6.1.1 ESG Risks and Their Determinants

Global attention to Environmental, Social, and Governance (ESG) factors has significantly increased in recent years, parallel to a growing sensitivity towards incorporating 'sustainable development'[1] as a central focus of political agendas and international development programmes. Sustainable development is defined as 'development that meets the needs of the present generation without compromising the ability of future generations to meet their own needs'.

Over the past decade, global institutions have acted with greater determination on these issues, initiating a regulatory process to guide the behaviour of governments and economic agents, aiming to promote a transition towards sustainability. In September 2015, the UN General Assembly established the Sustainable Development Goals (SDGs) through the 2030 Agenda. These 17 goals, further divided into 169 sub-goals, aim to combat poverty and inequality and promote social and economic development.

[1] First introduced in the report 'Our Common Future', published in 1987 by the World Commission on Environment and Development (Brundtland Commission) of the United Nations Environment Programme.

In the same year, 2015, the increasing awareness of the effects of climate change, both current and projected, led governments and major global institutions to undertake numerous initiatives to mitigate and adapt to these effects, signing the first legally binding international treaty on climate change, the Paris Agreement, which came into force in December 2016. The European Union, committed to achieving carbon neutrality by 2050, has positioned itself as a leader in promoting economic growth models that integrate environmental and social considerations. Since 2018, through the Commission's Action Plan on Sustainable Finance,[2] the EU has engaged the financial system, which—due to its capacity to mobilize large volumes of capital—is explicitly mandated to reallocate resources towards a more sustainable economy. The Action Plan on Sustainable Finance has the following three main objectives.

- Redirect capital flows towards a more sustainable economy.
- Integrate sustainability into risk management.
- Promote transparency and long-term vision.

The ten actions outlined in the Action Plan for Financing Sustainable Growth (European Commission's Action Plan, 2018)[3] have led, in subsequent years, to a comprehensive regulatory framework encompassing the entire financial system: banks and financial institutions, asset managers, investors, publicly traded companies and issuers of listed securities. The objective is to strengthen the 'sustainability measurement' and 'reporting' framework. In this context, the Regulation on Sustainability-Related Disclosures in the Financial Services Sector was introduced,[4] focused on transparency obligations towards end investors, aiming to integrate sustainability considerations such as 'sustainability risks, adverse sustainability impacts, sustainable investment objectives and the promotion of environmental or social characteristics' into the decision-making and advisory processes. A legally defined taxonomy of eco-sustainable activities

[2] https://finance.ec.europa.eu/publications/renewed-sustainable-finance-strategy-and-implementation-action-plan-financing-sustainable-growth_en.

[3] https://eur-lex.europa.eu/legal-content/EN/TXT/PDF/?uri=CELEX:52018DC0097&rid=4.

[4] Regulation (EU) 2019/2088 of the European Parliament and of the Council of 27 November 2019 on Sustainability-Related Disclosures in the Financial Services Sector.

has been established.[5] Additionally, the scope of companies required to produce non-financial reporting has been expanded by the *Corporate Sustainability Reporting Directive* (CSRD),[6] which also mandates the full inclusion of ESG factors in financial analysis, specifically in the 'Management Report', with the term evolving from 'non-financial reporting' to 'sustainability reporting'.

Alongside regulatory intervention and increased public awareness, investors are now equipped to consider sustainability factors when evaluating corporate performance and are increasingly inclined to allocate their capital responsibly, considering both financial returns and the environmental and social impact of companies. Companies, including banks, are incentivized to adopt sustainable practices, improve governance and provide ESG-related disclosures, as they tend to be rewarded by investors. Consequently, the number of companies voluntarily adopting ESG reporting, even before regulatory requirements, has been rising.

At the same time, the issue of 'greenwashing' or 'social washing' is becoming more prominent. ESG communication is intensifying, yet measuring the sustainability trajectory of banks and the financial system remains challenging. The factors considered and the metrics used are difficult to quantify and are often available only at the sectoral level rather than individually. European Supervisory Authorities, including the European Banking Authority (EBA), have issued technical standards requiring banks to disclose specific environmental and social sustainability indicators (the 'Pillar 3 disclosure on ESG risks'). The concern is substantial enough to initiate a call for evidence about greenwashing.[7]

To address the complexities associated with estimating ESG risks and their impact on traditional financial risks, we now present the main ESG factors and measurement metrics. EBA defines ESG factors as environmental, social or governance characteristics that may positively or

[5] Regulation (EU) 2020/852 of the European Parliament and of the Council of 18 June 2020 establishing a framework to facilitate sustainable investment.

[6] Directive (EU) 2022/2464 of the European Parliament and the Council of 14 December 2022 on Corporate Sustainability Reporting, known as the CSRD. This Directive, which must be implemented through transposition into national legislation, expands the scope of the NFRD (Non-Financial Reporting Directive), transposed in Italy by Legislative Decree 254/2016. The first European country to transpose the CSRD was France, on 7 December 2023.

[7] https://www.esma.europa.eu/press-news/consultations/esas-call-evidence-greenwashing.

negatively impact an entity's financial performance or solvency, whether that entity is sovereign, corporate or individual.[8] Similarly, the European Commission refers to ESG-related events or conditions that could adversely affect banks.[9]

The *Environmental* factor encompasses all aspects related to natural resources and their impact on the planet and human health. This includes, for example, clean water, accessible clean energy, responsible consumption and production, climate change mitigation, biodiversity in oceans and on land, food security, CO_2 emission reductions and minimizing natural resource use. The *Social* factor pertains to the societal impact of human activities, including goals such as eradicating poverty and hunger, ensuring health and wellbeing, providing quality education, achieving gender equality, promoting decent work and economic growth, and reducing inequalities. This factor relates to initiatives by economic entities that have a social impact. The *Governance* factor concerns the internal management of a company, specifically focusing on control mechanisms, internal policies, and objectives regarding areas such as anti-money laundering, anti-corruption, cybersecurity, risk management and privacy protection, all of which affect various stakeholders. Governance refers to how states, administrations, businesses and organizations, whether public or private, are managed and organized, impacting areas like innovation, sustainable cities and communities, peace, justice, strong institutions and partnerships for shared goals. For a company, including banks, Governance encompasses merit-based systems, board diversity policies, ethical compensation and anti-corruption efforts. Analyzing a company's governance structure also enables external stakeholders to assess its corporate identity, observing whether the company's behaviour aligns with ESG principles and a commitment to sustainable development supported by an appropriate internal organization.

The relevance of ESG factors for financial institutions depends on their business model and the nature of their assets (e.g., the sectors and geographical locations of counterparties) and liabilities (e.g., issued financial instruments). Given that ESG factors can influence financial institutions' performance, they intersect with traditional financial and

[8] EBA, Discussion Paper on Management and Supervision of ESG Risks for Credit Institutions and Investment Firms, October 2020, https://www.eba.europa.eu/calendar/discussion-paper-management-and-supervision-esg-risks-creditinstitutions-and-investment.

[9] European Commission, Delegated Regulation 2020/1817, 17 July 2020.

non-financial risk categories such as credit, market, operational, liquidity, and funding risks (see Sect. 5.3).

While ESG factors can have both positive and negative impacts, ESG risks are defined by the EBA as the negative manifestation of ESG factors on banks, 'in line with the regulator's prudential approach to risk management',[10] even though it is acknowledged that these factors may also have positive effects (e.g., mitigating liquidity risk from increased financial flows directed towards a bank perceived as 'green' within the sustainable finance context). ESG risks must be analyzed (and reported) under the 'double materiality' perspective:

- Financial materiality (outside-in) arises from the impact of ESG factors on a company's economic and financial activities through its entire value chain (both upstream and downstream), affecting the value (return) of those activities.
- Environmental and social materiality (inside-out) arises from the impact of a company's economic and financial activities on ESG factors, which in turn become financially material when their effects influence the company's asset value.

The Basel Committee classifies the transmission channels of ESG factors for financial intermediaries as follows.

- Microeconomic channels, through which ESG factors influence individual counterparties. These encompass both direct effects on banks (such as branch flooding due to extreme weather events) and indirect effects closely linked to the performance of financed entities, their behaviour, their exposure to these risks, and their ability to manage them over the short, medium and long term.
- Macroeconomic channels encompass the ways ESG factors influence macroeconomic variables, such as interest rates, inflation, commodities and GDP, which subsequently impact individual counterparties.

Through both transmission channels, ESG factors can have multiple impacts on intermediaries' 'traditional' risks (credit, operational, market,

[10] EBA/REP/2021/18, EBA Final Report on Management and Supervision of ESG Risks for Credit Institutions and Investment Firms, Par. 2.2. 'Definition of ESG risks'.

and liquidity risks), potentially leading to solvency challenges and, ultimately, increasing systemic risk. In recent years, all economic operators have shown a growing interest in these issues, recognizing that such factors are crucial for achieving sustainable economic growth. ESG dynamics can significantly affect corporate performance, influencing, to varying degrees, the risks companies face in their operations:

- Uncertainty in impact timing, as risks can materialize at any moment and have effects with indefinite timeframes.
- Measurement uncertainty: due to impacts that are difficult to identify and evaluate.
- Long-term negative economic externalities, as the cost of adverse effects is borne by society.
- Value chain impact, both upstream and downstream: this can be direct or indirect, depending on the stakeholders involved.
- High sensitivity to regulatory changes, as regulatory attention to ESG issues has increased over time, resulting in frequent and numerous interventions.

The *Environmental* factor underpins environmental and climate risk, understood as the negative impact that corporate activities can have on the environment and climate in the form of environmental degradation (e.g., air and water pollution, freshwater scarcity, soil contamination, biodiversity loss and deforestation) and climate change. Companies that inadequately manage these risks may face legal penalties, additional costs and reduced acceptance from savers and investors.

In banking, *environmental risks*, particularly those associated with climate change, are increasingly standardized in defining their core components. The ECB's guidelines on climate and environmental risks specify that these risks can be closely interrelated: climate change also drives environmental degradation, as an increase of only 1.5 °C is expected to have a significant impact on terrestrial and marine biodiversity and ecosystems. Financial risks faced by banks are both direct and indirect. Direct risks are those that banks may generate or experience as corporations, while indirect risks arise from exposure to clients who may contribute to or be affected by forms of environmental degradation. Climate risks refer to financial risks arising from exposures to counterparties that may contribute to or be impacted by climate change.

The last guidelines on the management of ESG risks (EBA, 2025) aim to direct banks towards environmentally responsible clients and incorporate the impact of these risks into pricing policies. Banks are also encouraged to identify key sectors and geographic areas potentially affected by environmental risks, considering the impact on the products/services they offer. Based on the ECB definition (ECB, 2020), climate risks manifest in the following three categories.

1. *Physical risk* involves potential negative economic and financial impacts arising from adverse climate events (acute risk) or gradually worsening climate conditions (chronic risk). For example, floods and earthquakes are acute risks, while rising sea levels and temperature increases are chronic risks. Physical risk encompasses the economic costs and financial losses due to the growing frequency, volatility and severity of climate-related weather events. Based on event type, physical risk is classified as 'acute' if stemming from extreme phenomena, and 'chronic' for gradual climate changes impacting economic performance over time. Physical risk estimates may vary by the business's geographic location; however, while acute risks are more easily identifiable and measurable, chronic risks pose greater assessment complexity. For instance, an agricultural business might be affected by flooding (acute physical risk) or by a temperature rise causing drought over time, impairing its repayment capacity (chronic physical risk).
2. *Transition risk* refers to financial losses that entities may incur directly or indirectly due to regulations promoting a more sustainable and low-carbon economy. The shift to new environmental norms increasingly involves adopting regulations to reduce CO_2 emissions and support renewable energy development. Consequently, businesses and intermediaries are significantly exposed to transition risk, tied to the costs companies must bear to comply with new ESG standards. For example, the mandated switch to electric vehicle fleets due to new emissions regulations banning the registration of internal combustion engine vehicles (diesel or gasoline) from 2035 represents a transition risk. If not promptly managed, this risk can lead to a business crisis. Unlike physical risk, transition risk is challenging to estimate and assess, as it requires companies to plan for the future and project into the medium to long term.

3. *Legal/reputational risk* pertains to potential losses or damage experienced by individuals or companies due to environmental factors. For instance, if a company becomes involved in litigation over environmental issues and the dispute becomes public, the company's reputation may suffer. Legal and reputational risks stem from possible financial losses resulting from behaviour that conflicts with ESG standards. Specifically, legal risk includes litigation expenses in the ESG domain, such as cases where a company fails to meet health and safety regulations, necessitating legal action. Reputational risk, on the other hand, concerns image damage resulting from such negative behaviour. For instance, if a company neglects employee health and safety standards, it may face reputational harm as clients and the general public lose trust in the company.

Social risks are more challenging to identify. The ECB (2020) defines them as risks arising from a bank's exposure to counterparties that social factors may adversely impact. Social factors can generate risks linked to labour regulations or interactions with clients and suppliers that must respect human rights. In other words, failing to respect the welfare and interests of people and communities interacting with a bank's clients can also negatively impact the bank. These social factors are increasingly incorporated into corporate strategies and operational frameworks by companies, banks and their counterparties and have garnered growing attention from supervisory bodies.

Finally, *governance risk* is linked to issues related to the structure and management of companies, such as poor management, conflicts of interest, lack of transparency, corruption, unethical behaviour and lack of accountability by executives. Ineffective corporate governance can lead to poor decision-making, financial losses, corporate instability and low investor confidence.

In conclusion, we summarize the impacts that the direct and indirect actions of ESG factors may have on the primary traditional risks faced by banks, including credit risk, funding risk, market risk, liquidity risk, operational risk and regulatory risk.

- *Credit Risk*: ESG factors can impact credit risk by increasing expected loss via a higher probability of default. Adverse weather conditions and/or substantial investment costs to transition to a sustainable economy could create financial difficulties for certain sectors/companies and deteriorate creditworthiness. Extreme environmental events could lead to unexpected adverse effects, increasing exposure at default, and the loss given default could be influenced by the erosion of collateral value due to adverse weather events. Generally, ESG risks challenge all phases of credit granting and monitoring processes, as environmental events frequently lead to financial distress for borrower companies, impacting their ability to repay and probability of default. Consequently, banks are increasingly integrating comprehensive internal ratings with environmental compliance scores/ratings for client credit evaluations.

- *Funding risk:* may increase if the expenses needed for a transition to a sustainable economy reduce depositors' savings or if the bank fails to adhere to ESG policies, damaging its reputation and resulting in a loss of depositor trust.
- *Market Risk*: ESG risks may reduce corporate value, which in turn leads to a devaluation of assets held by banks that have invested in such entities, possibly due to damage from extreme events, reputational damage from failure to adhere to social or environmental standards, etc. Physical events may also trigger market shocks, altering expectations and volatility, and potentially causing losses in certain economic sectors. ESG factors may affect the fair value of a portfolio of financial instruments, as purchasing equities in firms perceived as unsustainable makes the firm's stock more vulnerable to environmental and social factors, potentially reducing its value and causing losses on the bank's balance sheet. Supervisory authorities increasingly focus on sustainable investment levels, particularly through the Green Asset Ratio (GAR), a synthetic indicator measuring green assets relative to total bank assets. Introduced by the EBA under the EU Taxonomy framework, the GAR measures the proportion of a bank's assets that finance environmentally sustainable activities[11] and reflects the extent to which a bank's financing is aligned with the EU's environmental objectives, such as climate change mitigation or adaptation (EBA, 2021).
- *Liquidity Risk*: ESG risks may impact the asset side by reducing the value of financial assets, increasing illiquidity risk. For example, if

[11] The GAR is measured as follows: GAR = (Taxonomy-aligned assets)/(Total relevant assets).

a company in which the bank has invested experiences an adverse ESG event, the bank may face asset devaluation, harming liquidity. On the liability side, liquidity risk may arise from potential depositor runs due to unexpected environmental shocks or social unrest. ESG factors may also impact the availability and stability of funding sources due to more costly market access or changing depositor preferences in line with ESG principles.
- *Operational Risk*: closely relates to legal/reputational risk, as the bank's activities or those of its counterparties may harm its image due to ESG-related controversies. For example, financing activities for fossil fuel extraction companies may become publicly controversial, negatively impacting the reputation of the financing bank.
- *Regulatory Risk*: new ESG regulations may increase costs or reduce revenues, thus raising legislative risk. Errors and non-compliance in implementing ESG regulations may lead to fines, losses, or reputational harm, increasing compliance risk. For example, failure to comply with European board composition regulations may result in sanctions and reputational damage, leading to financial losses.

The Guidelines on the management of ESG risks issued by EBA (EBA, 2025) provide a structured framework for financial institutions to identify, measure, manage and monitor ESG risks. These guidelines, mandated by Article 87a of the CRD IV (Directive 2013/36/EU), aim to ensure the resilience and stability of institutions in response to the growing financial impact of ESG factors, particularly environmental risks associated with climate change and the transition to a sustainable economy.

The starting point is that the financial sector plays a crucial role in both supporting the transition to a sustainable economy and managing financial risks that emerge from ESG-related disruptions. Climate-related risks, social factors (e.g., human rights violations, demographic shifts) and governance issues (e.g., executive misconduct, corruption) increasingly threaten credit, market, operational, liquidity and reputational stability. The lack of historical data and methodological uniformity has led to a fragmented approach to ESG risk management across financial institutions, necessitating standardized regulatory guidance.

The guidelines build upon key legislative instruments such as CRD IV and CRR, which have been revised to integrate ESG considerations. The introduction of Article 87a in the CRD IV explicitly mandates financial institutions to develop robust strategies, policies and methodologies for ESG risk management. This framework aligns with broader European regulatory objectives, such as the European Green Deal and the Paris Agreement, and is consistent with international initiatives, including those of the Basel Committee on Banking Supervision (BCBS) and the Network for Greening the Financial System (NGFS).

The document prescribes minimum standards and reference methodologies for ESG risk assessment and integration into financial institutions' governance structures, and focuses on four key aspects:

1. *Identification and measurement of ESG risks*. Institutions must perform regular materiality assessments of ESG risks using both qualitative and quantitative methodologies. ESG risks must be analyzed in relation to credit, market, operational, liquidity and concentration risks over short (1–3 years), medium (3–10 years), and long-term (10+ years) horizons. Risk evaluation must incorporate scenario-based analysis, portfolio alignment methodologies and sector-based assessments to gauge ESG exposure.
2. *Risk management and monitoring*. ESG risks should be embedded in institution-wide risk management frameworks, including the ICAAP and ILAAP. Institutions must establish internal risk controls, ensuring that management bodies are equipped with the necessary expertise to oversee ESG risk strategies. Risk mitigation tools include engagement with counterparties, sectoral exposure limits and diversification strategies.
3. *ESG risk integration into business models and strategies*. Institutions should align business strategies with transition pathways and EU regulatory objectives, including the EU Climate Law (Regulation 2021/1119), which mandates carbon neutrality by 2050. ESG risk considerations must inform loan origination, investment policies, and credit assessments, ensuring that financial institutions do not expose themselves to high-risk counterparties. Risk appetite frameworks should set clear limits on ESG risk exposure, incorporating Key Risk Indicators (KRIs).
4. *Transition planning and supervisory expectations*. Institutions are required to develop transition plans addressing risks arising from the shift to a sustainable economy. These plans must include quantifiable targets, risk mitigation measures and scenario analysis in line with regulatory sustainability objectives. Supervisory authorities will

assess institutions' ESG strategies and test their resilience under different climate scenarios.

The guidelines adopt a proportional approach, allowing Small and Non-Complex Institutions (SNCIs) to implement simplified ESG risk frameworks. However, all institutions, regardless of size, must ensure sufficient preparedness for ESG-related financial risks. The implementation timeline mandates compliance by January 11, 2026, with an extended deadline for SNCIs until January 11, 2027. In conclusion, the last Guidelines on the management of ESG risks represent a critical regulatory advancement aimed at strengthening the financial sector's resilience against ESG-related challenges. By integrating ESG risks into prudential frameworks, the guidelines seek to enhance financial stability, promote sustainable economic transitions and ensure compliance with European and international climate and governance objectives. The standardized methodologies outlined in this report provide a comprehensive roadmap for institutions to systematically assess, manage and mitigate ESG risks in a forward-looking and risk-based manner.

6.1.2 Risk Data Aggregation and Risk Reporting (RDARR)

The Risk Data Aggregation and Risk Reporting (RDARR) principles emerged in direct response to deficiencies exposed by the 2007–2008 global financial crisis. During this period, many financial institutions revealed significant weaknesses in their ability to aggregate risk data efficiently and produce timely and accurate risk reports. Therefore, the financial crisis and subsequent global stress scenarios underscored the necessity of high-quality risk data to prevent significant financial losses and miscalculations in KRIs. These limitations prevented effective risk management and supervision, exacerbating financial instability. The RDARR framework was thus formally introduced by the BCBS through the document titled 'Principles for effective risk data aggregation and risk reporting' (BCBS 239), published in January 2013.

The RDARR focuses on improving the way banks collect, aggregate and report risk data and aims to enhance the quality and consistency of risk data, making it easier for banks to monitor and manage their risks, and it also seeks to improve the transparency of risk reporting, allowing supervisors to understand the risk profile of banks better. The ECB emphasizes the importance of RDARR as a fundamental prerequisite for sound risk governance, decision-making and regulatory compliance. The quality, completeness, timeliness, and accuracy of risk-related data directly impact an institution's ability to manage risk, ensure financial stability and adhere to supervisory regulations.

The RDARR was developed with the aim of: (i) enhancing banks' capabilities to aggregate risk data accurately and rapidly across their organizations; (ii) improving the timeliness and accuracy of risk reporting; (iii) strengthening governance and oversight, enabling senior management and supervisors to make better-informed risk management decisions; and (iv) ensuring that banks maintain resilience during periods of financial stress. These principles were initially mandatory for global systemically important banks (G-SIBs) and were intended to be implemented by January 2016. However, implementation has progressively expanded to other institutions.

The RDARR framework consists of 14 core principles grouped into four main areas:

(1) *Governance and Infrastructure*: clear responsibility of senior management and robust risk data infrastructure.
(2) *Risk Data Aggregation Capabilities*: accuracy and integrity, completeness, timeliness and adaptability.
(3) *Risk Reporting Practices*: accuracy, comprehensiveness, clarity and usefulness, frequency and distribution.
(4) *Supervisory Review and Evaluation*: supervisory review, providing oversight of banks' implementation.

RDARR is, therefore, a crucial aspect of effective risk management in financial institutions since it refers to the processes and systems that enable institutions to collect, aggregate and report risk data in a timely and accurate manner. The importance of RDARR was highlighted during the 2007–2008 financial crisis and, more recently, during the COVID-19 pandemic, when difficulties in data accuracy and adaptability were observed. From 2013 onwards, globally systemically important banks (G-SIBs) started aligning their internal processes to comply with RDARR principles. Although the original deadline was January 2016, many institutions have faced challenges, leading supervisors worldwide (including the ECB) to emphasize ongoing compliance and monitoring. The ECB has conducted a thematic review on RDARR, which revealed shortcomings in the effectiveness of data governance frameworks and the implementation of the BCBS 239 principles. In fact, even after the introduction of RDARR, banks continued to encounter challenges related to data governance frameworks, IT infrastructures and risk data aggregation capabilities.

The ECB has, therefore, developed a guide to assist institutions in strengthening their capabilities in this area (European Central Bank, 2024), with a strategic focus on compelling institutions to remedy structural deficiencies and achieve full adherence to the BCBS 239 principles. The guide outlines the ECB's expectations for RDARR, which include robust governance arrangements, effective data governance frameworks and integrated data architectures. Moreover, the guide provides detailed guidance on various aspects of RDARR, including the responsibilities of the management body, the scope of application of the data governance framework, data quality management and the timeliness of internal risk reporting. The guide also emphasizes the importance of effective implementation programmes to address any gaps and weaknesses identified in institutions' RDARR capabilities.

In particular, the ECB has outlined several supervisory expectations to enhance RDARR capabilities, grouped into seven priority areas:

1. Responsibilities of the management body, which must take full accountability for risk data quality and governance; RDARR should be a strategic priority, with adequate resources and governance frameworks in place, and a clear allocation of roles within the institution is required, ensuring robust oversight of data quality, IT infrastructures and internal controls.
2. Sufficient scope of application: RDARR frameworks should be comprehensive, covering all material legal entities, risks and business lines; the scope must include internal risk reports, financial reports, supervisory reports, KRIs and risk models.
3. Effective data governance framework: banks must establish clear responsibilities for data ownership and ensure robust monitoring mechanisms; a centralized data governance function should be implemented, supported by validation and audit mechanisms to prevent conflicts of interest.

4. Integrated data architecture: a unified data taxonomy and standardized data definitions must be implemented to ensure data consistency and traceability across the organization; data lineage tracking should be used to maintain visibility over data transformations and reporting processes.
5. Group-wide data quality management and standards; institutions should enforce uniform data quality controls across front-office and reporting layers; data quality indicators should be monitored systematically, with escalation procedures for material deficiencies.
6. Timeliness of internal risk reporting: institutions must optimize the frequency and speed of internal risk reporting to enable timely decision-making. ECB expects risk reports to be produced within 20 working days, with sufficient adaptability for stress or crises.
7. Effective implementation programmes: banks should establish implementation programmes to align with BCBS 239 principles, with specific targets, milestones and accountability mechanisms; management bodies must actively oversee the execution of RDARR remediation programmes, ensuring sustained progress.

Furthermore, the ECB has adopted a more intrusive supervisory stance, incorporating targeted reviews, benchmarking exercises and data quality assessments into its oversight activities. If institutions fail to comply with supervisory expectations, the ECB may:

- Impose qualitative requirements with strict deadlines for remediation.
- Apply capital add-ons, enforcement measures and sanctions.
- Reassess the suitability of management board members, including possible removals.

Overall, the ECB has adopted a supervisory approach to ensure that institutions comply with its expectations for RDARR, which includes targeted engagement with institutions, horizontal benchmarking of findings and an enhanced focus on the data quality of supervisory reporting. The ECB has also intensified its intrusiveness in the context of the annual Supervisory Review and Evaluation Process (SREP) and other supervisory activities. RDARR represents, therefore, a critical component of effective risk management in financial institutions.

6.1.3 The Impact of Digital Transformation on Credit Rationing

Technological advancements have significantly influenced the financial industry, particularly in mitigating credit rationing. By leveraging big data, machine learning, and financial technology (fintech), technology has transformed credit assessment processes, reduced information asymmetries and expanded access to credit.

One of the primary drivers of credit rationing is information asymmetry, where lenders lack sufficient information on borrowers' ability to repay. Technological advancements, particularly in data analytics and machine learning, have substantially reduced this gap. According to Frost et al. (2019), fintech companies utilize alternative data sources, such as social media activity, transaction history and online behaviour, to develop more accurate credit scoring models. These models provide a more comprehensive assessment of borrowers, especially those without traditional credit histories, thereby reducing the incidence of credit rationing.

Machine learning algorithms and artificial intelligence (AI) have revolutionized credit scoring by improving the accuracy and efficiency of risk assessment. Khandani et al. (2010) show that machine learning techniques can better predict default risks compared to traditional logistic regression models. These advanced models consider a wider array of variables and complex interactions, enabling lenders to differentiate between high-risk and low-risk borrowers more effectively. This precision reduces the likelihood of credit rationing, particularly for non-traditional borrowers who may have been underserved by conventional credit scoring systems.

Fintech innovations, such as peer-to-peer (P2P) lending platforms, have provided alternative avenues for borrowers to access credit. P2P platforms connect borrowers directly with individual lenders by bypassing traditional banking intermediaries. According to Duarte et al. (2012), these platforms leverage technology to assess credit risk and facilitate lending decisions. The transparency and efficiency of P2P platforms reduce transaction costs and broaden access to credit, particularly for small businesses and individuals who may be marginalized by traditional banks.

Blockchain technology has the potential to enhance credit transparency and trust in financial transactions. By providing a decentralized and immutable ledger of financial transactions, blockchain can improve the verification of borrowers' credit histories and reduce fraudulent activities. Chen et al. (2018) argue that blockchain-based credit reporting systems can offer a more reliable and tamper-proof record of borrowers' financial behaviour, thereby reducing the risk of adverse selection and moral hazard. This increased transparency can lead to a reduction in credit rationing as lenders gain greater trust in the accuracy of credit assessments.

While technology has significantly mitigated credit rationing, it is not without challenges. Data privacy concerns and the potential for algorithmic bias in credit scoring models are critical issues that need to be addressed. As pointed out by Hurley and Adebayo (2017), biased algorithms can perpetuate existing inequalities if not properly monitored and regulated. Therefore, it is essential to implement robust regulatory frameworks that ensure fairness and transparency in the use of technology in credit assessment.

Gambacorta et al. (2025) explore how AI-driven credit scoring interacts with relationship lending in the banking sector. Using a unique dataset on Italian banks, they examine whether AI complements or substitutes traditional lending practices and find that AI banks offer a more stable credit supply than traditional relationship lenders, reducing credit procyclicality. While relationship lending typically expands credit during crises and contracts it in normal times, AI lending is less sensitive to macroeconomic fluctuations. Instead, it reacts more to firm-specific conditions like transaction volumes and profitability. In normal times, AI banks reduce rent extraction, offering better credit terms regardless of relationship length, while during crises, relationship lending protects borrowers, but this effect is weaker for AI banks. AI investments help mitigate countercyclical effects on firms' credit supply, investment and employment. Overall, the study highlights a paradigm shift in financial intermediation, where data-driven lending challenges traditional, collateral-based models. The increasing reliance on AI in banking has important policy implications, requiring regulatory oversight to ensure fair and efficient credit allocation. The findings suggest that monetary policy and financial stability frameworks must adapt to this transformation.

Technology is, therefore, having a profound impact on reducing credit rationing by enhancing credit assessment processes, improving risk differentiation and expanding access to credit through innovative platforms. Nevertheless, while the benefits are substantial, it is crucial to address the challenges associated with data privacy and algorithmic bias to ensure that the advantages of technological advancements are equitably distributed. Continued innovation and thoughtful regulation will be key to maximizing the positive impact of technology on credit rationing.

6.2 The ICT Transformation Process and Its Regulation

The rapid evolution of the financial sector, characterized by increasing digitalization and the introduction of new instruments such as crypto-assets, has necessitated the implementation of new regulations to ensure the stability, integrity and efficiency of markets. In this context, the Digital Operational Resilience Act (DORA), the Markets in Crypto-Assets Regulation (MiCA) and the Artificial Intelligence Act (AI Act) represent important initiatives by the European Union to address the challenges posed by technological innovation in the financial sector.

6.2.1 The Digital Operational Resilience Act (DORA)

DORA is a regulation introduced in 2022 that aims to strengthen digital operational resilience in the financial sector, given the increasing dependence on ICT. The regulation establishes uniform requirements for the management of ICT risk, with a focus on the security of networks and information systems.[12] Regarding ICT risk management, financial entities are required to implement an internal governance and control framework for the effective management of ICT risk. This includes the identification, classification and documentation of all business functions supported by ICT, as well as information assets and dependencies related to ICT risk.

[12] Regulation (EU) 2022/2554 of the European Parliament and of the Council of 14 December 2022 on digital operational resilience for the financial sector and amending Regulations (EC) No 1060/2009, (EU) No 648/2012, (EU) No 600/2014, (EU) No 909/2014 and (EU) 2016/1011, Article 1: 'In order to achieve a high common level of digital operational resilience, this Regulation lays down uniform requirements concerning the security of network and information systems supporting the business processes of financial entities'.

DORA mandates the implementation of a digital operational resilience testing programme, which includes a series of assessments, tests, methodologies, practices and tools. Certain financial entities identified as significant will have to conduct advanced tests at least every three years. DORA introduces a supervisory framework for third-party ICT service providers deemed critical for the financial sector. This includes the designation of a 'Lead Overseer' responsible for monitoring critical third-party ICT service providers and the possibility of imposing sanctions in case of non-compliance. Finally, financial entities are required to report significant ICT-related incidents, including cyberattacks, to the competent authorities. The European Parliament and the Council—known collectively as European Supervisory Authorities (ESAs)—must develop technical standards for the harmonization of content and templates for ICT incident reporting.

The financial sector's increasing integration of ICT has led to significant advancements in efficiency, accessibility and innovation. However, it has also amplified the sector's exposure to a wide range of operational risks stemming from ICT disruptions. These risks include:

- Cyber-attacks: the threat of malicious cyber activities, such as data breaches, ransomware attacks and denial-of-service attacks, poses a significant threat to the confidentiality, integrity and availability of financial data and systems.
- ICT Failures: systemic failures due to software glitches, hardware malfunctions or network outages can disrupt critical financial services and undermine market confidence.
- Third-party concentration risk: the increasing reliance on third-party ICT service providers, including cloud computing providers, creates concentration risks and potential vulnerabilities if these providers experience disruptions.

DORA aims to mitigate these risks and ensure that financial entities can withstand, respond to, and recover from ICT-related disruptions, thereby maintaining financial stability and protecting consumers and investors. In particular, DORA establishes a comprehensive framework with several key components. First, financial entities are mandated to implement a robust internal governance and control framework for the effective management of ICT risk. This ICT risk management framework encompasses the following key elements:

- Identification and classification of ICT assets: financial entities must identify, classify, and document all business functions supported by ICT, as well as all information assets and dependencies relevant to ICT risk. This includes mapping critical processes, systems and data flows.
- Risk assessment: conducting thorough risk assessments to evaluate the vulnerabilities, threats and potential impacts of ICT disruptions.
- Implementation of security measures: establishing and maintaining appropriate security measures, including cybersecurity protocols, access controls and data protection mechanisms to mitigate identified risks.
- Business continuity and disaster recovery: developing and implementing comprehensive business continuity plans and disaster recovery procedures to ensure the timely recovery of critical functions in the event of an ICT disruption.

Furthermore, DORA mandates the implementation of a digital operational resilience testing programme, which requires financial entities to conduct a range of tests to assess the effectiveness of their ICT risk management framework. These tests may include:

- Vulnerability assessments: identifying weaknesses in systems and applications.
- Penetration testing: simulating cyberattacks to evaluate security defences.
- Scenario testing: assessing the ability to respond to and recover from various disruption scenarios.
- Advanced testing: certain significant financial entities will be required to conduct advanced testing, such as threat-led penetration testing (TLPT), at least every three years to assess their resilience against sophisticated cyber threats.

Finally, DORA introduces a supervisory framework for third-party ICT service providers that are deemed critical for the financial sector. This framework includes:

- Designation of critical providers: the designation of certain ICT providers as 'critical' based on their systemic importance to the financial sector.
- Lead overseer: the establishment of a 'lead overseer' responsible for supervising critical third-party ICT service providers. This overseer will have the authority to assess the providers' risk management practices and ensure compliance with DORA.
- Supervisory powers: the ability of the lead overseer to impose sanctions on critical third-party ICT service providers in case of non-compliance.

Financial entities are required to report significant ICT-related incidents, including cyberattacks, to the competent authorities. This aims to ensure timely awareness of major disruptions, to facilitate coordinated responses, and to enable the collection of data for analysis and improvement of resilience across the sector. DORA thus represents a significant step towards enhancing the digital operational resilience of the financial sector. Its implications include:

- Increased regulatory scrutiny: financial entities will face increased regulatory scrutiny and stricter requirements for ICT risk management.
- Enhanced resilience: the implementation of DORA should lead to a more resilient financial sector, better equipped to withstand and recover from ICT disruptions.
- Greater harmonization: DORA promotes greater harmonization of ICT risk management practices across the European Union.
- Focus on third-party risk: the regulation places a strong emphasis on managing third-party ICT risk, recognizing the interconnectedness of the financial ecosystem.

In conclusion, DORA signifies a paradigm shift in the regulation of operational resilience in the financial sector. By addressing the unique challenges and risks posed by ICT, DORA aims to ensure the stability and integrity of the financial system in an increasingly digital world.

6.2.2 *The Regulation on Markets in Crypto-Assets (MiCA)*

Besides the DORA, the MiCA regulation was approved in 2023[13] to create a harmonized regulatory framework for crypto-assets, defining them as 'a digital representation of value or rights that may be transferred and stored electronically, using distributed ledger technology or similar technology'. Prior to MiCA, the regulatory treatment of crypto-assets varied considerably across member states, creating legal uncertainty and hindering the development of a single market for these assets. The regulation introduces a series of obligations for issuers and service providers of crypto-assets, with the aim of protecting savers and preventing systemic risks. MiCA requires that offerors of crypto-assets publish a 'white paper' containing clear, correct and non-misleading information about the offered crypto asset. This document must include a statement warning potential buyers that the crypto asset could lose value. Additionally, the white paper must be prepared in a machine-readable format.

MiCA provides a classification of crypto-assets, distinguishing between Asset-Referenced Tokens (ARTs) and e-money tokens, each subject to specific requirements. The European Supervisory Authorities (ESAs) are tasked with issuing guidelines to support a uniform classification of crypto-assets. Issuers of ARTs and crypto-asset service providers must obtain authorization from the competent authorities of their home country. Supervisory authorities have the power to impose sanctions in case of violation of the regulation. Furthermore, MiCA provides procedures for cooperation between competent authorities and supervisory authorities of third countries.

MiCA's core objectives are:

- Legal certainty: providing a clear legal framework for crypto-assets, fostering innovation and investor confidence.
- Consumer protection: safeguarding consumers and investors from the risks associated with crypto-asset investments.

[13] Regulation (EU) 2023/1114 of the European Parliament and of the Council of 31 May 2023 on markets in crypto-assets and amending Regulations (EU) No 1093/2010 and (EU) No 1095/2010 and Directives 2013/36/EU and (EU) 2019/1937.

- Financial stability: addressing potential risks to the stability of the financial system arising from crypto-assets.
- Innovation: supporting the development of the crypto-asset market in a safe and sound manner.

MiCA imposes a set of obligations on issuers of crypto-assets and crypto-asset service providers (CASPs) to ensure market integrity and investor protection. Issuers of ARTs and CASPs are required to obtain authorization from the competent authorities in their home member state. This authorization process ensures that these entities meet specific prudential and operational requirements. Moreover, competent authorities are granted the power to supervise crypto-asset activities and enforce MiCA's provisions. They can impose sanctions in cases of non-compliance, which may include financial penalties and the withdrawal of authorization.

The ESAs play a crucial role in providing further guidance and ensuring a consistent classification of crypto-assets across the EU. MiCA establishes mechanisms for cooperation between competent authorities within the EU and supervisory authorities in third countries. This international cooperation is essential for addressing the cross-border nature of crypto-asset markets and ensuring effective supervision.

Although MiCA and DORA are distinct regulations, they are complementary in their goal of improving the stability and integrity of the financial sector in the digital age. While MiCA focuses on the regulation of crypto-assets, DORA aims to ensure that the sector's ICT infrastructures are resilient to operational incidents, including those related to crypto-assets, and also applies to services that support crypto-asset markets. Both regulations promote cooperation between competent authorities and provide for the possibility of consulting the ESAs to ensure a coherent approach.

The MiCA and DORA regulations therefore represent an important step towards creating a more robust and harmonized regulatory framework for the financial sector in the European Union. Their implementation will help protect savers, prevent systemic risks and promote responsible innovation in the digital financial sector. However, it will be crucial to closely monitor the evolution of the sector and make any necessary regulatory adjustments to adequately respond to new challenges posed by technological innovation.

6.2.3 *The Artificial Intelligence Act (AI Act)*

The Regulation (EU) 2024/1689, commonly known as the Artificial Intelligence Act (AI Act), constitutes a seminal legal framework aimed at establishing harmonized rules for artificial intelligence within the European Union. Its primary objective is to improve the functioning of the internal market while fostering the development and adoption of human-centric and trustworthy AI, ensuring a high level of protection for health, safety and fundamental rights as enshrined in the Charter of Fundamental Rights of the European Union. The AI Act seeks to mitigate potential harms posed by AI systems within the Union, concurrently supporting innovation.

The legal foundation of this regulation is primarily rooted in Article 114 of the Treaty on the Functioning of the European Union (TFEU), which pertains to the uniform protection of overriding reasons of public interest and the rights of individuals throughout the internal market. Additionally, specific rules concerning the protection of individuals with regard to the processing of personal data related to restrictions on the use of AI systems for remote biometric identification, risk assessments for law enforcement purposes, and biometric categorization for law enforcement are based on Article 16 TFEU.

The European legislator acknowledges the transformative potential of AI across various sectors but also recognizes the inherent risks and potential for harm to public interests and fundamental rights depending on the specific context of application, use and technological maturity. Such harm can be both material and immaterial, encompassing physical, psychological, social or economic damages. Given the significant societal impact of AI and the imperative to build trust, the development and regulatory framework of AI must align with the values of the Union articulated in Article 2 of the Treaty on European Union (TEU) and the fundamental rights and freedoms enshrined in the treaties and the Charter. A foundational principle is that AI should remain a human-centric technology, serving as a tool to enhance human wellbeing.

The AI Act adopts a 'risk-based approach', wherein the stringency and nature of the regulatory requirements are modulated according to the level of risk that AI systems may pose. This approach categorizes AI systems into different levels of risk, ranging from unacceptable AI practices, which are prohibited, to high-risk AI systems, which are subject to specific obligations and requirements, and finally to AI systems with limited risk, for which primarily transparency obligations are stipulated.

Unacceptable AI practices are delineated in Article 5 and are consequently forbidden within the European Union. These include the placing on the market, putting into service, or use of an AI system that employs subliminal techniques beyond a person's awareness, or intentionally manipulative or deceptive techniques, with the objective or effect of materially distorting the behaviour of a person or group, thereby significantly impairing their ability to make informed decisions and causing them to take a decision they would not otherwise have made, resulting in or being reasonably likely to result in significant harm.

Beyond prohibited practices, the AI Act identifies a category of 'high-risk AI systems'. This category comprises two main types of systems:

- AI systems intended to be used as 'safety components of a product' or the AI system itself as a product, covered by Union harmonization legislation listed in Annex I, where the product or AI system is subject to a third-party conformity assessment prior to being placed on the market or put into service.
- AI systems 'listed in Annex III' of the regulation. This annex includes use cases in sectors such as education, employment, access to essential private and public services, law enforcement, management of migration, asylum and border control and administration of justice and democratic processes.

However, a derogation from classification as high-risk is provided for AI systems listed in Annex III if they do not pose a significant risk of harm to the health, safety or fundamental rights of natural persons, including by not materially influencing the outcome of decision-making. This applies under specific conditions, such as when the AI system is intended to perform a narrow procedural task, improve the result of a previously completed human activity, detect decision-making patterns or deviations without replacing or influencing human assessment, or perform a preparatory task for an assessment relevant to the use cases in Annex III. Notwithstanding these conditions, an AI system referred to in Annex III is always considered high-risk if it performs profiling of natural persons. Providers who consider their Annex III AI system to be non-high-risk must document their assessment and register the system in the EU database.

Providers of 'high-risk AI systems' bear several obligations to ensure compliance with the requirements set out in Sect. 6.2 of Chapter III of the AI Act. These obligations include ensuring the high-risk AI system complies with the relevant requirements, indicating the provider's details on the system or its documentation, having a 'quality management system' in place, keeping the technical documentation and automatically generated logs, undergoing the relevant conformity assessment procedure, drawing up an 'EU declaration of conformity', affixing the CE marking, complying with registration obligations, taking necessary corrective actions and providing required information, demonstrating conformity upon request from competent authorities, and ensuring compliance with accessibility requirements.

Deployers of high-risk AI systems also have distinct obligations. They must take appropriate technical and organizational measures to use the systems in accordance with the instructions for use. Deployers are required to assign human oversight to individuals with the necessary competence, training and authority. Where the deployer exercises control over input data, they must ensure it is relevant and sufficiently representative for the intended purpose of the AI system. Certain deployers—particularly public bodies, private entities providing public services, and deployers of specific high-risk AI systems listed in Annex III (e.g. in banking or insurance)—are obligated to conduct a fundamental rights impact assessment prior to putting the system into use. This assessment aims to identify specific risks to the rights of individuals or groups likely to be affected, and to determine measures to be taken if those risks materialize.

For certain AI systems, regardless of their high-risk classification, the AI Act mandates 'specific transparency obligations'. Providers must ensure that AI systems intended to interact directly with natural people are designed and developed to inform individuals that they are interacting with an AI system, unless this is reasonably obvious. Furthermore, providers of AI systems—including general-purpose AI models that generate synthetic audio, image, video or text content—must ensure that the outputs are marked in a machine-readable format and detectable as artificially generated or manipulated. This obligation aims to enhance transparency and address the risks of misinformation and manipulation.

The AI Act also introduces specific provisions for 'general-purpose AI models', particularly those deemed to present systemic risks due to their high-impact capabilities or significant market reach. Providers of general-purpose AI models are required to formulate and maintain technical documentation, provide information to downstream providers, and publish a sufficiently detailed summary about the content used to train the model. Models meeting a specified threshold for computational power used in training are presumed to present systemic risks.

The governance of the AI Act is structured at multiple levels, with the establishment of the 'AI Office' at the Union level to develop expertise and support the implementation of the regulation. A board composed of representatives from member states, a scientific panel and an advisory forum involving stakeholders are also part of this governance framework. Member States are responsible for designating national competent authorities to supervise and enforce the regulation, ensuring they have adequate resources and expertise.

To ensure the effective application of the AI Act, a robust post-market monitoring system is mandated for providers of high-risk AI systems to track performance and identify potential issues. Providers are also obligated to report serious incidents resulting from the use of their AI systems to the relevant authorities. The AI Act also establishes mechanisms for conformity assessment, which, for certain high-risk AI systems, may involve notified bodies. In cases of non-compliance, the AI Act stipulates administrative fines that may be significant, depending on the nature of the infringement and the size of the undertaking. These fines are intended to be effective, proportionate and dissuasive.

In conclusion, the AI Act represents a comprehensive and multifaceted regulatory framework designed to govern the development and deployment of AI systems within the European Union. By adopting a risk-based approach and establishing clear obligations for providers and deployers, the Act aims to harness the benefits of AI while mitigating its potential risks to fundamental rights, safety and the integrity of the information environment. Its provisions on prohibited practices, high-risk systems, transparency and governance mechanisms signify a concerted effort to shape a future in which AI is trustworthy and aligned with European values.

References

Bonfim, D., Nogueira, G., & Ongena, S. (2021). 'Sorry, we're closed' bank branch closures, loan pricing, and information asymmetries. *Review of Finance, 25*(4), 1211–1259.

Chen, M., Xu, L., Lu, Y., & Chen, N. S. (2018). Exploring blockchain technology and its potential applications for education. *Smart Learning Environments, 5*(1), 1–10.

Degryse, H., Morales Acevedo, P., Ongena, S., & Osberghaus, A. (2025). Competition in banking: When banks compete with non-banks. In A. N. Berger, P. Molyneux, & J. Wilson (Eds.), T*he Oxford handbook of banking* (4th ed., pp. 265–296). Oxford University Press.

Duarte, J., Siegel, S., & Young, L. (2012). Trust and credit: The role of appearance in peer-to-peer lending. *Review of Financial Studies, 25*(8), 2455–2484.

European Banking Authority (EBA). (2021). Advice to the commission on KPIS and methodology for disclosure by credit institutions and investment firms under the NFRD on how and to what extent their activities qualify as environmentally sustainable according to the EU taxonomy (EBA/Rep/2021/03).

European Banking Authority (EBA). (2025). Guidelines on the management of environmental, social and governance (ESG) risks (EBA/GL/2025/01).

European Central Bank (ECB). (2020). Guide on climate-related and environmental risks. Supervisory expectations relating to risk management and disclosure.

European Central Bank (ECB). (2024). Guide on Effective Risk Data Aggregation and Risk Reporting.

European Commission. (2018). Action plan: Financing sustainable growth.

Frost, J., Gambacorta, L., Huang, Y., Shin, H. S., & Zbinden, P. (2019). Big Tech and the changing structure of financial intermediation. *Economic Policy, 34*(100), 761–799.

Gambacorta, L., Sabatini, F., & Schiaffi, S. (2025). Artificial intelligence and relationship lending. Bank of Italy Temi di Discussione (Working Paper) No, 1476.

Hurley, M., & Adebayo, J. (2017). Credit scoring in the era of big data. *Yale Journal of Law and Technology, 18*, 148–216.

Khandani, A. E., Kim, A. J., & Lo, A. W. (2010). Consumer credit-risk models via machine-learning algorithms. *Journal of Banking & Finance, 34*(11), 2767–2787.

Vives, X. (2019). Digital disruption in banking. *Annual Review of Financial Economics, 11*, 243–272.

Weber, A. M., Mittwoch, A. C., Herbet-Homenda, W., & Stefaniuk, W. (2024). Digitalizing the commercial banking business model: Vanishing bank branches and the risks of financial exclusion of the elderly. In M. Bodellini, G. Gimigliano, & D. Singh (Eds.), *Commercial banking in transition: A cross-country analysis*. Springer International Publishing.

Weber, O. (2021). The banking sector and the SDGs: Interconnections and future directions. In O. M. Lehner (Ed.), *A research agenda for social finance* (pp. 175–198). Edward Elgar.

CHAPTER 7

Conclusions

Multiple interconnected factors—including informational asymmetries, financial constraints, regulatory transformations and technological innovation—have profoundly influenced the evolution of the bank-business relationship. This book has examined the core mechanisms through which banks allocate financial resources, assess credit risk and adapt to regulatory pressures, ultimately shaping the dynamics of corporate finance and the broader financial system.

A central theme throughout this work is the tension between market imperfections and financial regulation—particularly in the context of credit rationing, relationship lending and financial stability. Theoretical models and empirical evidence demonstrate that asymmetric information remains a fundamental challenge in bank–firm interactions, necessitating risk management strategies, regulatory oversight and innovative financing approaches to improve credit allocation and ensure systemic resilience (see Chapter 2). In addition to analyzing these structural issues, the book also explored the implications of the 'twin transition' in the banking sector, i.e., the simultaneous push for digitalization and sustainability, which is reshaping traditional banking models (see Chapter 6). As banks navigate these transitions, they must balance profitability, compliance and technological adaptation while responding to shifting corporate financial needs, regulatory expectations and macroeconomic uncertainties.

P. Brighi and M. Mussoni, *The Bank-Business Relationship*,
https://doi.org/10.1007/978-3-031-91068-5_7

One of the fundamental insights from this work is the persistence of credit rationing and asymmetric information: credit rationing often remains a pervasive issue, particularly for SMEs, start-ups, and R&D-oriented firms (see Chapter 3). While neoclassical financial theory suggests that interest rate adjustments should equilibrate the supply and demand for credit, empirical evidence confirms that adverse selection and moral hazard distort the efficiency of credit markets, leading banks to ration credit rather than raise lending rates to compensate for higher risk. To mitigate these inefficiencies, financial institutions rely on screening, monitoring and information-sharing mechanisms, such as credit registries, rating agencies and collateral-based lending. However, despite these efforts, information gaps persist, especially for firms lacking established financial histories or operating in high-risk sectors. Future research should continue to explore alternative mechanisms—such as AI-driven credit scoring models, decentralized financial systems and open banking frameworks—to reduce informational frictions and improve credit access.

The literature reinforces the view that relationship lending serves as a key mechanism for overcoming informational asymmetries and fostering long-term trust between banks and firms (see Chapter 4). Unlike transaction-based lending, which relies on standardized credit assessments, relationship lending allows banks to gather proprietary 'soft information' about borrowers over time, enabling them to offer more favourable lending terms and reduce credit constraints for financially opaque firms. However, the benefits of relationship lending come with potential risks and trade-offs. Borrowers engaged in long-term banking relationships may face switching costs and reduced bargaining power, potentially leading to lock-in effects and inefficient credit allocation. At the same time, the rise of fintech, alternative lending platforms and AI-powered credit assessment models is challenging the traditional dominance of relationship lending, creating new opportunities for digitalized and data-driven credit markets. Future research should assess how technological advancements affect the balance between relationship- and transaction-based lending models and how firms navigate their funding strategies in this evolving landscape.

Under this point of view, the corporate banking landscape has undergone a significant evolution and transformation—particularly in how firms engage with multiple financial intermediaries. Traditional corporate banking models, historically characterized by long-term bank–firm relationships and centralized financing strategies, are increasingly being replaced by multi-banking lending arrangements, in which firms diversify their funding sources across multiple banks and financial institutions. Several factors drive the shift towards multi-banking:

- Risk diversification: by maintaining relationships with multiple banks, firms reduce their dependence on a single financial institution—lowering their exposure to idiosyncratic bank risks.
- Improved credit access: multi-banking relationships allow firms to tap into a broader range of financial products and lending conditions, increasing their negotiating power.
- Regulatory and compliance considerations: stricter prudential regulations—particularly under Basel III and Basel IV—have led banks to reassess corporate lending strategies, often resulting in more selective credit allocation.
- Technological advancements and financial innovation: the rise of fintech platforms, supply chain finance solutions and alternative lending markets has facilitated access to non-traditional funding sources, reducing reliance on any single banking partner.

However, while multi-banking offers greater financial flexibility, it also introduces new challenges, such as increased administrative costs, information asymmetry across lenders and increased complexity in credit monitoring and risk management. Banks must adapt their business models to accommodate this shift, leveraging advanced data analytics, AI-driven risk assessment tools and digital lending platforms to remain competitive in the evolving corporate banking landscape.

Regulation has always been a fundamental tool for managing problems related to information asymmetries. The evolution of banking regulation—from Basel I to Basel IV and the recent Loan Origination and Monitoring (LOM) Guidelines—has significantly shaped financial institutions' risk management strategies and lending practices (see Chapter 5). Prudential supervision, capital requirements, and liquidity controls have become central components of modern financial regulation aimed at ensuring financial stability while balancing economic growth objectives. However, while regulatory measures are necessary to prevent excessive risk-taking and systemic crises, they also introduce compliance costs and potential unintended consequences, such as reduced credit supply, procyclicality in lending decisions and constraints on financial innovation. The future of banking regulation must strike a balance between risk mitigation and financial inclusion, particularly in the context of SME financing, fintech integration and sustainable finance.

One of the most transformative developments in the financial sector (see Chapter 6) is the concurrent shift towards digitalization (fintech and AI-driven banking models) and sustainability (ESG integration). The transition to environmentally and socially responsible banking practices is being driven by global climate goals (EU Green Deal, Paris Agreement) and regulatory mandates (EU Taxonomy, ESG disclosure requirements). At the same time, the digitalization of banking services is altering the traditional mechanisms of credit intermediation. The rise of blockchain, AI and decentralized finance (DeFi) is challenging conventional banking models, introducing new credit risk assessment tools, digital lending platforms and algorithm-driven credit allocation mechanisms.

While these technologies may offer greater efficiency and financial inclusion, they also introduce new risks related to cybersecurity, operational resilience and data governance. The banking sector must, therefore, navigate the dual pressures of sustainable finance and digital transformation, balancing innovation, risk management and regulatory compliance in an increasingly complex financial landscape.

The overall picture that can be drawn from this book suggests several key policy implications and avenues for future research. Policymakers should focus on enhancing credit market efficiency—that is, on reducing informational asymmetries by improving credit registries, promoting open banking initiatives and fostering the development of AI-driven credit risk models. Expanding public–private partnerships in credit assessment and risk-sharing mechanisms could further enhance the efficiency of lending markets.

Future regulatory frameworks should balance prudential regulation and financial innovation by seeking balance between ensuring financial stability and allowing room for innovation. This includes rethinking capital requirements, adopting dynamic stress-testing methodologies and integrating fintech-driven solutions while maintaining strong consumer protection measures. Furthermore, given the increasing importance of ESG risks, banks should foster sustainable finance and climate risk management by integrating sustainability considerations into credit risk assessment and lending policies, while policymakers should provide a simpler regulatory framework on ESG risk disclosures, climate stress-testing and sustainable finance incentives to support the transition to a greener economy. There is still much to understand about how fintech, AI and decentralized finance will impact the stability and competitiveness of traditional banking institutions. Under this point of view, regulators should ensure that digital finance ecosystems remain secure, resilient and inclusive, minimizing systemic vulnerabilities while fostering financial innovation.

As the financial sector continues to evolve, driven by technological advancements, regulatory shifts and macroeconomic uncertainties, banks must adapt by developing resilient, data-driven and sustainable business models. The challenges ahead require an ongoing dialogue between academics, policymakers and financial practitioners to ensure that the banking system remains efficient, inclusive and responsive to emerging financial risks. As relationship lending coexists with digital finance and as regulatory demands intensify alongside market innovations, the future of banking will depend on its ability to balance stability, flexibility and strategic foresight.

Ultimately, the bank–business relationship will continue to evolve in response to economic, technological and societal changes, and financial institutions that are capable of successfully integrating risk-aware, technology-enabled and sustainability-driven strategies will be best positioned to navigate future challenges and drive long-term economic prosperity.

Index

P. Brighi and M. Mussoni, *The Bank-Business Relationship*, https://doi.org/10.1007/978-3-031-91068-5

The manufacturer's authorised representative in the EU is Springer Nature Customer Service Centre GmbH, Europaplatz 3, 69115 Heidelberg, Germany. If you have any concerns regarding our products, please contact ProductSafety@springernature.com

Printed and bound by CPI Group (UK) Ltd, Croydon, CR0 4YY

01/10/2026

02225954-0001